INCA ARCHITECTURE

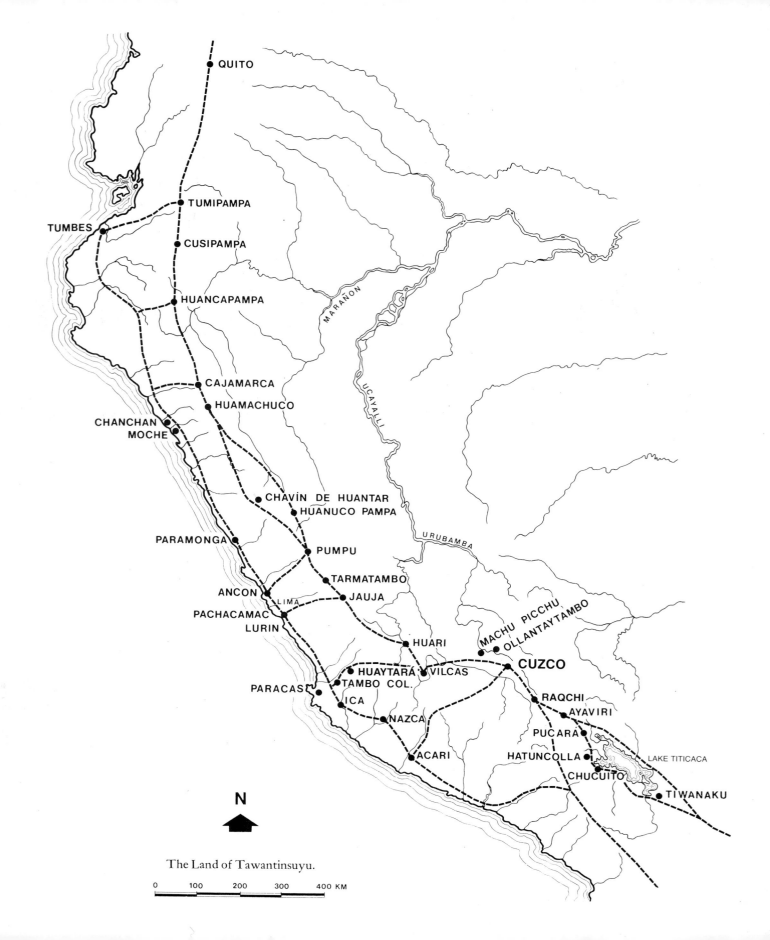

QUITO

TUMIPAMPA

TUMBES

CUSIPAMPA

HUANCAPAMPA

MARAÑON

UCAYALI

CAJAMARCA

HUAMACHUCO

CHANCHAN
MOCHE

CHAVÍN DE HUANTAR

HUANUCO PAMPA

PARAMONGA

PUMPU

URUBAMBA

TARMATAMBO

ANCON
LIMA

JAUJA

PACHACAMAC
LURIN

HUARI

MACHU PICCHU
OLLANTAYTAMBO

CUZCO

HUAYTARÁ
VILCAS

PARACAS

TAMBO COL.

ICA

RAQCHI

AYAVIRI

NAZCA

PUCARA

ACARI

HATUNCOLLA

LAKE TITICACA

CHUCUITO

TIWANAKU

N

The Land of Tawantinsuyu.

0   100   200   300   400 KM

INCA ARCHITECTURE

BY

Graziano Gasparini & Luise Margolies

Translated by Patricia J. Lyon

Indiana University Press • Bloomington

LIBRARY OF CONGRESS CATALOGING IN PUBLICATION DATA

Gasparini, Graziano.
  Inca Architecture.

  Translation of Arquitectura Inka.
  Includes bibliographical references and index.
  1. Incas—Architecture. 2. Indians of South America—Architecture. 1. Margolies, Luise, joint author. II. Title.
F3429.3.A65G3713   722′.91   79–3005
ISBN 0–253–30443–1   2 3 4 5 88 87 86 85 84

To ABRAHAM GUILLÉN,
whose extraordinary photographic activity
has enriched our understanding of pre-Columbian
and colonial Peru during the last fifty years.

Contents

FOREWORD

There is no end to books about the Incas—what does surprise and even exasperate the student of that remarkable Andean state is how little each new title contributes to what we already know. If we compare Prescott's readable account of the conquest of Peru, which he wrote some 140 years ago, with what can be asserted with some confidence today, the relevations are few.

What has been accomplished in the study of Tawantinsuyu, the Inca state, has followed three approaches:

1. Surveys of the administrative and storage centers, of the roads, agricultural terraces, and temples, whose incredible size, beauty, and efficiency, and the architectural skill involved, have attracted the admiration of outsiders ever since 1532. Not only the adventurers who witnessed their destruction but also the nineteenth-century scholars who were the first to measure, draw, photograph, and even excavate the monuments agreed that in the Andes we confront a human achievement that requires fresh scrutiny.

2. Utilization of the dynastic oral tradition, which stored the deeds of legendary, but also historical, kings, and which in passing described some of the Inca institutions. This was collected within the first two or three decades after the invasion by European writers like Betanzos, Polo, or Cieza. While fragmentary, the information provided by such primary sources about the economic, social, and political organization is frequently useful as we strive to understand the meaning of the public works and monuments of this civilization.

3. Utilization of Andean and Inca data for comparative interpretations. In the eighteenth century the comparisons stressed what seemed to be the utopian, welfare features of Andean social organization. In recent decades, fashion has shifted rapidly: a "slave society" or a "feudal" one, a "totalitarian state," an "Asiatic mode of production," or a "socialist empire"—each of these labels has had its partisans, searching in other latitudes when not in outer space, for models to explain the extraordinary phenomena documented for us by architectural or ethnohistoric details.

In ideal circumstances, each of these three approaches could make a contribution: each one and the three in interaction could sponsor the search for new information and its prompt verification. Alas, in practice, each has fallen into the hands of specialists who do not always value, nor always know how to utilize, information provided by the other two.

One of the assets of Gasparini and Margolies's work is their consistent attention to two of these tactics in their study of Tawantinsuyu: they pool and contrast the information emerging from sixteenth-century eyewitness accounts with what their own observations and measurements in the field have told them and what little can be learned from the excavations of Inca settlements and administrative centers. If Garcilaso de la Vega offers a description of the shrine at Cacha, allegedly dedicated to Wiraqocha, Gasparini and Margolies visit the site, measuring, surveying, and photographing what is supposed to be that very monument. A newcomer to Andean studies may think it an obvious step: as early at the nineteenth century, some of our forerunners like Squier or Bandelier had taken it. In our time, Luis E. Valcárel and John H. Rowe have followed this "method" in Cuzco. But in most cases, coordination of the several tactics and their verification through excavation run into stubborn and manifold obstacles.

A good example of the inadequacy of single-tactic attempts to answer some of the better questions in the study of Tawantinsuyu will be found in Gasparini and Margolies's third chapter, where they deal with domestic architecture. Household and village matters, away from Cuzco and far from the *qhapaq-ñan*, the royal road, still await archaeological attention. As knowledgeable an archaeologist as Wendell C. Bennett mused that in much of the territory reported by oral tradition as incorporated into the Inca realm, one was unable to find any physical trace of such an occupation.

The research conducted in the Huallaga Valley of Huánuco by the Institute of Andean Research (1963–65), based on sixteenth-century written sources, told us that the valley's inhabitants had served their *mit'a* turns at such nearby state installations as Huánuco Pampa or Pumpu but also in faraway Cuzco. At the first survey, no Inca remains could be identified in the valley. When the archaeological data was confronted with the house-by-house survey of a 1562 inspection and with information provided by the present-day inhabitants interviewed by the Institute's ethnologists, we learned that:

1. The present-day "ruin" at Ichu was in ceremonial use as recently as 1950. It had once been the seat of power for the whole valley, but nothing about its exterior condition would have suggested it. Once it was identified by the ethnologists, the archaeological determination of the most complex domestic compound allowed the location of a unique, if small, assemblage of Cuzco pottery—thus confirming and extending archaeologically what had been claimed by the sixteenth-century text.

2. It was possible to locate Inca state installations in the Huallaga Valley, away from the royal road. Among them were such diverse occupations as a shrine of the Cuzco solar cult and the hamlets where the Incas had relocated the households of the "thirty couples" sent into this territory to man the "fortresses" deemed necessary by the state. We still do not know who the enemies were; unfortunately, such provincial state installations, as well as others described by Gasparini and Margolies, remain unexcavated.

Another contribution of the present work is its participation in an effort that in recent years has attempted to understand Andean civilization through minute research into particular human activities, in this case building and architectural technology.

It is not a matter simply of providing better catalogues of the materials resulting from metallurgical, textile, ceramic, and agricultural technologies, or inventories of the ways used to preserve and store, although such compilations would be very useful. What is being reached for is a perception of the whole of Andean technology—the result of thousands of years of a local praxis, obviously successful under extremely difficult environmental circumstances, without parallel on other continents. If we seriously aim to fathom this achievement, in ways to allow comparison with, let us say, the one recorded by Joseph Needham for China, we will have to go beyond the data provided by pollen analysis or thermoluminescence. We will require parallel efforts to understand the economic, social, and political formations that allowed the efficient use of human energy in the Andes.

In this light, architecture and building technology are welcome additions to such disciplines as linguistics, archaeology, contemporary ethnography, and the so-called ethnohistory. All of them deal with fragmentary materials, rarely cumulated and suffering from insufficient critical confrontation; one hopes these are no more than the limitations inherent in a very recent research design. Once they are coordinated, the study of construction design and techniques, and also of the builders, promises to allow the crossing of new thresholds in our understanding of the achievements of Andean man.

JOHN V. MURRA
Cornell University

PREFACE

In 1972 the Consejo de Desarrollo Científico y Humanístico of the Universidad Central de Venezuela approved a grant for our research project, "Inca Architecture." This support enabled us to increase the time devoted to documentation and to extend our travels in Ecuador, Peru, and Bolivia.

The idea of undertaking a study of Inca architecture—analyzing the form, volume, and spatial arrangements as well as trying to understand state regulation of building activities—originated in the late 1960s and was finally decided upon in 1970, when we attended the 39th International Congress of Americanists in Lima. We immediately began to structure the program and establish the precise limits of the points to be covered. We agreed that a portion must be devoted to urban centers, for example, and that areas related to other cultural expressions would not be dealt with.

As students of pre-Columbian art and architecture, we have long noted the lack of attention to Inca architecture. Although books on Inca culture are numerous, they almost always focus on the totality of cultural and artistic manifestations. Architecture finds an obligatory place in a few apologetic pages only because the most obvious, tangible, and important testimony remaining from that culture cannot be ignored.

It should also be noted that most of the authors who have dealt with Inca architecture are archaeologists, historians, or art historians. Indisputably qualified specialists in their own fields, they are sometimes unacquainted with the language and interpretation of the architectural historian. The language of the architectural historian would be dry and dull, however, without the strong input of anthropological interpretation. Hence the reason for the collaboration.

Recognized Peruvian scholars, like Emilio Harth-terré, Santiago Agurto, Fernando Belaunde Terry, Víctor Pimentel, José García Bryce, Héctor Velarde, Manuel Chávez Ballón, Oscar Ladrón de Guevara, and many others, have made such valuable contributions to the study of this material that it might seem pretentious for us to attempt such a project. Therefore we should note that we have been motivated by our deep admiration for the Andean peoples and for the architectural manifestations of a culture that left an indelible mark from Ecuador to Bolivia, as well as the respect we bear toward the city that boasts eight centuries of uninterrupted life and is, at the same time, the most admirable and stirring example of historical and architectural stratification in America: Cuzco.

This book has some of the defects and errors that might be expected from any study that undertakes for the first time to develop a single theme extensively and dedicates its entire content to material previously treated summarily with other aspects of Inca culture. The major defect of which we are aware is that much remains to be done before the work may be considered complete. Consequently this is not to be regarded as a definitive study. Quite the contrary, it is rather a new endeavor that seeks to stress the great value of architecture, an invitation to continue investigating and—above all—a call to preserve an irreplaceable patrimony that, deplorably, is being destroyed by neglect, indolence, ignorance, lack of funds, poorly planned tourism, and improvised restorations.

The completion of this book was possible thanks to the help that, in one form or another, we have received from persons and institutions. In the first place we must thank the Consejo de Desarrollo Científico y Humanístico of the Universidad Central de Venezuela. The most valuable scientific aid, however, was provided by John H. Rowe, who, displaying great friendship and collaboration, read the entire text and furnished observations and suggestions of incalculable value. The same was done by John V. Murra, whose knowledge of the Andean world was of great help to us.

We are also grateful to Craig Morris for assisting us with material referring to Huánuco Pampa; to the architects Teresa Gisbert and José de Mesa, who provided data and photos for Bolivia; to the Instituto Nacional de Cultura del Perú and José Correa Orbegoso, who provided us with plans and assistance; and to the Department of Anthropology of Yale University, which provided us with several photographs and plans from the Bingham Collection. Speaking of photographs, we must thank Abraham Guillén, who provided us with various photos from his fabulous archive, an inexhaustible source for all investigators who during the last fifty years have needed photographs of pre-Columbian and colonial Peru. Nor can we fail to acknowledge our gratitude for the help that, in various ways, we were given by José and Rosalía Matos Mar, Manuel Chávez Ballón, Emilio Harth-terré, Santiago Agurto, Alberto Rex González, Luis Guillermo Lumbreras, Fernando Cabieses, Hernán Crespo Toral, Ann Kendall, Elías Mujíca, Emma Velasco Cáceres, and Geraldine Byrne de Caballero.

The Spanish version of this book was first published by the Universidad Central de Venezuela in 1977. We are especially indebted to Patricia J. Lyon for her perceptive and dedicated translation and for extending her collaboration to include a meticulous revision of the bibliographic references. We greatly benefited from her incisive understanding of Andean culture. To all, our sincere gratitude.

Graziano Gasparini and Luise Margolies
Caracas, 1978

INCA ARCHITECTURE

1

Technical and Formal Antecedents

The descriptions of urban centers and Inca structures left to us by sixteenth-century chroniclers are frequently eyewitness accounts. Many of these writers knew and described various complexes that have since disappeared or have been badly damaged, altered, or ruined. The temples, dedicated to an idolatrous worship unacceptable to the fanatically religious Spanish of the Counter-Reformation, were destroyed and their cut stones used to build Catholic churches or the conquerors' dwellings. Nevertheless, numerous remains of Inca construction have survived to the present because of their location in remote or poorly known regions. Other structures are preserved because their sites were abandoned or because they were sometimes used by the Spanish for their own purposes. The city of Cuzco itself is a good example of cultural stratification. Other constructions managed to survive the destruction occasioned by the conquest and the long colonial period but suffered the deterioration caused by the elements, landslides, vegetation, prolonged abandonment, and human ignorance.

Some chroniclers and government inspectors, besides recounting the deeds of the conquest, gathering information for intended historical-chronological reconstruction of the Incas, and expatiating on their inspection trips, noted down the characteristics of the urban settlements and the constructions that they saw in the course of their travels through the highlands and along the coast. They observed building systems, urban plans, and house forms; they were astounded by the size of the stones and praised the perfect union of the blocks. In the sixteenth century the structures must have afforded a clearer understanding of the complex functions and uses for which they were intended, but we have little information on these points. While recent research in various urban complexes and architectural units has allowed us to establish formal and spatial characteristics, the determination of the use of many components of the small *tampu* or great administrative centers of Tawantinsuyu is more questionable and frequently hypothetical.[1] The variety of types of structures has impeded our ascertaining the activities that were carried out in their interior spaces. The typology of the storage structures, or *qollqa*, is more readily identifiable[2] than that of the domestic architecture, which is represented by a great diversity of rectangular compounds of varying dimensions. The variable number of buildings grouped together in the *kancha* system is easily identified on the basis of form. Nevertheless, it is difficult to determine which structures served as dwellings and what functions were assigned to those that did not. Buildings used as common facilities, such as the great halls, sometimes called *kallanka*, as well as the spaces used for temporary occupancy during fulfillment of the *mit'a* obligation, have given rise to differing functional interpretations. Archaeology and ethnography are contributing to the clarification and identification of use and have so far achieved results that are satisfactory though limited. The repetitive character of the form and function of Inca architecture is of considerable help to the historian of this material. This pattern is manifest in both those works modeled directly on the city of Cuzco[3] and those following the guidelines of a technique that was institutionalized and then applied throughout the conquered highlands. We should note at the outset that Inca architecture on the coast has a different character because it assimilated and adapted the experiences of the local cultures. It is also possible that limited construction techniques and the similarity of state guidelines for all the works may have contributed still more in establishing this repetitive character.

Although the chroniclers' observations on urbanism and architecture are only descriptive, they constitute a source of firsthand data that is of maximum utility in those cases where the same urban center or monument attracted the attention of several writers at different time periods. The descriptions are very heterogeneous, ranging from the briefest mention to long-winded, detailed reports. The data on the city of Cuzco or on the Qorikancha have been of great help in attempts at hypothetical reconstructions of the Inca capital and its principal temple.[4] The number of references may be increased by adding the accounts of nineteenth-century travelers to the earlier sources. The series of illustrations made in the last century by Squier and Wiener, as well as Angrand's admirable drawings,[5] provide a valuable contribution to the better understanding of many architectural works, documenting the state of preservation of many monuments more than a century ago and confirming, unhappily, that destruction and decay have not been arrested.

It goes without saying that the scientific investigations carried out in the last four decades provide the most reliable material for our true understanding of the Inca world.

Speculation abounds regarding the antiquity of some structures in Cuzco and its environs. Comparisons between the great stone blocks of Tiwanaku and Saqsaywaman, supposedly demonstrating their simultaneous existence during some alleged "megalithic" period, are entirely outdated since, more than thirty years ago, Rowe established the time period during which Inca architecture was produced.[6] Likewise, the antiquity of the Inca realm based on legends transmitted by professional "rememberers" has been disproved by irrefutable archaeological evidence. The irresistible territorial expansion of the Incas began with the victory of Pachakuti over the Chanka, achieved, according to Cabello Valboa, about 1438.[7] Before that date the frontiers of Inca territory must have been located near Cuzco. Thus it was about the middle of the fifteenth century when Pachakuti began the remodeling and reconstruction of the city of Cuzco and, in passing, the building activity that was continued by his successors, Thupa Inca and Wayna Qhapaq. We may suppose, therefore, that the Inca architecture related to the "Cuzco style" appeared suddenly and with characteristics different from those found in the Valley of the Huatanay River before the victory over the Chanka. It follows that Pachakuti can be considered the originator of the repetitive character of that architecture. The works executed after his death, first under Thupa Inca and then under Wayna Qhapaq, or from about 1478 to 1525, repeated and diffused the same characteristics of a standardized model. In the course of some eighty years (1450–1530) almost all the works related to the Cuzco style were completed. As far as Ecuador to the north and Bolivia to the south, the shape identifying the Inca presence —the trapezoid—was imposed as the seal of the conquering culture (fig. 1). If the chroniclers of the sixteenth century expressed their astonishment at the size of the stones and the perfect union of the blocks, today one is amazed by the incredible building activity undertaken in such a relatively short time. If one then adds to the architectural works all the stone-paved roads, bridges, irrigation canals, agricultural terraces, river canalizations, etc., it is clear that such results were possible only through the impressive

1. The identifying shape of the Incas–the trapezoid–marks the
   presence of the conquering culture from Ecuador to Bolivia.

organization of a system based on rigorous state control over the
rhythm and nature of the *mit'a*, or tributary labor.

Nevertheless the formal unity evident in the buildings the
Incas raised throughout the conquered highland regions could not
have developed without the artistic and technical influences of
other cultures. The Incas assimilated and developed these influences, finally transforming them into an independent expression.
The reports of the chroniclers and, especially, the questionnaires
of the government inspectors, reveal the great cultural mosaic that
existed before the Inca conquest. Earlier cultures with different
traditions and experiences surely provided new knowledge to the
Incas. Rowe has indicated how the urban solutions of the Chimú
kingdom involving great rectangular walled enclosures could have
influenced the rectangular design of the Inca living compounds.[8]
Also, expert artisans in metallurgy and ceramics were sent from
the coastal Chimú kingdom to work and teach in Cuzco and
other highland centers. The later tendency of the Incas to lay
out settlements in a grid plan with straight streets and rectangular
solutions could have derived from Chanchan and other coastal
centers and, more likely, from neighboring Pikillaqta and other
Wari sites.

Although it is clear that Tiwanaku has nothing to do with
Saqsaywaman from the artistic point of view,[9] we cannot fail to
note a continuity between Tiwanaku technique and form and
Inca architecture. Tiwanaku monuments are of unequaled technical and artistic quality. If the conquest of the Lake Titicaca
region, which includes Tiwanaku, was accomplished by Pachakuti
about 1450,[10] it is probable that the Inca planner would have been
impressed by the excellence of the Tiwanaku monuments. According to Bernabé Cobo, Pachakuti ordered his companions to
study that perfect technique, unknown to the Incas, with the
idea of applying it in the Cuzco region. It is probable, therefore,
that Tiwanaku architectural influence manifests itself in Inca
works through two channels of transmission: first, through the
introduction of high quality stoneworking; and second, through
the acceptance by the Incas of some elements of form and aesthetics that, although reworked into a new expression, allow one
to identify their origin.

7

Let us examine this argument. First we shall try to determine how the technique of fine stoneworking could have appeared in the constructions of the new Cuzco. Besides the supposed interest demonstrated by Pachakuti toward the Tiwanaku lithic technique, we now know that Lupaqa stoneworkers from Qollasuyu were in great demand and that their contribution possibly represented the fulfillment of the obligatory labor tribute, *mit'a*. The demand for Qolla artisans to work in stone is documented in the report of the government inspection trip made to the province of Chucuito by Garci Diez de San Miguel in 1567.[11] This report, which Murra considers "the earliest and most detailed sixteenth-century source on Qollasuyu that has been found so far . . . ,"[12] provides very valuable ethnohistorical data. Garci Diez questioned Pedro Cutinbo, previously governor of the principal *cacicazgo* of the Anansaya division of Chucuito, about the tribute rendered to the Incas. "Asked what tribute they gave to the Inca in Inca times and of what things, he said that they gave him three thousand Indians for war sometimes, other times they gave him all the Indians he wanted for making walls and houses. . . ."[13] The principal men of the Urinsaya division of Chucuito, when "asked what tribute and other things they gave to the Inca in Inca times, said that they gave the Inca Indians for war and Indians to make houses in Cuzco . . . and that they gave Indians for *mitimaes* in Jauja and in Llajapallanga and in La Banda in the province of Quito and in Vilcas and in Andahuailas and in Cuzco and in Yucay and in Caracara and Ayaviri and in Pacari and in Cochabamba and in the Chiriguanes and in Tarabuco and in Pocona and in Chocollabamba and in Topisa which is more than two hundred leagues from this province. . . ."[14] When the principal men of the Anansaya division of Acora "were asked what tribute this town [Acora] and its subjects paid and in what form in Inca times, they said that they gave many Indians for war and to make houses and cultivated fields in Cuzco . . . and Indians to put as *mitimaes* in many places. . . ."[15] Francisco Vilcacutipa, principal *cacique* of the Anansaya division of Ilave declared he was one hundred years old and had fought with Guainacaua (Wayna Qhapaq) against the Indians of Tumipampa. Regarding tribute, he said that "they gave him Indians for his *mitas* to build him

8

houses in Cuzco. . . .''[16] Also the principal Indians of Juli said that "they gave him . . . Indians for war . . . and other Indians to make him houses in Cuzco. . . .''[17] The synthesis of answers about tribute written by the inspector Garci Diez says "that all Indians in general declare that in Inca times they gave the Inca . . . all the Indians for war that he asked for and they say that for a war against those of Tomebamba which is in the district of Quito more than three hundred leagues from the aforementioned province [of Chucuito] they gave him six thousand Indians and that likewise they gave him Indian men and women and children for his service and to mine gold and silver and to build him houses in Cuzco. . . .''[18] That is, all the principal men of the Lupaqa of Qollasuyu declared that they gave Indians to build houses and walls in Cuzco.

There are other inspection reports. For example, during his inspection of Cajamarca in 1540, Cristóbal de Barrientos inquired about the tribute given by that province to the Inca state. According to his report, "the aforementioned lords of Caxamarca declared that some of them served the Inca with men of war, with maize and sheep [native camelids: llamas or alpacas] and woolen clothing and potatoes and *chuño* and coca and sandals and armaments: and that the men of war were given by some of the aforementioned divisions. And all served as declared above and that they gave these things in quantity.''[19] In Barrientos' report there is no mention of tribute in manpower for house construction in Cuzco. On the other hand, in the inspection that Juan de Mori and Hernando Alonso Malpartida made in 1549 in the province of the Chupacho, the principal men "said that four hundred Indian men and women remained continuously in Cuzco to make walls. . . .''[20]

Of fundamental importance for ethnohistory is the detailed report of the inspection carried out by Iñigo Ortiz de Zúñiga in 1562 in the province of León de Huánuco.[21] The inspector collected great quantities of information during his visit to the Chupacho, the Yacha, and the Cuzco *mitimaes*. It is interesting to note that among all those interviewed, only one, Cristóbal Xulca Condor, said that "they gave masons to build the Inca's houses in Cuzco and in other places where they were made and for this purpose they gave three Indians, one from each *pa-*

chaca. . . ."[22] All the rest reported that they gave men for war, to care for bridges, maintain roads, and man fortresses, and that they also gave carpenters, bearers, potters, weavers, etc. Xulca Condor states that besides sending masons to Cuzco they were also sent to other places where houses were being built, that is, to those sites where the Incas built *tampu* or administrative centers like the one at Huánuco Pampa. Thus we note that in Garci Diez's inspection of the Aymara-speaking Lupaqa, almost all of those interviewed stated that one of the services most frequently required to fulfill the *mit'a* obligation was the sending of stonemasons to build houses in Cuzco, whereas the reports of the inspections in other regions show rare use of local manpower on Cuzco constructions. This observation leads us to suppose that the stonemasons of Qollasuyu had not lost their reputation as expert artisans and, therefore, it is very possible that Qolla technical experience is present in the most representative buildings of Cuzco. There is, we should note, no other highland region with monuments comparable to those of Tiwanaku. Even at Chavín the quality of the lithic technique is inferior to Tiwanaku. Besides, the antiquity of Chavín eliminates any possible survival of craft experience among the ethnic groups whom the Incas found there in the course of their territorial expansion. In other words, those people from the north, like the Chupacho, who went to Cuzco to work on houses lacked a developed technical tradition in stoneworking. Their buildings were made of fieldstone as were those of the Wanka, the Chanka and, surely, the people of Cuzco themselves before Pachakuti.

There is, however, a problem in demonstrating the continuity of stonemasonry even among the Lupaqa masons who went in such great numbers to Cuzco. In fact, between the Tiwanaku monuments and the Inca constructions there lie several centuries without buildings of cut stone. Indeed there are no examples of that technique during the entire Late Intermediate Period. Therefore, the Lupaqa also had to learn stonecutting, since they were not building with quarried stone. It is, however, probable that the inhabitants of the Titicaca region were preferred because in that area there were several fine examples of the earlier domination of the art of stonemasonry. If they were so able in the past, they

3. Tiwanaku. In the base of the structure called the Akapana are stone blocks in the form of parallelopipeds with smooth faces and perfect joining. They are similar to those the Incas made much later for the Qorikancha.

could surely be so again to satisfy the exigencies of the Incas. Besides, they had the models in plain sight.

The base of the wall of the structure at Tiwanaku called the Akapana has cut and polished stone blocks very similar in shape to those that were used, much later, in the Qorikancha, with smooth rather than rounded faces (*fig. 3*). Courses of regular and interlocking stone blocks are known from various walls of the surviving monuments at Tiwanaku. If, as it appears, the technique of perfectly fitted stonework appeared suddenly in Cuzco, we may certainly consider the transmission of the experience of Tiwanaku to the ambitious works of the renovator Pachakuti.

Cieza de León as well as Cobo gathered accounts indicating the possible influence of Tiwanaku architecture on Inca construction. Cieza says that "he heard Indians state that the Incas made the great buildings of Cuzco on the basis of the form of the wall that is to be seen in this town: and they say still more: that the first Incas discussed making their court and seat of government in this Tiaguanaco."[23]

Nevertheless, it seems that the excellent stone finishing must

4. Pukara. Remains of a doorway with a double jamb and a double lintel.

have made more of an impression than the building techniques. In fact, the technique the Incas later developed for containing earthen platforms employed different solutions from that of Tiwanaku, with its great vertical monoliths sunk into the ground. Those evenly spaced monoliths insure the greater stability of the smaller stones set between them.

In addition to the interest shown toward stoneworking technique, which could have contributed to improving the coursing of the Cuzco walls, it is possible that some Tiwanaku formal elements may have served as "inspiration" in the formation and proliferation of the formal elements we now identify as Inca. Here we refer only, however, to architectonic-ornamental elements and not to volumetric aspects of the monumental complexes. In Inca architecture there appeared no structures similar to the Kalasasaya, the Akapana, the "semisubterranean temple" or Puma Punku, nor did the elaborate decoration of the Gateway of the Sun and other Tiwanaku monuments serve as a model. Possibly the different religious concepts of the Incas prevented the acceptance of foreign iconographic symbols.

The few formal components of Inca architecture also appeared already formed, thus complicating any effort to trace their development in the area where the Cuzco style originated. An architectural expression shunning ornamentation and identifying itself by a vigorous simplicity permits comparison with similar foreign forms. It is thus quite possible that the frequently repeated double jamb of Inca doorways may have its formal antecedents in the architecture of Qollasuyu. We need not look only at Tiwanaku, however, for there are much earlier examples at sites such as Chiripa and Pukara (*fig. 4*). There are more than twenty centuries between the Chiripa examples and those of the Cuzco style, which shows the continuity and popularity of certain formal elements. In the palace of Pilco Kayma, an Inca work in Qolla territory (Island of Titicaca in Lake Titicaca), is to be seen the most illustrative example of the Tiwanaku-Inca combination. The typical Tiwanaku double-jamb rectangular doorway takes on the Inca trapezoidal shape (*fig. 5*), retaining on both ends of the lintel the "stepped sign," which so frequently decorates the doors, windows, and niches of Tiwanaku monuments

13

5. The rectangular doorway with a double jamb and "stepped sign," typical of Tiwanaku, assimilates the Inca trapezoidal form, which results, during the occupation of the Qolla territory, in a shape combining the two experiences.

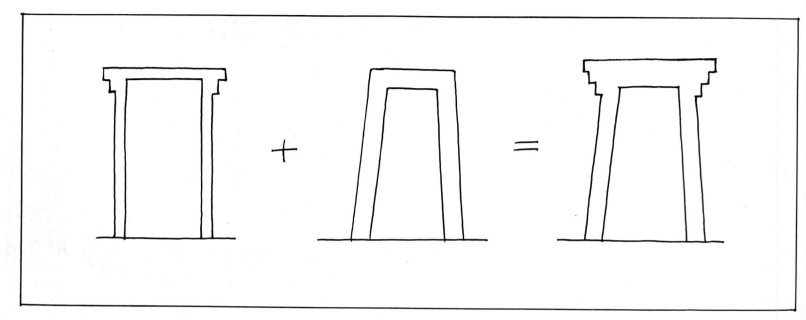

(*fig. 6*). The decorative use of niches, as seen at Puma Punku, could also have contributed to the decision to consider as ornamental an element that had been utilitarian since very early times.

The difference between Tiwanaku doorways and Inca ones lies in the shape: the former rectangular, the latter trapezoidal. It is hazardous to assert that the trapezoidal shape is of Inca origin. On the other hand, it can certainly be said that the Incas transformed this shape into their identifying mark. We need not indulge in new speculations and interpretations regarding the "stepped sign," which also appears frequently in works that are totally Inca (*fig. 7*). It doubtless had a constant and notable symbolic significance in the various cultures that used it before the Incas, but there is no reason to believe it was invented only once.

While it is hardly incumbent upon this work to present a detailed description and analysis of Tiwanaku, since we have a good and unusually complete photographic record of this complex, we have included several illustrations and limited ourselves to a brief commentary.

The documentation for this important center, which rose in the Early Intermediate Period, reaching its peak and beginning its

14

6. Tiwanaku. The "stepped sign" on one of the fragments of the doors of the Puma Punku complex.

7. Ollantaytambo. The "stepped sign" on an Inca structure.
8. Tiwanaku. The monoliths of the "balcony wall" that Squier called "the American Stonehenge."

decline in the Middle Horizon, is greater in quantity than in quality. Leaving aside the fantasies of Posnansky, the classification and sequences proposed by Bennett are also erroneous in many respects. These errors have not been corrected by the publications of Ponce Sanginés, who appears to be using the same units with different names.[24] In fact, our knowledge of the archaeology of Tiwanaku is minimal.

Not all the monuments of Tiwanaku have been studied. For example, there are only some unconvincing hypotheses about the Akapana and Puma Punku. The "semisubterranean temple" is the most thoroughly studied, and the most disfigured is the Kalasasaya; its famous "balcony wall," which Squier called "the American Stonehenge,"[25] has been violated and put to scorn by additions unrelated to any principle of restoration (*figs. 8, 9*). The entrance to the interior courtyard of the same monument has been reconstructed, resulting in a version that is pure fantasy (*figs. 10, 11*). The marks indicating the width of the doorway were evident on the top landing of the stairway, like a floorplan, but there was no further indication of the original appearance of the entrance and, hence, no justification for erecting it. Such meddling, rather than saving the monument, submits it to capricious and irresponsible deformation.

9. The unacceptable recent reconstruction of the "balcony wall" of the Kalasasaya. An example of how a monument can be distorted when treated without the slightest concept of archaeological restoration.

10. Tiwanaku. The entrance to the Kalasasaya in a 1910 photograph.
11. Tiwanaku. The present appearance of the same entrance.

12. Hypothetical reconstruction of the Puma Punku complex according to Ponce Sanginés.

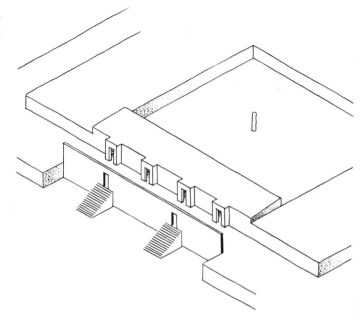

Puma Punku is the unit that has attracted the most attention from those visiting the ruins of Tiwanaku. The extraordinary size of its stones, the unrivaled technique used in the perforation of doors and windows in finely worked monolithic pieces, and the exquisite taste of the ornamentation suggest the importance the structure must have had and attest to the ability reached by the stonemason-artists. Various investigators have attempted to interpret the structures related to the stone platform that is still preserved, and d'Orbigny, Posnansky, Kiss, Torres de Kuljis, Mesa, and Ponce Sanginés have presented hypothetical reconstructions of the monument (figs. 12, 13).[26] Each of these is different and all rely on chroniclers and nineteenth-century travelers to support the proposed solutions. Nevertheless, it seems that these writers have paid little attention to the architectural characteristics repeated in other Tiwanaku monuments, which would have been useful for typological orientation. The idea of symmetry, for example, must have had a very precise value in composition: such, at least, is indicated by the Kantatayta stone, which seems to be a model, the entrance to the "semisubterranean temple" placed on the long axis, and the entrance to the Kalasasaya, also on the same axis. These axes, besides establishing a symmetrical division, set up definite visual guides. In the Kalasasaya, for example, the stairway, the doorway, and the monolith in the interior courtyard form a sequence governed by the symmetrical axis. Thus it is strange that in Ponce Sanginés's proposed reconstruction, the two axes of the stairways have no continuity and run into a transverse wall. Another observation not taken into account in the proposed reconstructions is the form of the stairways. The three stairways presently known, the one leading down into the "semisubterranean temple," the entrance stairway to the Kalasasaya, and the stairway on the west side of that monument (fig. 14), all adopt the same solution; they are all set into the earthen platform rather than abutting the retaining wall. That is, the continuity of the retaining wall is interrupted to leave space for the stairs. It is, therefore, possible that the most frequent "type" of Tiwanaku stairway was inset and not abutting as proposed by Ponce Sanginés.

There are other reconstruction hypotheses that could be

13. Different hypothetical reconstructions of the Puma Punku stone platform: *A.* Base plan with the four segments   *B.* According to d'Orbigny   *C.* Kiss's complex proposal   *D.* Torres de Kuljis's version   *E.* According to the Mesas   *F.* Ponce Sanginés's proposed solution.

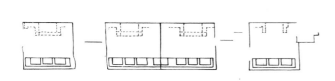

A

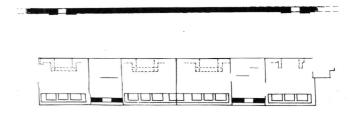

B

C

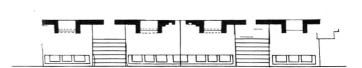

D

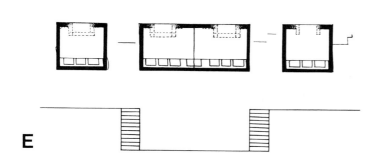

E

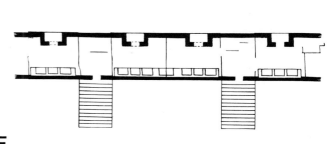

F

14. Tiwanaku. The three known stairways are the same type, set
into the earthen platform rather than abutting the retaining wall.
The stairway on the west side of the Kalasasaya, the one leading
down into the "semisubterranean temple," and the entrance to
the Kalasasaya present the same solution.

15. Tiwanaku. Block 11 of Puma Punku segment 3, in a 1906
    photograph.

16. Tiwanaku. In the foreground the blocks of segment 2; in the background segment 1.

suggested for the Puma Punku complex. All must remain in the realm of speculation, however, until the completion of archaeological research that does not aspire simply to "restore" the monument.

The remains of stone portals found at Puma Punku suggest that the doorway was cut in a monolithic piece preserving the threshold at the bottom. It is likely that the so-called Gateway of the Sun (*fig. 17*) also had a threshold at the base of the doorway forming a compact whole with the rest of the portal (*fig. 18*). On the basis of old photographs showing the breaks in the lower part of the jambs or doorposts (*figs. 19, 20, 21*), it is possible to determine the thickness of the threshold. Those breaks were filled with cement when the door was set in its present location (*fig. 22*). Today the door appears as if its monolithic form were that of an inverted U. Cieza, referring to the doors at Puma Punku, says that the portal and its jambs and thresholds were a single piece.[27] The Gateway of the Sun is now located in the northwest corner of the Kalasasaya, but the general opinion is that this was not its original placement. In the course of the work done in 1908 to set it upright, no vestige of foundations appeared.

In summary, we suggest that the architecture of Tiwanaku may have impressed the Inca conquerors, at the same time inspiring the intention to develop fine stonemasonry, which perhaps was not practiced prior to Pachakuti. It should be emphasized that the quality of finish on masonry has no chronological implications. Although all the finely finished structures in the Cuzco area seem to belong to the period of Pachakuti or later, the rustic *pirca* technique was the most commonly used in all times and places. As will be seen later, the hierarchy of quality is closely linked to the use and meaning of the structure.

17. Tiwanaku. The Gateway of the Sun.

18. *Left,* the Gateway of the Sun as we know it today. *Right,* as it could have been originally, that is, with a stone threshold at the base of the doorway.

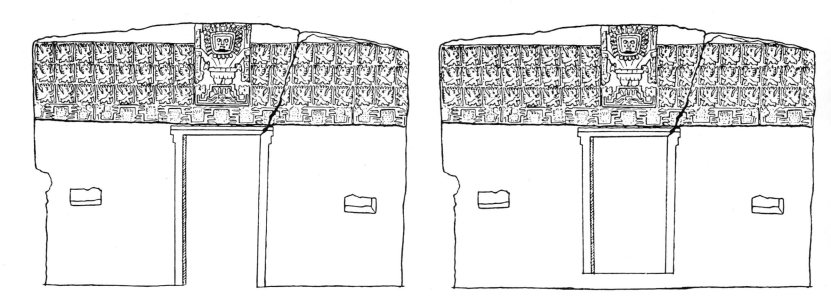

19. Tiwanaku. The front of the Gateway of the Sun in a photograph taken before 1908, the year in which it was excavated.

20. Tiwanaku. The back of the stone portal before 1908.

21. Tiwanaku. 1908. A rare graphic document showing the actual
    excavation of the monument. No stones appeared that might have
    represented a foundation to bear the weight of the monolithic
    portal. On the two lower extremes of the doorway, the break
    of the possible threshold can be clearly seen. The accompanying

drawing, made with a transparent overlay from the photograph,
suggests the possible thickness of the threshold.

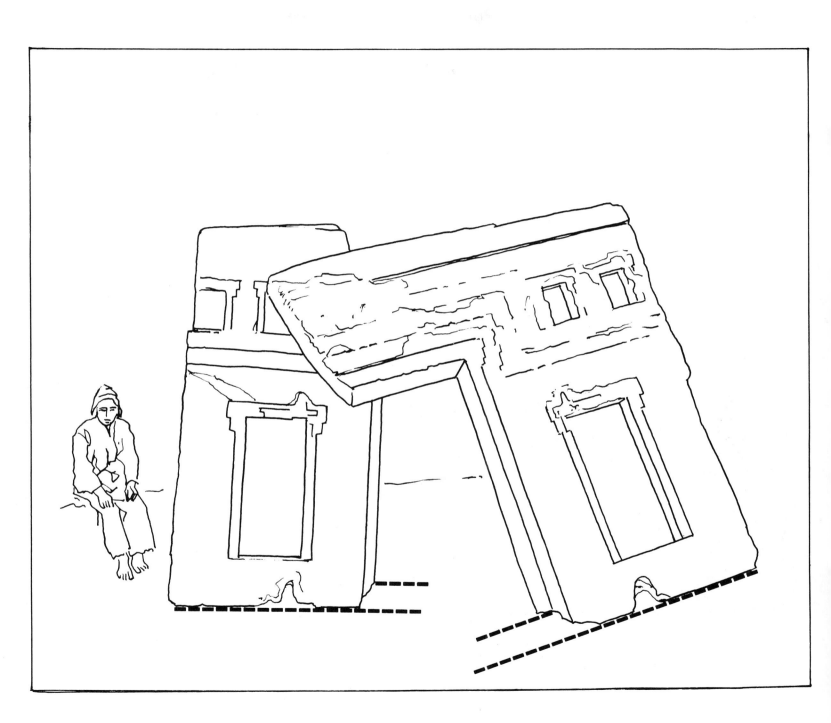

22. Tiwanaku. Photograph of the Gateway of the Sun taken about 1910. The base of the left side of the doorway still shows the break of the possible threshold. The right-hand base was already filled with cement.

23. Tiwanaku. The central figure of the Gateway of the Sun.

2

Urban Settlements

Wari

Edward Lanning asserts that there were no cities in southern Peru from the fall of Wari and Tiwanaku around the end of Epoch 2 of the Middle Horizon, about 800 A.D., until the rebuilding of Cuzco initiated toward the middle of the fifteenth century. During this period of almost seven hundred years, the population seems to have lived in small rural villages.[1] Tiwanaku, Pukara, and Wari are the three southern cities that were formed in the Early Intermediate Period and two of them, Tiwanaku and Wari, exercised a cultural influence that reached north to Cajamarca and the Piura Valley. Pukara, according to Lanning, had a shorter life, not more than two hundred years.[2] This suggests that the height of Pukara culture occurred at least five hundred years before classic Tiwanaku.

There are different opinions and interpretations regarding the great similarity that exists between the various artistic manifestations of Wari and Tiwanaku, but everyone recognizes the resemblance. This likeness has resulted in calling Wari works "Expansive Tiahuanaco," "Peruvian Tiahuanaco," and "Tiahuanacoid." According to Lumbreras, although "Tiahuanacoid" was interpreted by some as meaning "derived from," it actually meant "similar to" or "in the form of," at the same time as "not Tiahuanaco."[3] Actually, the continuing acceptance of so vague a definition as "it is and it isn't" is very little help and promotes confusion. Cultural transmission always results in derivation and similarity, while differences arise from interpretations removed from the cultural centers of original production. Also, anyone intentionally copying or imitating elements from another culture almost always produces a different result because of differences in world view. What is important is to indicate the origin of the transmitting sources and to explain the reason for the acceptance and diffusion of their creations in areas that previously had different expressions and manifestations. The example of popular architecture in the colonial eighteenth century in southern Peru may serve to explain a phenomenon with similar implications.[4]

Dorothy Menzel, avoiding earlier terminology, is very clear when she says, referring to the representational themes of Wari

35

ceramics, "[they] resemble so closely mythical representations at Tiahuanaco in Bolivia, particularly those carved in relief on the Monolithic Gateway or incised on some of the larger statues, that a close connection is obvious."[5] The Mesas, however, do not seem to share the valuable contribution that Menzel has made to the study of Wari culture, and accuse her of being "responsible for causing the term Expansive Tiahuanaco to be replaced by Wari, with the subsequent confusion."[6] We do not consider it to be "confusion," but rather a compromise proposed in order to clarify the contacts that, even while recognizing the pan-Andean prestige that Tiwanaku may have had, must reveal the lack of Tiwanaku remains in the "tiwanacoid" production area. It is thus clear that the importance of the phenomenon lies in the contacts, in the transmission channels, in the common religious beliefs, and in the fact that, according to Menzel, no whole or fragmentary specimen of pottery belonging to ordinary-sized Tiwanaku vessels has been found to the north and west of the departments of Arequipa and Puno.[7]

For William H. Isbell, "The kind of contact suggested seems to be only that resulting from intensive trade in consumer items or raw materials, and possibly through priest-missionaries who converted the populations visited to their new religion, totally erasing the local culture."[8] Dorothy Menzel rejects military conquest and suggests a purely religious movement reinforced by "a very small number of individuals [who] actually traveled between the area of Ayacucho and Huari and the source of the new ideas. Such traveling as did occur may have been done either by missionaries from the Tiahuanaco center or by men from the area of Ayacucho and Huari who learned the new religion abroad and brought it home."[9]

The cultural connections between Tiwanaku and Wari and the acceptance of the Tiwanaku religion in Wari are still largely areas of conjecture. Conquest with a strong religious stimulus is possible, but it is unclear how a very small number of priest-missionaries could prompt a sudden mastery of stoneworking equal in quality to that of Tiwanaku, as in the subterranean chambers of the Cheqo Wasi sector at Wari (*figs. 25, 26*). The technique differs not at all from that of the tombs found at Ti-

25. Site of Wari, Ayacucho. Two views of a subterranean chamber in the Cheqo Wasi sector.

wanaku. There is no doubt that the new religion and its images were widely accepted and spread, as shown by the pottery that appears at Wari without antecedents. It is also possible that, besides iconographic transmission through religious channels, there may have been the transmission of experiences by coercion. In addition to acceptance, there seems to have been an imposition of standards of form and technique in some areas of construction. If not, there is no explanation for the fact that high quality stonework is limited to the subterranean chambers and did not appear in the other buildings. It is hard to accept that the superior technique was concentrated only on the tombs of important persons. Tombs of the priest-missionaries, perhaps? Actually, the hypothesis explaining the similarities and contacts via traveling missionary activity is not very satisfactory or convincing. The conquest was probably not as peaceful as some would have it. On Tiwanaku pottery there frequently appears a warrior holding an enemy trophy head in one hand. Perhaps a missionary?

Continuing investigations have revealed more and more marked differences between Tiwanaku and Wari iconography, so that the derivation of Wari religion from Tiwanaku, as Dorothy

37

26. Site of Wari, Ayacucho. Another subterranean chamber in the Cheqo Wasi sector.

27. Quinua, Ayacucho. Wari sculpture beside the church.
28. Site of Wari, Ayacucho. Wari sculptures.

Menzel proposed some years ago, is increasingly problematical.

Wari stone sculpture does not bear comparison with that of Tiwanaku, although they are closely related as shown by the statue beside the church at Quinua near Ayacucho (*fig. 27*). Wari sculpture does not display the same mastery of the craft as Tiwanaku, and thus could be judged "peripheral" to the center of cultural radiation, which would explain why it exhibits an expression typical of undeveloped artistic phases that are late recipients of the formal transmitted elements (*fig. 28*). It may be, however, that the porous stone used for the Wari sculptures would not permit fine work. On the other hand, this same porosity is very well suited to receiving a clay plaster on which fine painted or incised drawings could be executed. Obviously it is the green stone miniatures, such as those found at Pikillaqta, that show the finest quality of Wari sculpture.

The site of the city of Wari is very extensive. There is not yet a study of its urban characteristics or a plan to help understand the complex. The construction remains (*figs. 29, 30*) have fieldstone walls varying in height from six to twelve meters and freestanding walls up to a hundred meters long, which seem to have served to enclose sectors of the city. The monumental character of the complex can be explained on the basis of the requirements of a new power center. It is hard to tell if the urban form of Tiwanaku exerted any influence on the planning of Wari. One shared feature is their use of right angles. On the other hand, the building technique is very rustic at Wari and unrelated to the quality of the Tiwanaku monuments. All Wari urban centers used uncut fieldstones in their buildings, a technique very similar to that used in many villages during the Late Intermediate Period.

Wari expansion reached Piura in the north and Ocoña in the south. "Great complexes of storage buildings at Wiraqocha Pampa, near Huamachuco, and Pikillaqta, in the lower Cuzco Valley, provide additional evidence of Huari rule and suggest a centralized administration such as the Incas established later, with similar concern for the collection and redistribution of goods and supplies."[10] The long high walls of Wiraqocha Pampa and Pikillaqta are similar in construction to those of Wari, with fieldstone laid in clay and an absence of windows. In both centers the plan

39

is regular, with straight streets meeting at right angles (*fig. 31*). This similarity permits us to infer that in the Middle Horizon there were also intrusive and compulsory establishments like those of the Inca state.[11] Rowe also has noted that "The existence of these ... complexes provides evidence that the expansion of Huari was not simply a matter of peaceful penetration or raiding. It represents the formation of an imperial state with a well organized administration."[12]

General features of the period of Wari expansion include "the introduction of great planned settlements with enclosure walls having few entrances and no windows forming houses around courts, with streets, and almost always associated with very high walls made of irregular stones and clay"[13] (*figs. 32, 33*).

Rowe and Lanning note the presence of possible Wari influence on the planning of the great northern cities.[14] The large walled enclosures of the city of Chanchan repeat criteria of the Wari centers. The difference lies primarily in a change of building materials, from stones to very large adobes made of sandy earth. Although antecedents are known, the concept of sectors and units enclosed by high walls may have been spread by the Wari culture. Consequently, even if the Inca rectangular compounds derive from a Chimú loan, they may also be related to the characteristics of planned sites of the Wari culture like Pikillaqta. At Tiwanaku, in contrast, walls that form enclosures are retaining walls, as in the Kalasasaya and the "semisubterranean temple."

In the preceding chapter we noted some aspects of Tiwanaku architecture with the intention of indicating probable formal influences of that culture on some features of Inca architecture. In this chapter, our brief introduction to the "urbanizing" nature of Wari culture is of interest for a better understanding of Inca urban centers. The Wari expansion brought about the appearance of several centers that continued during the Late Intermediate Period, mainly on the central and north coasts. During that period, from 1000 A.D. to the rise of the Incas, occurred the urban phenomenon of Chanchan, the largest city built in ancient Peru. On the central coast, Pachacamac and Cajamarquilla were other

30. Site of Wari, Ayacucho. Wall in the "capilla" sector.

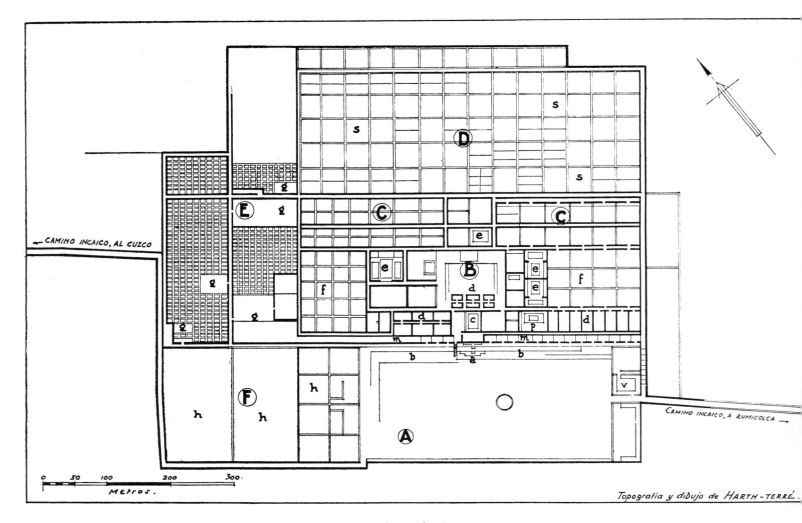

← CAMINO INCAICO, AL CUZCO

CAMINO INCAICO, A RUMICOLCA →

0 50 100 200 300·
Metros.

Topografía y dibujo de HARTH-TERRÉ.

large urban establishments.[15] In contrast, after the fall of Tiwanaku and Wari, urban centers did not appear in the south until the rebuilding of Cuzco; life was essentially rural and Art did not again produce works comparable to Tiwanaku.

Cuzco

What were the characteristics of the human groupings surrounding Cuzco during that long interregnum of almost seven hundred years? In the central highlands between the Pampas and

42

32. Pikillaqta. A sector of this ancient Wari center in a 1934 photograph.
33. Pikillaqta. Detail of wall construction.

Apurímac rivers was the area of the Chanka culture, whose expansionist aspirations were crushed in the attempt to conquer Cuzco. The rout of the Chanka and the conquest of their territory initiated the uncontrollable expansion of the Incas. Further north, in the region of the Mantaro River, lay the seat of the Wanka. This was the Andean group that, in an effort to free themselves from the domination of Cuzco, a power they saw as usurping and exploitative, most fully collaborated with the Spanish in their fight against the Incas.[16] Chanka and Wanka centers had much in common: closely packed house groups forming compact nuclei on mountainsides or hilltops. Several small villages are known, as well as settlements of considerable size like the Wanka site of Tunan Marka, one of the most extensive complexes. There are remains of both circular and rectangular buildings, with the former predominating. We shall discuss these in the following chapter dealing with houses. There is still much research to be done on the characteristics of the central highlands, that culture area which bordered the Cuzco region. We can already state without question, however, that Wanka and Chanka settlements had no influence on the urban design of the Cuzco seen by the Spanish when they reached that city in 1533. It is also probable that the Qolla, Lupaqa, and other post-Tiwanaku lacustrine kingdoms had more influence on the political organization of Cuzco, based on a dual division of power, than on its urban forms. Rowe notes that many signs of "tiwanacoid" or Wari influence have been found in the Cuzco region, but much still remains to be discovered.[17]

The beginnings of Cuzco, from the viewpoint of its urban appearance, must not have been very different from those of any highland village like the Wanka and Chanka ones. The great change took place in the second half of the fifteenth century, during and after the reign of Pachakuti, the Inca reformer and conqueror. With Pachakuti, the small domain of Cuzco was transformed into an empire and the village of clay and straw into a planned capital with stone buildings. How can we explain so sudden and radical a change in the urban design adopted by the Incas? What are the outside experiences that influenced the new planning criteria applied by the Incas? Everything suggests that the sudden appearance of the new urban design criteria that replaced those of the primitive village, of new spatial concepts like the *kancha* compounds, of new techniques, and of the high quality in stone finishing are due to contacts that the Incas experienced as they established relations with other cultures during their territorial expansion. The monumentality of Wari, the grid plan of neighboring Pikillaqta, the compounds of Chanchan, and the fine stonework of Tiwanaku probably contributed to the formation of the Inca expression. Pachakuti must have been a good observer with a talent for planning. He conceived and developed the "idea" of the new capital, taking into account those experiences he considered valid and useful. According to Betanzos, "thus it was done; Inca Yupanqui [Pachakuti] planned the city and ordered clay figures made just as he thought to build and make it. . . ."[18] He adds that the Inca ordered the village of Cuzco evacuated to lay out the plan of the new city.[19] So was born the city the Spaniards saw.

Although Cuzco was burned and partly destroyed in 1535, during the Inca attempt to reconquer the city, surely the worst damage to the original urban plan was caused by the distribution of house lots, begun by the conquerors in 1534, within the area built by the Incas. Thus, the plaza of Cusipata was broken up and other sectors of the city altered, opening and closing off streets. In spite of these changes, part of the complex of streets and plazas of the Inca zone of Cuzco is still identifiable by its plan as part of the original work, persisting into today's urban context. The modifications imposed during the colonial period were generally adapted to the plan of the Inca capital. It is a good example of the persistence of a plan, as well as the oldest document of Pachakuti's design. The five short descriptions of Cuzco before the 1535 burning are very brief and do not provide any fundamental contribution to our understanding of the "idea" of the city. Obviously the vision that greeted the first Spaniards to enter Cuzco was not properly transmitted. Certainly the results of recent investigations have permitted the elaboration of a more precise "idea." What was lost in the 1535 fire was mainly wooden structural members and thatched roofs. In contrast, the plan, which can still be experienced and is the urban element most resistant to obliteration, has been the irreplaceable foundation for urban research.

The city was located between the Tullumayo and Huatanay rivers, which run from northwest to southeast. It had the form of a puma, the head coinciding with the "fortress" of Saqsaywaman and the tail with the confluence of the two rivers, a place that still bears the name of Pumac Chupan, meaning puma's tail. Rowe indicates that the space between the front and back legs corresponds to the plaza of Haucaypata. He further observes that, between being adapted to the topography and to the puma shape, the layout of the streets produced not one square block and a great variety of sizes.[20] Although there are a great many straight streets, which suggests the intention of imposing principles of order on the urban context, it is hard to know whether the intention was to achieve a rectangular layout. The blocks were probably of different sizes not only because of the difficulties

35. Plan of Inca Cuzco: 1. Kiswarkancha   2. Cuyusmanco
    3. Coracora   4. Cassana   5. Amarukancha   6. Aqllawasi
    7. Pucamarka   8. Qorikancha   9. Hatunkancha   10. Yacha
    Wasi.

36. Cuzco. Aerial view of the city. The zone delimited by the
    Huatanay and Tullumayo rivers is clearly visible.

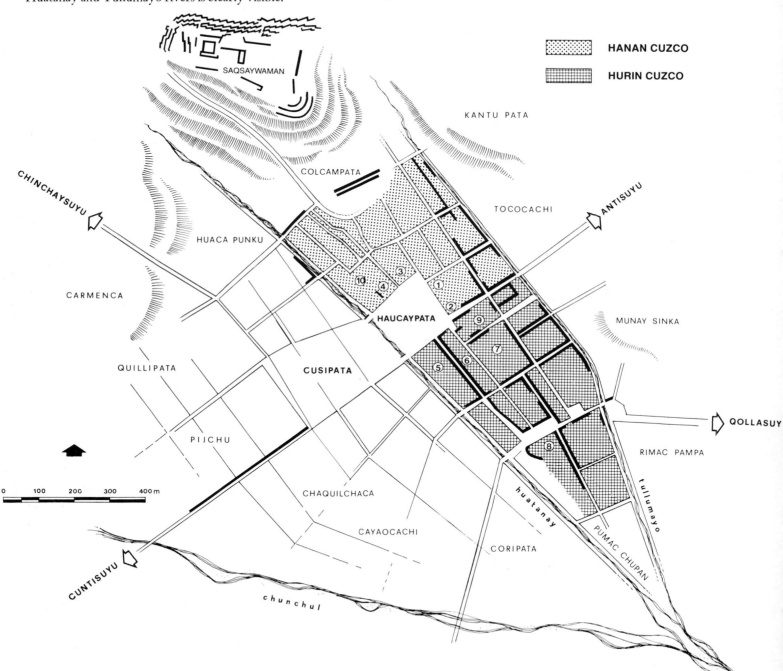

HANAN CUZCO

HURIN CUZCO

SAQSAYWAMAN

KANTU PATA

COLCAMPATA

CHINCHAYSUYU

TOCOCACHI

ANTISUYU

HUACA PUNKU

CARMENCA

MUNAY SINKA

HAUCAYPATA

QUILLIPATA

CUSIPATA

QOLLASUY

PIJCHU

RIMAC PAMPA

CHAQUILCHACA

CUNTISUYU

CAYAOCACHI

CORIPATA

huatanay

tullumayo

PUMAC CHUPAN

chunchul

0   100   200   300   400 m

46

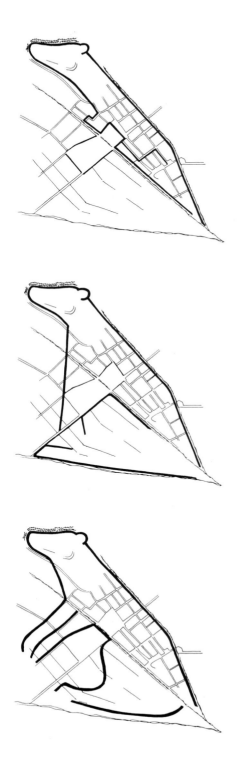

posed by the topography but also because they had to satisfy the
requirements and rank of the different *panaqa*. The puma shape
suggested by Rowe (*fig. 37*) lies between the Huatanay and Tullumayo rivers, the sacred precinct of the city, which has a relatively small area. If Pachakuti thought of Cuzco as the capital for
the future, it seems improbable that he would not have provided
areas for further expansion. We must not forget that the city
planned by Pachakuti was only some sixty or seventy years old
when the Spanish arrived—very young for a city conceived with
long-term ambitions. That it was a city with a view toward
growth is shown by Garcilaso when he states, "to the west of the
[Huatanay] river the Inca Kings had not built; there were only
the surrounding outlying settlements that we mentioned. That
site was set aside so that the succeeding Kings might build their
houses. . . ."[21] This logical anticipation of future expansion shows
that Pachakuti provided for the growth of Cuzco in his planning
program. We are faced, then, with the following question: Was
the puma shape planned to take into account the size the entire
city would reach, or was it limited to the "sacred" zone? Stating
the problem this way suggests other alternatives to the puma shape
suggested by Rowe. The size of Rowe's puma is small for the
great city conceived by Pachakuti, the growth of which was pre-
maturely ended by the conquest.

South of the Huatanay and Tullumayo rivers is another, the
Chunchulmayo, which also flows into the Huatanay. Its name
means "gut river," in other words, the puma's belly. Using this
fact, we can try another version of the puma shape while leaving
the head and tail in the same place. What changes is the feline's
position; instead of a long, crouching puma, we now have a
seated puma like the one published by Squier and the sculpture
found at Wari (*fig. 38*). This proposed shape considerably en-
larges the area of the city. Another possible shape might be a
puma lying on its side, which would also increase the urban area.

Between the Huatanay and Tullumayo rivers were the
temples, royal palaces, and palaces of the preceding royal *ayllu*
under the care of the various *panaqa*. But the urban area must
have been much larger and composed of several districts, which
are listed by Garcilaso.[22] According to Rowe, some of these names

38. Two depictions of a seated puma: an engraving from Squier
   and a Wari sculpture

refer to habitation sites, while others appear to be "place names added for symmetry."[23] Nonetheless, the city seen by the Spaniards before the 1535 fire must have given the impression of a very dense urban complex, otherwise the author of *Noticia del Perú*, who saw the city at the same time as Pedro Sancho, would not have said that the Huatanay is a "river that passes through the city. . . ."[24] He then adds, "This was a great city, extensive, with many outlying settlements where many lords had houses; it was very compact with fine buildings."[25] Pedro Sancho says that "there are many houses on the hillsides and others below on the plain."[26] From Saqsaywaman he saw "surrounding the city many houses to a quarter of a league, half a league, and a league, and in the valley in the middle there are more than a hundred thousand houses surrounded by hills. . . ," including storehouses.[27] The number of inhabitants surprised Pedro Pizarro: "It was astonishing to see the people in Cuzco. . . ."[28] In 1553 Cristóbal de Molina says that the city "was very large and very populous, with large buildings and outlying settlements. When the Spanish first entered it there was a great quantity of people, it was probably a town of more than forty thousand citizens in the city alone, with suburbs and outlying settlements around Cuzco to 10 or 12 leagues, I believe there must have been 200,000 Indians, because it was the most populous of all these kingdoms."[29]

The fact that the author of the *Noticia* indicated that the river passed "through the city" suggests that the terracing to the southwest of the Huatanay must have appeared to be an integral part of the inhabited area. Furthermore, the houses of the hillside districts, those in the suburbs, and the great number of *qollqa* to the southeast of the city must have enlivened the planned urban area and had great visual impact. Sancho estimated the number of houses in the valley as a hundred thousand and Cristóbal de Molina the number of its inhabitants as forty thousand citizens, which would be equivalent to a population of 200,000. Inflated figures like these, surely derived from approximations based on initial impressions, help little today in formulating a more accurate estimate.

Noted modern researchers state that the Incas were not city builders and that their activity in this area is not to be compared

39. Cuzco. Oblique view of the city. In the foreground is the complex of Saqsaywaman, then the Inca urban zone delimited by the Tullumayo and Huatanay rivers and terminating in Pumac Chupan.

40. Cuzco. View of the city from the complex of Saqsaywaman.
41. On the streets of Cuzco

with that of the Middle Horizon and Late Intermediate Period cultures.[30] Hardoy notes that it is easier to establish criteria for defining Teotihuacán, Tenochtitlán, the Maya centers, or Chanchan as cities than it is to do so for Cuzco.[31] There are disagreements regarding the specifications necessary to define a city. The number of inhabitants, density of dwellings, variety of activities, social heterogeneity, permanence of location, concentration of supplies, the nature of the urban structure, and many other factors have been considered indispensable for differentiating city life from rural life. These are concepts that help increase the precision of our generalized idea of the city and that are probably not all applicable to the "idea" of city that Pachakuti had in mind when he rebuilt Cuzco. Pachakuti may have thought more of building

42. Cuzco. The street of Hatunrumiyoq.

a physical representation of power rather than a "city" in the sense of our definitions. In other words, more than a city, he wanted to build a capital. The Cuzco-capital as an Inca urban form was the monumental embodiment of the "seat of power." Cuzco was unquestionably the seat of political and religious power, so it can also be considered a ceremonial center. If Cuzco could achieve this high prestige and urban rank in no more than seven decades, we may, without worrying about all the definitional postulates, consider it a city. And as a city it was defined by Pedro Sancho, the first person to write about Cuzco.

The appearance of Cuzco must have been quite uniform, since all the houses, temples, and palaces had only one story and all the roofs were thatched. And since there was no structure like the Mexican pyramids to impose its mass and stand out as an important visual reference point, the relationship of the volumes of the buildings was even. It was the topography that gave movement to the urban texture, and the great open space produced by the union of the two plazas, Haucaypata and Cusipata (*figs. 43, 44*) was clearly the most important urban episode in the city. Thus, the location of greatest prestige within the urban setting was established on the basis of space rather than volume.

The plaza of Haucaypata was surrounded by edifices of great symbolic and representative significance within the Inca politico-religious structure. These buildings are dealt with in chapter 4 in an attempt to capture the architectural form of these great halls called *kallanka*.

On the north side of the plaza were the buildings related to the "lineage" of the Inca Wiraqocha, Kiswarkancha and Cuyusmanco. The relationship between the two names is not clear. Nevertheless, several accounts say that the Temple of Wiraqocha, "the creator," was in Kiswarkancha, and that Cuyusmanco, situated where the Cathedral now stands, was the building where the Spaniards took refuge during the rebellion of Manco Inca. On the northwest side of the plaza there were two other great halls, Cassana and Coracora. Remains of the walls of Cassana, robbed of their original dignity, today decorate the interior of a restaurant. According to Garcilaso, the great hall of Cassana had an

43. Cuzco. Possible dimensions of the plazas of 1. Haucaypata and
2. Cusipata. *Inca period: a.* Cuyusmanco   *b.* Kiswarkancha
c. Coracora   *d.* Cassana   *e.* Yacha Wasi   *f.* Amarukancha
g. Aqllawasi   *h.* Hatunkancha   *i.* Pucamarka.   *Colonial period:*
A. Cathedral   *B.* Triunfo   *C.* Sagrada Familia   *D.* La
Compañía   *E.* La Merced   *F.* San Francisco   *G.* House of
Garcilaso.

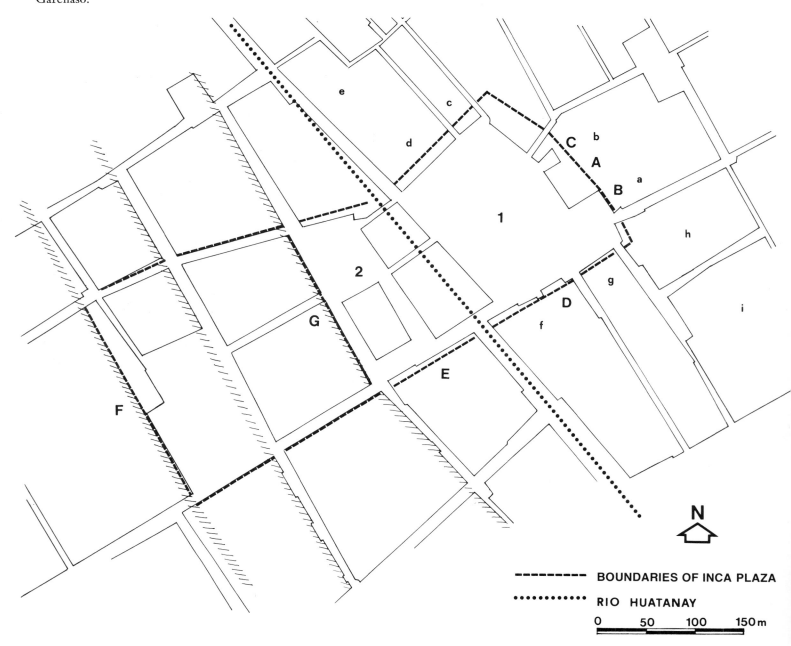

N

- - - - - - - - BOUNDARIES OF INCA PLAZA

• • • • • • • • • RIO HUATANAY

0   50   100   150m

44. Hypothetical perspective of the two plazas separated by the Huatanay River: 1. Plaza of Haucaypata 2. Plaza of Cusipata A. Present site of the church of San Francisco B. Present site of the house of Garcilaso.

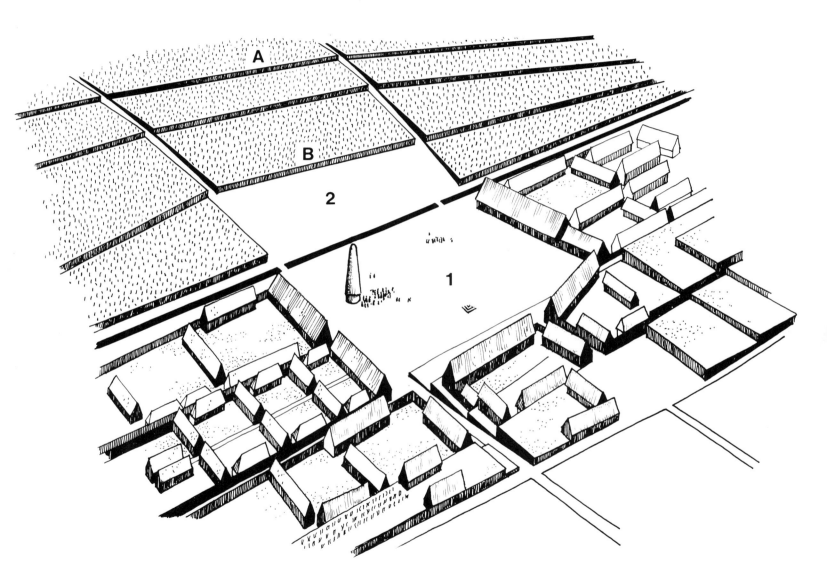

enormous roofed space; it could shelter three thousand people and was the site of the Franciscan monastery. Behind this great hall were the buildings of the Yacha Wasi, the school of the nobles. The existence of that school is somewhat dubious; Garcilaso is the only author to mention this establishment, which is probably the fruit of his imagination.[32] He wanted to give Cuzco a "university" to exalt it and, at the same time, to impress his European readers. On the southeast side of the plaza, where the Spanish built the church of the Compañía, one of the outstanding examples of Latin American colonial architecture, was the Amarukancha compound belonging to the "lineage" of Wayna Qhapaq. Separated from it by the present Callejón de Loreto was the Aqllawasi compound, where the convent of Santa Catalina is today. And still further along was the great Hatunkancha enclosure. To the south, where the Huatanay River runs, there were no buildings because the plaza of Haucaypata meets the plaza of Cusipata. This great urban space was broken up and parceled out starting in 1534, when the distribution of house lots to the Spaniards began. According to Garcilaso, in the plaza of Haucaypata, opposite the Amarukancha, there was a building with a circular plan, "a most beautiful circular tower"[33] with a high conical roof, which must have been the *sunturwasi*. Its form established the only vertical element within a horizontal complex.

There are no reliable data on the size of the plaza of Cusipata. It is customarily considered to have extended from the Huatanay River to the present site of the monastery of San Francisco. Nevertheless, it is possible that the plaza devoted to public activities may not have extended beyond the area today defined by the house of Garcilaso. From there on there were certainly cultivated terraces or "maize fields" according to the information provided by the documents on the distribution of house lots.

Betanzos says that Pachakuti ordered the canalization of the Huatanay and Tullumayo rivers before undertaking the rebuilding of the city, to avoid possible flooding in the urban area.[34] This magnificent engineering work, visible until a few decades ago (*fig. 45*), continues to accomplish its drainage functions beneath the present streets of the city. Beyond the town of San

45. Cuzco. Canalization of the Huatanay River at Saphi Street in the center of the city. The photograph is from 1934 when the river was open. Today the entire course of the river through the city is covered.

Sebastián, some ten kilometers from Cuzco, portions of the Huatanay canalization are still preserved (*fig. 46*). According to the author of the *Noticia del Perú*, the Huatanay River, "from where it rises, for more than twenty leagues down that valley, where there are many settlements, is paved on the bottom and the vertical sides of its bed are faced with dressed stone, something never [before] seen nor heard."[35]

Although some writers consider the Huatanay River to have been the dividing line between upper (*hanan*) and lower (*hurin*) Cuzco, it is certain that the symbolic division of the urban area in two halves passed through the plaza in a northwest-southeast direction along the axis that coincides with the roads that lead to Cuntisuyu and Antisuyu. The moiety system, or dual division, was widespread throughout the Andes and is still operating in many highland communities. *Hanansaya* and *hurinsaya* were the terms in *runasimi*, the official language of the Incas. In *haqaru*, the language of the Aymara and other ethnic groups of Qollasuyu, these divisions were called *alasaa* and *masaa*. The upper, or *hanan*, moiety has been considered of higher prestige than the lower, or *hurin*. There is no general agreement on the origin of this dual organization. It has neither place nor date of birth in the Andean world. It almost seems as though it had always existed, from the moment that the people cultivating the high-altitude lands realized they could not survive without certain controls and contacts with the lowlands and vice versa. The dual division could have originated from the need to establish contact between the different ecological zones. The two parts meet in a symbolically agreeable place, *tinkuy*, which does not exclude rivalries because the division was associated with very clear-cut power structures.

In Cuzco the division was more sophisticated. The two halves were identified with the same number of "lineages" or royal clans; the oldest were those of *hurin* Cuzco, succeeded by those of *hanan* Cuzco. Recent speculations have posited possible rivalries between *hurin* and *hanan*; the possibility that two kings governed simultaneously, one in each moiety; the "doubling" of rulers to "make up" the dynastic sequence; and other suggestions related to aspects of the dual division that are less than clear.

For the present study, the moiety system of *hanan* and *hurin*

46. Cuzco. Remains of the canalization work on the Huatanay
    River some 10 kilometers from the city.

is of interest primarily because it is related to the urban organization of Cuzco as well as other settlements founded by the Incas.

From Cuzco four highways led to the four divisions (Chinchaysuyu, Antisuyu, Qollasuyu, Cuntisuyu) that together formed the four-part empire, Tawantinsuyu (*fig. 47*). The location of the four *suyu* does not derive from a division based on the four cardinal points, but rather one that probably permitted control over economy and manpower in ecologically similar zones. Each of the four main highways led to a different *suyu*. In the administrative centers and *tampu* founded by the Incas all along the *qhapaq-ñan*, the highway passed through each settlement and continued on to the next. In Cuzco, on the other hand, the roads

47. Cuzco. Relationship between the cardinal points and the departure of the four highways toward the four *suyu*.

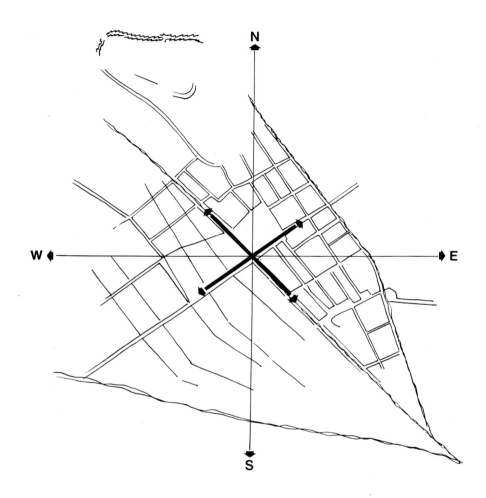

originated as well as terminated. That is, the roads not only depart from Cuzco, but also arrive at the capital city from the entire empire, somewhat like the saying that all roads lead to Rome.

Besides the three principal temples dedicated respectively to the Sun (Qorikancha), Wiraqocha creator (Kiswarkancha), and Thunder (Pucamarka), Cuzco contained a great number of sacred places distributed along imaginary lines, or *ceque*, which radiated out from Qorikancha.[36] In this work we do not intend to deal with the complex significance and organization of the *ceque* because we do not think that their religious and calendric implications caused any changes in the urban layout, even though they were related to the system of spatial organization of Cuzco.

The austerity of the walls and lack of ornamentation on all the façades must have unified the appearance of the Cuzco streets and limited visual experiences. In addition to the great urban space formed by Haucaypata and Cusipata, there were other lesser plazas, and there was considerable regularity in the layout of the straight, narrow streets. Pedro Sancho noted that the streets were made "crossing at right angles, very straight, all paved with stone and in the middle of each one runs a water channel lined with stone. Their defect is in being narrow, since only a single horse-man can go on one side of the channel and another on the other side."[37] In spite of the narrow streets, the layout of Cuzco met the requirements of the Spaniards, who felt no need to introduce substantial changes in the original plan. Reducing the great open space of Haucaypata-Cusipata was the principal modification to the plan. The two combined plazas were undoubtedly considered excessively large for the early sixteenth-century European mind. In Spanish cities of medieval structure with Muslim influence, such as Cordoba, Seville, Toledo, and more, narrow streets abound and plazas are few and small. In Madrid itself, the Plaza Mayor was begun in 1617, and it was necessary to demolish a densely built-up area of appropriate size to acquire the requisite space. In other words, the large European plazas are an urban phenomenon prompted by the Renaissance. It is not surprising, therefore, that the first house-lot distributions entailed the parti-tioning of the great Inca plaza. The size of the plaza of Huánuco Pampa must have been considered equally excessive, since it was in that open space that the Spanish began to build their houses.

In summary, Cuzco's urban form, dignified with "monu-ments" because of its condition as capital and seat of government, may be considered the resultant of the sum of various experiences adapted to the needs of the politico-religious structure. The fact that some of these experiences represented loans from Chanchan, Wari, or Tiwanaku did not prevent the formation of a unified expression that is identified as Inca in the morphological analysis of the city.

One is constantly struck by the fact that we have no plan

48. Cuzco. Callejón de Loreto. The wall belongs to the ancient
    Aqllawasi compound.

of Cuzco made during the three centuries of the colonial period. While various plans of Mexico City, Lima, Puebla, and many other cities are known, it is strange that Cuzco, a city of such importance in the history of the conquest and colonial period, is represented by none. We know of graphic versions of México-Tenochtitlán that provide an idea of what the Aztec capital was like in the sixteenth century. Such a document would be highly useful to us today in our attempts to understand the Inca plan, but Cuzco is instead represented by numerous descriptions, which seem to have inspired several "bird's-eye" views of the city. The latter are actually totally fantastic European interpretations based on a formula probably originated in Italy by Ramusio about 1556 and then repeated for three centuries. This widely disseminated "scene never seen" first appeared in the book of Antoine du Pinet (1564) as a double-page xylograph crowned by an Italian legend reading: "Il Cuscho città principale della provincia del Peru" (*fig. 49*). The city is perfectly rectangular; the straight streets have water channels in the center; there is a city wall with towers and a great domed "palace." In the plaza some men are bearing a litter with a personage identified as *Atabalipa* (Atawallpa).[38] While trying to portray the straight streets with the water channels, walls, and palaces mentioned in the chroniclers' descriptions, this image of the imaginary city, placed in a conventional landscape, is also adapted to the ideas of order and regularity typical of Renaissance writers. What is curious is that this view, with minor variations, is repeated for three centuries. Some seventeenth-century engraver apparently wanted to introduce new data gathered from other sources, and so, in 1673, the illustration in Dapper's book (*fig. 50*) embellishes the hills with some little towers that might well be either *qollqa, sucanka*, or *chullpa*.[39]

In the British Museum in London there is a plan that is striking for its unrealistic Hippodamic regularity (*fig. 51*). Although the size of Cusipata recalls the Inca period dimensions, the plan seems to be from the end of the seventeenth or early in the eighteenth century.

Not until 1821 do we find the first plan of Cuzco, mapped by Pentland with instruments.

The chroniclers frequently note that Cuzco served as a

49. Imaginary view of Cuzco according to a European engraver. It was published in 1564 in the book of Antoine du Pinet.

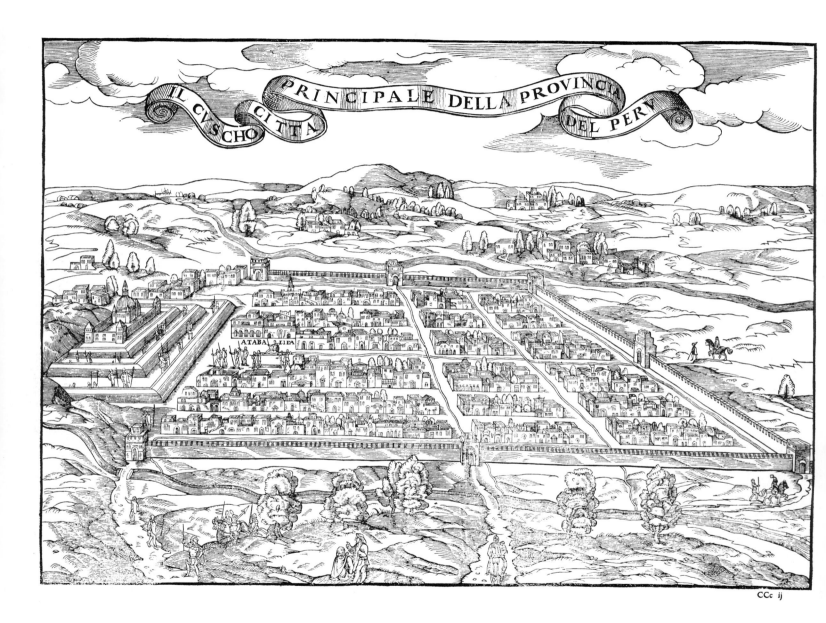

50. The same scheme of urban regularity is repeated in Dapper's
    engraving, published in 1673.

CUSCO

51. Plan of Cuzco in the British Museum, London, showing an angular regularity that never existed.

model for building new settlements. Nevertheless, if the plans of the settlements built along the *qhapaq-ñan* and those in the central Inca zone are compared with the plan of Cuzco, one immediately sees that there is no formal similarity between them. The city of Cuzco was used as a model for the functional, ritual, and symbolic elements of the system but not for its shape and physical appearance. No other urban center repeated the puma shape. The meaning and function of the forms, rather than the forms themselves, were taken from the model. For example, near a new settlement there was often a hill named Huanacauri, after the name of the famous hill-sanctuary near Cuzco. And in founding a new settlement, an area with topography reminiscent of Cuzco was sought. Referring to the administrative center of Tumipampa, Cieza says, "The buildings of Tumebamba are situated at the confluence of two small rivers . . . ,"[40] seeking perhaps, a setting similar to Cuzco, which is situated at the confluence of the Tullumayo and Huatanay rivers. Bonavia has noted that there is no similarity between Inkawasi in the Lunahuaná Valley and Cuzco when the plans are compared, "but if one begins to analyze the component elements of the city, one by one, forgetting their location within the general plan, then we do indeed find that they coincide."[41] In fact, independent of the actual form of the settlements, patterns identifiable with the Cuzco model are repeated with considerable insistence. The division into *hanan* and *hurin*, the presence of a principal and secondary plaza, the great halls (*kallanka*) on the plaza, the *usnu*, the *inkawasi*, the *aqllawasi*, the temple of the sun, and the storehouses, or *qollqa*, are found in almost all the best-preserved administrative centers, and they were probably not absent in those settlements of which only a few ruins remain.

Nevertheless, there are certain elements that differentiate the populated centers in, at least, four territorially defined regions of Tawantinsuyu: (1) the central region near Cuzco; (2) the territory along the *qhapaq-ñan* toward Quito; (3) the coastal region; (4) the Qollasuyu region. For example, in the administrative centers and *tampu* along the *qhapaq-ñan* the quantity of *qollqa* is much greater than that found in the settlements of the central region, perhaps because the administrative centers had a more artificial urban character and depended largely on the storehouses for survival. In contrast, in the central region *qollqa* are few because the nature of the settlement is firmer and more deeply rooted. There was a greater equilibrium between production, consumption, and stable population than there was in the administrative centers that had a floating and transient population. In the Pisaq area it is startling to see the great number of agricultural terraces and cultivated fields compared to the few structures considered to be for storage. At the administrative center of Huánuco Pampa, in contrast, the five hundred *qollqa* suggest completely different patterns of supply and organization.

The *kallanka*, those great halls so frequently mentioned by the chroniclers, appear more consistently in the settlements along the *qhapaq-ñan* than in the central region, that is, where there was movement of great masses of people, armies or *mitimaes*, that needed temporary shelter and provisioning. On the coast, mainly in the north, existing settlements were used, which, although different urbanistically and architectonically from Inca settlements, served to control the region and, at the same time, to give the impression of "respect" toward structures of the subject cities.

The Incas were not city builders. With the exception of Cuzco, the known examples tend to give the impression of a limited urban concept. The lack of cities may, however, result from a planned policy of territorial control. It seems that the nucleus of control was more important than the great city. Otherwise it would be hard to explain how a presumed lack of urban concept could exist together with such a broad concept of territorial control.

Settlements of the central region

In the environs of Cuzco there exists a vast quantity of archaeological remains testifying to the building activity of the Incas. Most of these remains do not appear to be population centers and will, therefore, not be treated in this chapter. We find it more interesting to analyze the forms and criteria involved in the formation of the inhabited centers. Although the settlements of the central region are very different from one another, a great ability to adapt to and take advantage of the difficult topography is evident in all of them. Considering the complexes of Machu Picchu, Patallaqta, Pisaq, Ollantaytambo and others, one is struck by the way in which steepness is dominated, ruggedness is used, and irregularities are turned to advantage. There was no site, however difficult, that could discourage the determination to build once it was considered to be convenient.

Ollantaytambo, in the Urubamba Valley, is a unique case of regular planning laid out on a grid (*figs. 52, 53*). The complex has a trapezoidal shape, like the niches, and as a consequence the longitudinal streets fan out toward the Urubamba River. This peculiarity does not, however, detract from the almost rectangular character, since the cross streets are parallel to one another. The grid forms several blocks, each of which contains two indepen-

52. Plan of the Ollantaytambo complex: 1. Plaza of Maniaraki
2. Religious sector   3. Residential sector with regular plan.

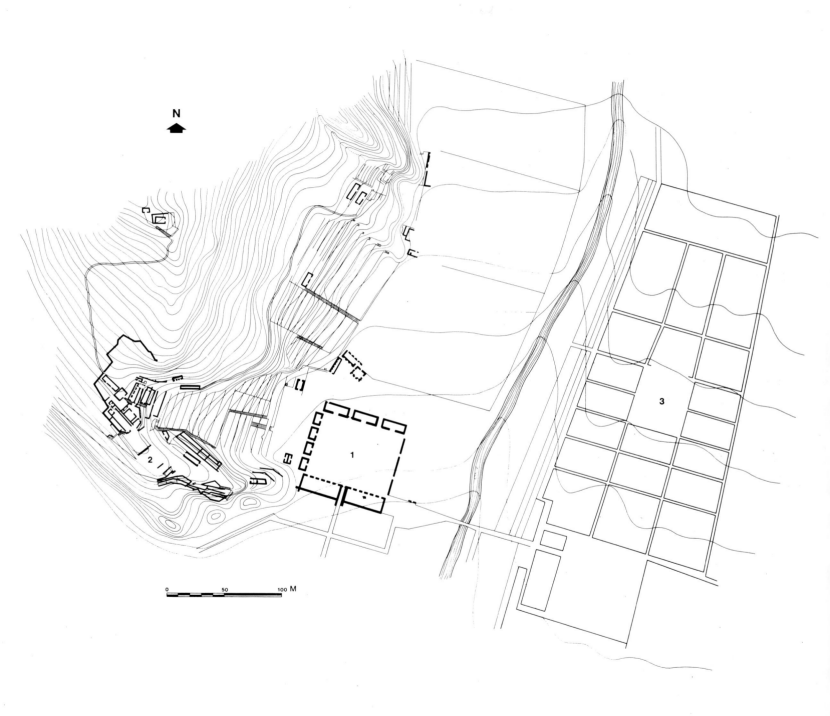

53. Ollantaytambo. Plan of the residential sector drafted by Hiram
    Bingham in 1911.

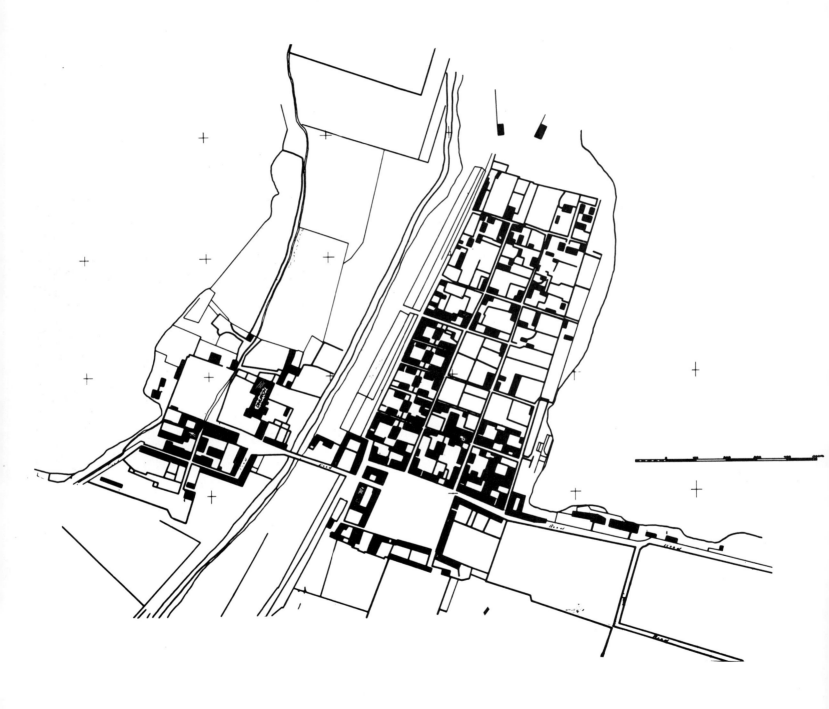

dent habitation units. In the following chapter this type of unit will be discussed when we deal with the *kancha*.

In the center of the trapezoidal complex there was a plaza the size of two blocks that in colonial times was occupied by other buildings that eliminated that space. Water channels were built down the longitudinal streets, taking advantage of the slight slope toward the river and passing in front of the doors of each habitation unit—an elementary solution, but extremely efficient in providing each *kancha* with fresh, clean water (*fig. 55*). Today, as in Inca times, one can see a person appear in a doorway to fill a pitcher with water from the canal.

The grid-plan zone was never completed. The entire Ollantaytambo complex was under construction at the moment of the conquest. Thus, we are dealing with an urban concept of the final years of the Inca empire, and the regularity of the plan may possibly suggest a groping toward increasingly precise and rigid principles of order. By pure chance, in Europe, at the same time, Renaissance urbanism was turning toward certain principles of order, which were then applied in the colonial cities founded by Spain in America.

The Patakancha River divides the Ollantaytambo complex in two: on the east the regular planned sector and on the west the representative-ceremonial sector with various buildings around three sides of the plaza of Maniaraki. The adobe walls with large doorways and monolithic lintels (*fig. 57*) are clear evidence of the importance of this space. From the plaza one passes on to the so-called fortress zone and the Temple of the Sun, located high on a steep rocky scarp, where there are impressive remains of incomplete stone structures. Enormous stones were apparently brought from the Cachikata quarry located on the hill across the Urubamba River.

All the architecture of Ollantaytambo exhibits a quality and proportions that prevent our considering it to be an agricultural center inhabited by a farming population. Yet, again, the difficulty in attributing functions to the buildings is due to the lack of archaeological research.

In many respects the plan of Chucuito (*figs. 61, 62*) is quite similar to that of Ollantaytambo. This ancient and important seat

55. Ollantaytambo. A channel in the longitudinal streets still supplies
 fresh water to the occupants of the *kancha*.

56. Ollantaytambo. Recent additions to buildings have not altered the regularity of the original plan.

57. Ollantaytambo. Houses of adobe with stone lintels on the Plaza of Maniaraki. 1951 photograph.

58. Ollantaytambo. Entrance to the "religious zone."

59. Ollantaytambo. Double-jamb doorway on the Plaza of Maniaraki.

60. Ollantaytambo. Uncompleted structures on the heights of the "religious zone." Monoliths up to six meters long were used.

61. Chucuito. Aerial view of the town. This is not an oblique view,
as can be seen from the roofs of the two churches; in an oblique
view the walls would be visible.

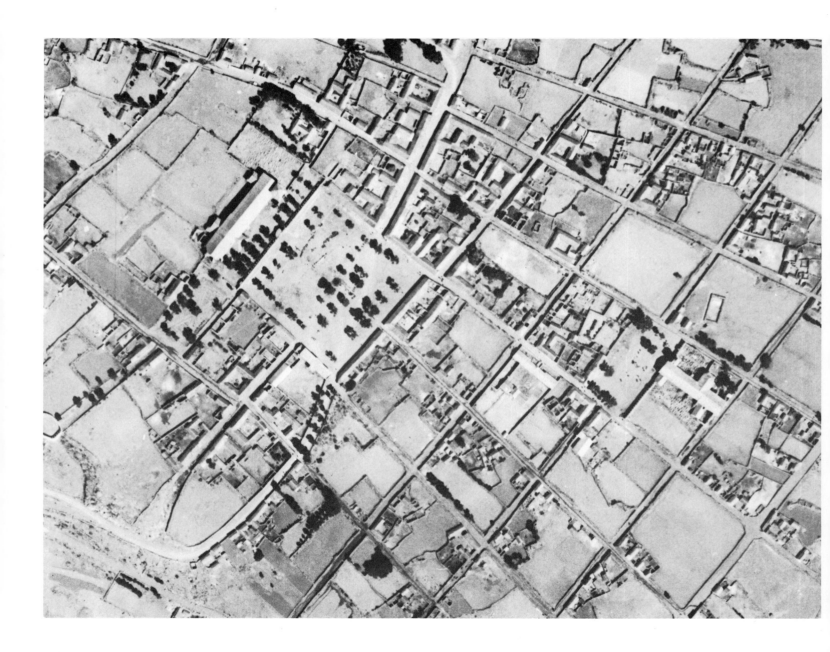

62. Possible plan of Chucuito under Inca domination. The two plazas are conspicuous.

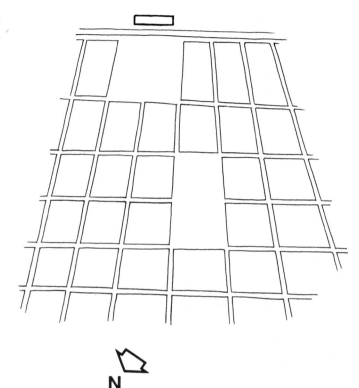

N

of the Lupaqa on the shore of Lake Titicaca also has long streets fanning out as they lead down toward the lake, while the cross streets are parallel. At its southern extreme is a large plaza that surely had a temple at its end in the same place where the sixteenth-century Catholic church stands today. As in Ollantaytambo there is another plaza the size of two blocks, further north toward the lake. Another Catholic church was built in this plaza, which probably belonged to the *masaa* division of the community.

There are no documents to confirm the Inca origin of this plan. Nevertheless, Chucuito may have been remodeled under the Incas, considering how important the entire lake region, and especially the subjection of Chucuito, was to the Inca economy. The planning of Chucuito may also have been earlier than that of Ollantaytambo, so the latter could be interpreted as an improved version. In any case, the idea of Spanish influence on this type of radial plan can be discarded for two reasons: first, because we know the plan of Ollantaytambo is Inca, and second, because the many examples of Spanish planning never depart from a rigidly squared grid plan. None of them is similar to Ollantaytambo and Chucuito.

Between Ollantaytambo and Machu Picchu lies the valley of the Cusichaca River, a tributary of the Urubamba. In this area are many Inca ruins, among which the planned complex of Patallaqta is outstanding. Hiram Bingham drafted the first plan of this settlement in 1911 (*fig. 63*). Ann Kendall has recently completed a detailed study of the architectural characteristics of the settlement and of the clusters of ruins in the entire Cusichaca area.[42] According to Kendall, Patallaqta was an important administrative center surrounded by satellite groups with functions related to the principal center. It has 112 buildings forming *kancha* of different sizes. In order to derive maximum use from the valley land, Patallaqta was located on a hillside on a large, artificially leveled platform skillfully adapted to the topography. Twelve terraces repeat the undulating form of the hill on the side of the valley, descending like a flight of steps to the level farmlands (*fig. 64*). The road crosses the entire built-up area and passes through the two plazas, of which the larger is trapezoidal and the smaller rectangular. Apparently the majority of the

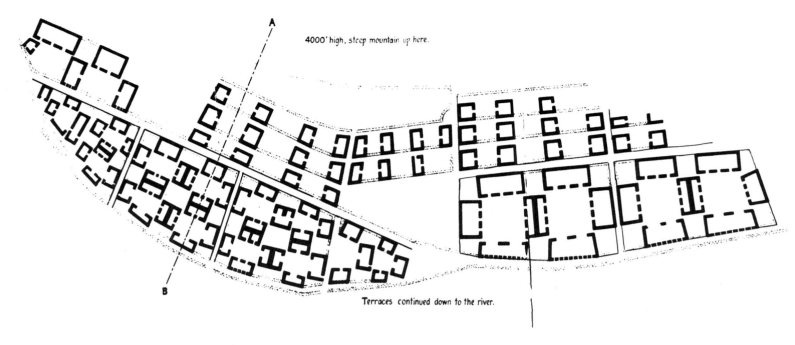

A

4000' high, steep mountain up here.

B

Terraces continued down to the river.

78

63. Patallaqta. Plan of the settlement drafted by Hiram Bingham in 1911.

64. Patallaqta. Panoramic view of the Patallaqta complex, Cusichaca.

buildings were residences or work areas. The different sizes of the houses and *kancha* suggest a difference in rank among the occupants. There are no buildings that suggest ceremonial use; the masonry is uniform and no structure stands out.

The entire Urubamba region, from Pisaq to Machu Picchu, contains a quantity of ceremonial centers, small residential clusters, and great expanses of terraces that, as in Pisaq, seem to be extensive agricultural works (*fig. 65*). The function, or functions, of Pisaq are difficult to determine from observing its multiple structural groupings, walls, gateways on the roads, circular towers, tombs, residential areas, and shrines. The structures exhibit a great variety of techniques, from finely finished walls like those of the *intiwatana* group (*fig. 66*) to *pirca*. None of the chroniclers mentions this place and no special studies have yet been made of it. Rowe has suggested that Pisaq was Pachakuti's private property.[43]

The original function of the constellation of centers near Machu Picchu remains a mystery. We know very little of Inkaraqay, Chachabamba, Sayacmarka, Puyupatamarka (*fig. 67*), Wiñay Wayna, and Choquesuysuy in spite of the work of Hiram Bingham and Paul Fejos.[44] These are complexes with few houses accommodating a maximum of fifty people. The complexes are well built and the houses have high stone gables. Wiñay Wayna, for example, comprises a group of no more than twenty rooms, a series of "baths" stepped down the hillside, a semicircular tower, and a great many terraces. The complex suggests a combination of profane and sacred architecture, an exalted rural village, and a ceremonial center for the worship of water and earth, but never an urban center (*figs. 68–71*).

Machu Picchu (*fig. 72*) is the Inca settlement about which we have the most interpretations and publications. Since its discovery by Hiram Bingham in 1911, its popularity has continually increased until it has become one of the most visited monumental complexes of Latin America. The beauty of this center lies in the aggregate rather than in the individual structures taken separately. The whole is more impressive than the detail, not so much for the spectacular beauty of the site as for the integration of architecture and environment. The fame of Machu Picchu has led

65. Pisaq. Some of the agricultural terraces.
66. Pisaq. View of the "Intiwatana."

67. Puyupatamarka. View of the complex. In the foreground, a
    sequence of "baths."

68. Wiñay Wayna. The house group with high gables.

69. Wiñay Wayna. Interior of one of the houses.

70. Wiñay Wayna. Wall between the two sectors of the settlement.

71. Wiñay Wayna. View of the sector with residential characteristics.

72. Machu Picchu. Panoramic view of the urban settlement.

73. Machu Picchu. The complex seen from the peak of Huayna Picchu.

to an abundant literature describing the ruins, starting with Bingham's publication of the results of his research and interpretations, many of which are still valid.[45] Attempts to explain the function of this complex have given rise to the most varied attributions. Machu Picchu has been considered a fortified city, an outpost toward the tropical forest, a frontier citadel, a sanctuary dedicated to the moon, a work center for women supervised by *aqllakuna* or "Chosen Women," a great and select ceremonial center, the last refuge of the Incas, and the seat of the "University of Idolatry" of which Fray Antonio de la Calancha spoke.

Thoughts of fortifications and military use are evoked by the solid stone construction and the inaccessible location. Nevertheless, the walls and abysses hinder access more than providing

74. Machu Picchu. The high quality of the construction. Wall with the "door of the serpents."

a defensive vantage against enemy attacks; they seem to guard a site into which not everyone might enter. Several of the buildings of Machu Picchu seem to have a religious and ceremonial quality, although dwellings are also numerous. Valcárcel considers that Machu Picchu was essentially sacred.[46] It is clear that its functions cannot be understood by persisting in the use of names like "mausoleum," "house of the *ñusta*," "watchtower," "*intiwatana*,"

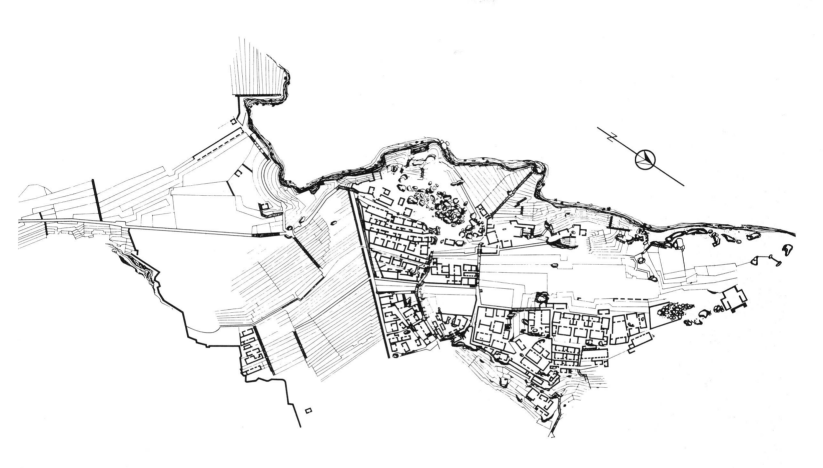

"jails," and so forth. The high quality of the masonry in all the buildings is one striking aspect of Machu Picchu that cannot be questioned (*fig. 74*), as is the lack of adobe construction. These features might indicate a ceremonial center of great importance, but, besides noting that stones are abundant there while earth is relatively scarce, we might also suggest that the state wanted to show the neighboring peoples its firm intention to remain in the area. We must not forget that there are only two or three months of good weather at Machu Picchu; the rest of the year is cold and wet and not conducive to easy living. A stable state installation could mean security to the farmers of the five fertile valleys near Machu Picchu.[47]

The settlement, surely built with *mit'a* labor, repeats Cuzco characteristics in its architecture and in the plan (*fig. 75*), which

76. Machu Picchu. The so-called Temple of the Three Windows.

is divided into *hanan* and *hurin*. Entrance to the complex is on the south end of the residential zone and leads into the *hanan* sector. Besides this entrance, and following the outside of the wall, a broad stairway descends to where there might have been an entrance to the *hurin* sector.

Machu Picchu contains various buildings displaying excellent stonework. The Temple of the Three Windows (*fig. 76*) (there were really five, but the two end windows are blind), the Temple of the Altar, the Watchtower (*fig. 77*), the Mausoleum, and the Intiwatana (*fig. 79*) are all works revealing the versatility, skill, and aesthetic sense of the stonemasons. It is evident that the entire complex was planned; the precise separation between the agricultural and residential zones (*fig. 78*), the location of the plaza to divide *hanan* from *hurin* (*fig. 80*), and the clever use of irregularities in the land for placing buildings show that the plan was deliberate and not achieved by chance.

But Machu Picchu does not have the characteristics of a city. Its two hundred buildings allow for a population of about one thousand inhabitants, a very small unit to merit this urban rank.

The town of Chinchero, in the province of Urubamba, lies at 3,762 meters above sea level. According to Alcina, Chinchero was a small courtly establishment set in a rural environment and was probably founded by Thupa Inca as a place for rest and relaxation. It is hard to say if it had a truly urban structure. Nevertheless, the archaeological site of Chinchero "has an extraordinary area, including not only the entire old center of the settlement, but also a considerable surrounding zone, especially to the north and northeast. Most of the modern settlement is located on top of the Inca site, so that the Christian church, for example, rests on a building which is not yet identified but is apparently of the very first importance judging by the style of the walls that are still preserved. . . ."[48] Another historical detail reported by Alcina is that Chinchero was destroyed in 1540 by Manco Inca II. Evidence of burned roofs appeared frequently in the excavations.

The complex shows a studied planning in both the location of the buildings and the use of the irregular terrain. We find here, also, two large plazas. The larger, today called Capellanpampa, is

91

79. Machu Picchu. Southwest side. Terraces that culminate in the "Intiwatana" platform.
80. Machu Picchu. The central zone with the plaza that separates the *hurin* and *hanan* sectors.

81. Chinchero. The buildings on the south side of the great plaza
   now called Capellanpampa.

some 60 meters wide by 114 long and has three buildings lined up
along the south side (*fig. 81*). We will discuss their architectural
characteristics in chapter 4. On the north and west the plaza has
a free and open view and communicates with the bottom of the
ravine via a series of terraces. The other plaza, the one belonging
to the present town, has two levels: the higher is the present
atrium of the church, and the lower is the plaza proper (*fig. 82*).
The division is emphasized by a retaining wall adorned with
twelve great niches and topped by a series of fifty-eight cap-
stones (*fig. 83*). It is most probable that this wall was built during
the colonial period, in the second half of the sixteenth century, at
the time of the construction of the Catholic church. In fact, in
the sector of the church atrium there were several Inca houses
that had been filled in with earth to provide an open space on a
higher level. It is also possible that part of the niched wall was
original and that some of those niches were doors later closed up
as a result of the filling.

To the east of town there is a great expanse of terraces that,
while following the contours of the land, form great angular
amphitheaters (*fig. 84*). The masonry of the retaining walls of
these terraces is the same quality as that of the buildings. The
entire zone has, besides, a quantity of great carved rocks that may
have been *wak'a* and *usnu*.

82. Chinchero. The second plaza is the present town plaza. In the background is the niched retaining wall defining the two levels: the upper corresponds to the atrium of the church; the lower is the marketplace.

83. Chinchero. The niched wall separating the two levels of the plaza.

84. Chinchero. Terraced area adjoining the town.
85. Limatambo. Stairway leading to the upper platform.

Retaining walls with large niches are also found in other centers: Tampumachay near the complex of Saqsaywaman, Limatambo, and Vilcashuamán. Tarawasi at Limatambo has a great platform that is reached by a central stairway that breaks the continuity of the magnificent retaining wall (*fig. 85*). At the back of this platform, another retaining wall is enriched by a series of niches that emphasize the plastic value of the sober and austere composition (*fig. 86*) Little remains in Limatambo to permit us to determine its functions and decide whether it had an urban structure. We do know that it was one of the first *tampu* near Cuzco on the road to the north.

The niched wall in the town of Vilcashuamán has small niches alternating with the large ones. We shall deal with ancient Willka Waman in the analysis of the administrative centers founded along the *qhapaq-ñan*.

Other urban establishments of the Inca central region deserve mention, but the lack of plans and research makes this task difficult. The majority of such places repeat architectural characteristics already noted. At Mawk'allaqta (Paruro),[49] for example, the streets with a central water channel recall the first descriptions of Cuzco (*fig. 87*); buildings with double- and triple-jamb niches and doorways remind one of Chinchero; the great surrounding wall with an entrance to one sector of the settlement is similar to that of Wiñay Wayna (*fig. 88*); and the stonework of the retaining walls is identical to that of Limatambo and Chinchero.

At Huchuy Cuzco (*fig. 89*), the *kallanka* and the large plaza also display repetitive patterns that are probably present in other centers of this region, which is so rich in evidence of the Inca presence.

Settlements along the qhapaq-ñan

The administrative centers and *tampu* found along the road between Quito and Cuzco were the first settlements the Spanish encountered during their reconnaissance following the events in Cajamarca.

Cieza de León followed the entire *qhapaq-ñan* to Cuzco, and,

86. Limatambo. The great platform and, beyond, another retaining
wall with large niches.

87. Mawk'allaqta. Street with steps and a drainage canal.

88. Mawk'allaqta. Retaining wall. At the end an entrance to one sector of the settlement.

89. Huchuy Cuzco. View of the complex. In the foreground, the *kallanka* with doorways onto the plaza.

although he found it almost entirely destroyed, he refers to Quito as "founded on some ancient buildings that the Incas had ordered built there during their reign. . . ."[50] At Latacunga he also found large buildings "as great as those of Quito. And despite their ruined condition, the grandeur of these buildings is apparent. . . ."[51] Near the Ambato River were the "sumptuous structures of Mocha, so many and so large that I was amazed at the sight of them; but now, with the fall of the Inca kings, all the palaces and buildings, with other of their mighty things, have fallen into ruin and there stands only enough to see the outlines and part of their structures. . . ."[52] The edifices of Riobamba "are no less to see than those of Mocha . . . ,"[53] and the famous ones of Tumebamba, "head of a kingdom or bishopric . . . were some of the most splendid and luxurious in all of Peru. . . ."[54] The store-houses contained "woolen clothing . . . that was so much and so rich, that if it were kept and not lost, it would be worth a great treasure."[55] Continuing south, Cieza passed through the province of "Guancabamba" and arrived in Cajamarca. The Incas "held [Cajamarca] in high esteem and ordered their palaces built there and constructed [a] temple for the service of the sun, of very high rank, and there were great numbers of storehouses."[56] "In that place they call Guanuco [Huánuco Pampa] there was a royal house of marvelous construction because the stones were large and set very evenly. This palace or seat was head of the provinces bordering on the Andes [the eastern tropical forest], and next to it was the temple of the sun with numerous virgins and ministers; and it was so important in Inca times that there were continually, solely for its service, more than thirty thousand Indians."[57]

Beyond "Bombón" and "Tarma," "following the royal highway of the Incas, one arrives at the large and beautiful valley of Jauja, which was one of the great things in Peru."[58] Further along are "Guamanga" and "Bilcas" (Vilcashuamán), "which was the middle of the domain and kingdom of the Incas; because from Quito to Bilcas, they state, is as far as from Bilcas to Chile. . . ."[59]

These brief excerpts from Cieza's report, limited to a few of the population centers, give an idea of the impressive chain of *tampu* and administrative centers that formed the long rosary of the *qhapaq-ñan*.

We must quote one more chronicler, Cristóbal de Molina, who confirms the organization and control that the administrative centers exercised:

> . . . in every one of the towns in this land, and especially in those on the two royal highways [coast and highland], there is or were royal quarters of the Inca or Sun, with his retinue of Indian men and women to serve him and the nobles and captains and messengers that he sent here and there, and quarters and houses of worship for the Sun, with its retinue of women called *mamacunas*, who were like holy women who remained chaste. . . . They were very meticulous, and in the tribute to the Inca such accounts [were kept] that each town of these provinces had accountants who kept account of the tribute and of what tribute each Indian gave and served, so that the work might be allocated and no one serve more than any other. . . .
>
> Likewise each town of these had a great quantity of storehouses wherein were gathered the maize and other supplies that were paid in tribute to the Inca, and the clothing and looms where the rich clothing for the Inca and *caciques* and the other common cloth for the warriors was woven and many storehouses of wool for it. . . .[60]

As we noted earlier, the urban character of the administrative centers was more artificial than that of the settlements in the central region, largely because of their floating population and great dependence for sustenance on the products stored in the *qollqa*. There are, however, other factors that indicate the special nature of these settlements. In the first place, there is the pattern of "compulsory" or "imposed" urbanism, which, according to Morris, can arise in response to centralized planning or directed migration.[61] In fact, the state, whose economic and political actions were related to the conquest and control of a constantly growing territory, had to resort to the formula of "imposed" settlements that could be rapidly built and enlarged to support its expansionist tactics. The number of new installations founded by the Inca state in the seven decades preceding the conquest was impressive and extraordinary when compared to expansionist feats of other ancient cultures. This very fact may have contributed to doubts regarding the chronology of the rapid Inca expansion. For example, Ake Wedin has objected to the chronology formulated by Rowe but suggests nothing to replace it and only notes that the time was very short.[62] If we take into account the *nature* of the Inca conquest, however, we can see that it actually could have been accomplished at an accelerated rate. It has been shown that in a large part of the territory known to have been included in Tawantinsuyu there is no archaeological evidence of the Inca presence. Only along the *qhapaq-ñan* or where there were *miti-maes* were there *tampu* and urban centers. If we accept that the model for Inca military conquest was archipelagic, that is that the objective was control of certain ecological zones and strong points rather than conversion of every last peasant to the solar cult, then we see that it could have advanced very rapidly indeed.[63]

Morris, besides pointing out the intrusive nature of the centers along the *qhapaq-ñan*, evident in the great difference between local and "imperial" architecture, indicates six characteristics typical of such establishments:

1. The surprising difference between the "state pottery" found in the administrative centers and that of the local ethnic groups.

2. The sudden appearance of these establishments on the archaeological scene.

3. The evident preoccupation with the storage of a wide variety of products. In Huánuco Pampa there are 497 *qollqa* with a capacity of 38,000 cubic meters. The primary function of these goods was to supply the needs of the settlements themselves. A second function may have been related to redistribution.

4. The architecture of these complexes includes various buildings apparently intended for temporary occupation by transients and for activities that were not basically residential.

5. Another factor asserting the "artificiality" of these settlements is the speed with which they were abandoned after the fall of the Inca state.

6. The apparent lack of cemeteries also indicates the short life of these centers.[64]

The establishment and rapid growth of so many installations on the network of roads in the territory incorporated into Tawantinsuyu was essential to expansionist policy and territorial control. The state was supported by conscripted work, not tribute in kind. The primary source of labor was the *mit'a*, temporary labor service performed on a rotating basis. This service could explain the nature of these settlements, planned to accommodate great masses of transients or temporary residents. Probably a high percentage of the population was composed of *mit'a* laborers in constant rotation.

In most of the administrative establishments that extended from Cuzco to Quito almost all the structures built by the Incas in the Cuzco style have disappeared. In many cases destruction, abandonment, and the growth of a colonial city on top of the Inca site have obliterated the evidence. Nothing remains to be seen of Inca Quito. Tumipampa (today the city of Cuenca in Ecuador) was shown by the excavations and studies of Max Uhle to have architectural characteristics similar to those of other, better preserved, installations.[65] For example, a great rectangular building, 72 meters long by 12 wide, with eleven doors opening onto the plaza, has measurements almost identical to those of the *kallanka* occupying one side of the plaza of Huánuco Pampa. Uhle suggests it was a temple dedicated to Wiraqocha and compares it to the one at Raqchi, but that hypothesis is now harder to test. Behind this great rectagular building are two large courtyards and some buildings recalling a similar arrangement of courtyards and buildings behind the two *kallanka* at Huánuco Pampa. The trapezoidal form of the plaza at Tumipampa, the *usnu*, and a further large rectangular structure on another of the sides of the plaza suggest the application of patterns that are repetitive although different formally.

There is also almost nothing remaining of Inca Cajamarca. We know some of its characteristics from the descriptions of the chroniclers who entered it with Francisco Pizarro in 1532. We know of the "triangular" (possibly trapezoidal) plaza, of the three great halls on the plaza, and of the *usnu*, which the Spanish called a "fortress" and which they could not climb because Atawallpa forbade it.

In the northern highlands, centers like Marka Wamachuku and Wiraqocha Pampa reveal pre-Inca origins. They were surely remodeled by the Incas to maintain the occupation of the sites. Wiraqocha Pampa in many respects recalls the plan of Pikillaqta and suggests Wari relationships.

Huánuco Pampa, also known as Old Huánuco, is the best preserved Inca administrative center and, therefore, the one most helpful in comprehending the plan. Located some 3,700 meters above sea level, Huánuco Pampa has preserved a great number of its original buildings, mainly because of two factors: first, it was rapidly abandoned upon the fall of the Incas; second, the attempt to found a Spanish city on the Inca one failed. Probably the settlement was abandoned so rapidly because the majority of its inhabitants were *mitimaes* whose homes were elsewhere. The destruction occasioned by lack of care and the peasants' use of material from the site to build houses and enclosures has been, in all cases, much less extensive than in other centers that served as the seat of colonial settlements.

Huánuco Pampa, like the other administrative centers, contains no structures that could be interpreted as defensive military works: no fortresses, no walls, no trenches. The complex has a "peaceful" and "open" layout, accessible from any of its sides. From the fact that such settlements are located in regions conquered and incorporated into Tawantinsuyu, it appears that the system of territorial control was not based on military domination. Surely the prompt movement of *mitimaes* and colonists from Cuzco was the mechanism that permitted the continuing pacification of the conquered ethnic groups—a policy needing bureaucratic apparatus more than military installations to maintain territorial control and utilize the newly acquired manpower.

The plan of the administrative center of Huánuco Pampa (*fig. 90*) shows more than a thousand structures framing an enormous rectangular plaza more than 540 meters long by 370 meters wide. Each of the four sides of the plaza is related to one or more *barrios*. The *qhapaq-ñan* crosses the plaza diagonally, southeast to northwest.

Within the criteria regulating urban planning, the spatial concept displays a preoccupation with dimensionality that surely linked design values and symbolism. In fact, if Inca urbanism did indeed place primary importance on the plaza as a space of multiple significance within the urban context, then possibly the dimensions of the plazas of the administrative centers may have attained proportions symbolically comparable to the greatness of the power that had conquered those territories. The plaza of Huánuco

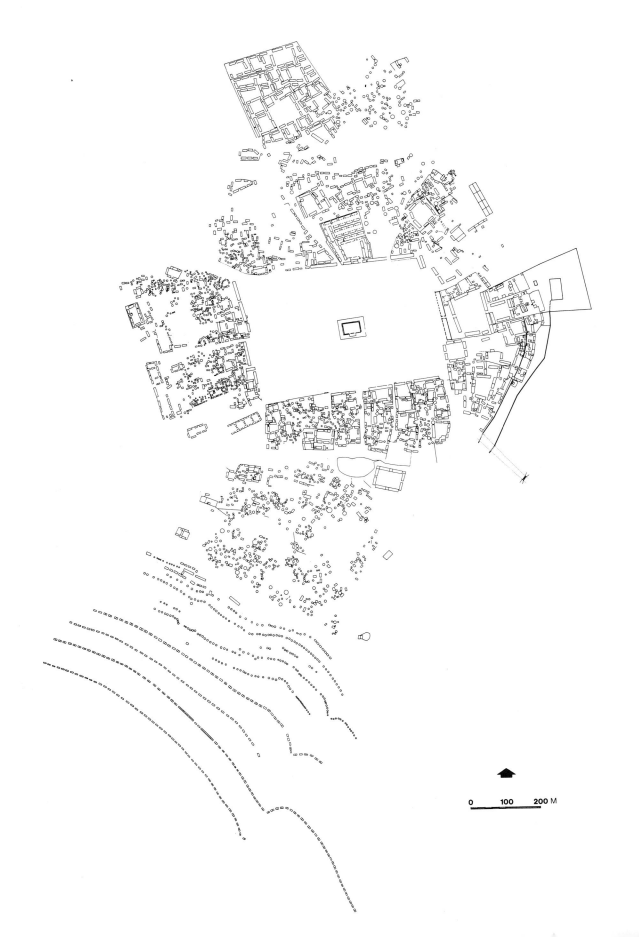

0   100   200 M

90. Huánuco Pampa. Complete plan of the Inca administrative
    center. The great rectangular plaza with the *usnu* in the center
    is prominent. To the south is the *qollqa* sector.

Pampa is, doubtless, the most important urban episode of that administrative center, and its prestige is enhanced by the austere volume of the *usnu* located in the exact center. A plaza more than 500 meters long is enormous anywhere, and in the case of Huánuco Pampa the sensation of vastness must have been intensified by the fact that the buildings surrounding it were only one story high. There was a very sharp delimitation of the space without changes of volume, permitting an almost limitless view toward the hills and the sky. This spatial experience immediately cries for comparison. Where is there anything similar? Teotihuacán is different: the volumes are imposing and the views obligatory. At Chanchan the high walls of the enclosures break up space, producing different perceptions. In the plaza of Chichén Itzá architectural form is emphasized. Perhaps Monte Albán, although its morphology is more strongly felt, produces sensations joining the urban spatial continuity to the natural surrounding space. All are interesting cases, but the magnificent spatial generosity of Inca urbanism is a case that must provoke further and more intensive investigation.

On the eastern side of the plaza lies the complex probably intended for the authorities sent from Cuzco. It is called *inkawasi* and its entrance lies between the two *kallanka* that face on the plaza (see chapter 4). The doorway "street" begins at the separation between the two great halls. Actually, there is no street, but rather a sequence of courtyards with doorways that respect the perfect alignment established by the central axis common to all of them (*fig. 91*). From the plaza the effect of perspective is striking and was observed in the early seventeenth century by Vázquez de Espinoza, who says that "all the doorways could be seen from outside. . . ."[66] Interestingly, the prolongation of this axis into the plaza coincides exactly with the midpoint of the *usnu* (*fig. 92*).[67] Only the doorways are of fine Cuzco-type masonry; the rest of the walls are rustic. Other examples of good masonry are to be found in some buildings located at the far end of the *inkawasi*, where the "small temple," which seems never to have been completed, is also found. The fact that only in this sector of the urban installation are there walls with fine stoneworking supports the hypothesis of its higher status; it may be

91. Huánuco Pampa. The sequence of doorways located on the same axis.

92. Huánuco Pampa. The perfect alignment of doorways on the same axis. The prolongation of the axis coincides with the midpoint of the *usnu*. The east-west axis of the doorways was probably meant to be perpendicular to the north-south orientation.

93. Huánuco Pampa. The "barracks" sector on the north side of the plaza.

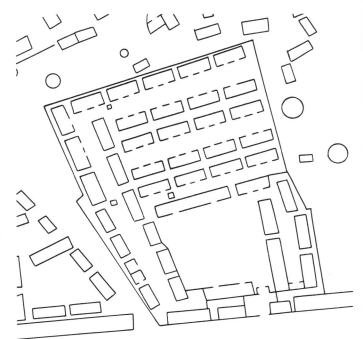

that the ceremonial compounds and the representatives of the administrative center were located here.[68]

In the northern *barrio* the most striking feature is the ordered placement of some fifty buildings that Harth-terré has called barracks (*fig. 93*). Certainly the arrangement of so many rooms of similar size within an enclosure having a single entrance has contributed to the interpretation of this sector as barracks or dormitories for the city garrison. Recent archaeological research by Craig Morris has demonstrated, however, that the complex served for the production of cloth under the supervision of *aqllakuna* completing their labor obligation.[69]

To the south of the urban center is the hill with 497 *qollqa*, whose importance for the sustenance of the administrative centers has already been mentioned. We shall discuss the architecture of the storehouses in chapter 4.

Another interesting point about Huánuco Pampa is the evidence of the brief Spanish occupation. As in Cuzco, the Inca plaza was considered excessively large, and it was probably there that the distribution of house lots began. It appears that the first houses were laid out on a grid plan based on a measurement of 110 *varas*, as suggested by the alignment of the ruins, which seem to outline blocks (*fig. 94*). The Spanish plaza must have been planned to occupy the space to the west of the *usnu*, and the platform of the *usnu* would surely have served as a base for the Catholic church, which, fortunately, was never built (*fig. 95*).

From one administrative center to another was about four or five days' travel, but at the end of each day was a *tampu*, located to facilitate movement along the *qhapaq-ñan* as well as for territorial control. The installations at these lesser centers were much more modest and certainly contained buildings for the accommodation of those in charge of the *tampu* and for transients. That, at least, is what is suggested by the plan of the *tampu* of Tunsukancha, near Huánuco Pampa, studied by Morris.[70] Here also the *kallanka* around the plaza seem to have served as lodging for people in transit. We still know very little, however, about the functioning of the *tampu* and the criteria used in their planning.

Pumpu (*fig. 96*) is the administrative center that follows

94. Traces of the first Spanish occupation are concentrated in the
plaza and seem to adopt a grid plan.

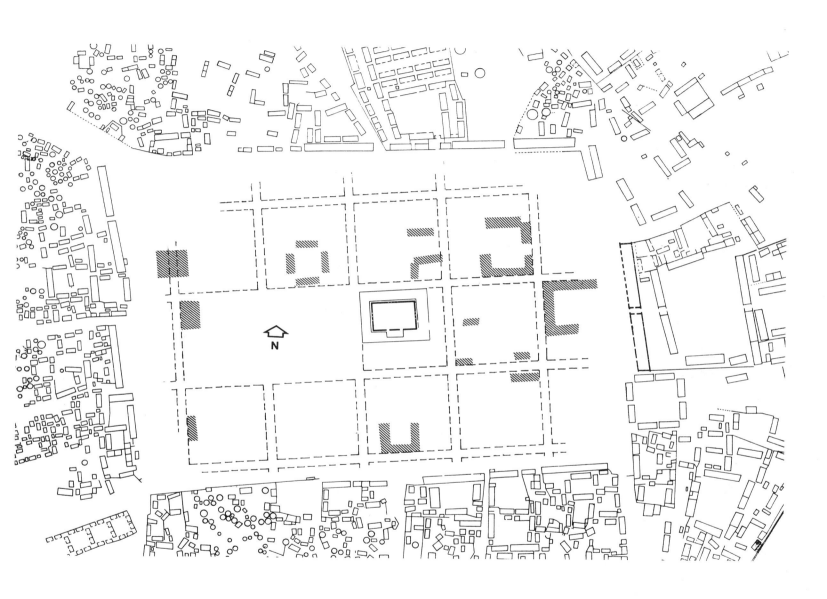

95. Huánuco Pampa. The *usnu* in the center of the plaza.

96. Pumpu. Aerial photography of the administrative center. The great plaza is conspicuous, with the *usnu* in its center. Part of the buildings are submerged because a dam was built recently. In the lower left-hand corner is the hill with the *qollqa* on it.

Huánuco Pampa to the south. It is not as large, nor does it have any structures with fine stonework. Toward the north end of the settlement is a great trapezoidal plaza, completely open on one of its sides. In the center of the plaza the *usnu* platform is repeated, but with *pirca* construction. On the east and south sides of the plaza are the ruins of great rectangular enclosures that were surely *kallanka*. Unfortunately, a great many of the buildings of Pumpu have gone to provide material for the construction of a modern dam; today part of the Inca administrative center is underwater. On the hill to the southeast are the remains of *qollqa* built in rows, but many fewer than those at Huánuco Pampa. In Pumpu the size of the plaza seems disproportionate to the number of buildings that surround it; furthermore, its one open side prevents it from achieving the spatial value of the Huánuco Pampa plaza.

Another administrative center that must be noted because it preserves so much valuable information on the Incas is Willka Waman (*figs. 97, 98*). In contrast to Huánuco Pampa and Pumpu, for both of which we have valuable studies, there is not even a superficial study of Willka Waman. Although various investigators have turned their interest to the central highlands, the Inca architecture of Willka Waman is known only from brief descriptions of the chroniclers and of nineteenth-century travelers and from a few recent comments of little relevance.

The town of Vilcashuamán, or simply Vilcas as its inhabitants call it, is located 80 kilometers southeast of the city of Ayacucho, in the district of Huambalpa, province of Cangallo, department of Ayacucho, in what was previously Chanka territory. Most of the present houses occupy the site of the Inca installation. The area of the modern plaza is less than that of the Inca one because houses have been built within this space, principally on the south and west sides, that is, opposite the Temple of the Sun and the *usnu*. These two monuments, in spite of their advanced state of destruction and deformation, are the most significant remains of Willka Waman. Many houses built in relatively recent times have in their walls quantities of stone blocks torn from the Inca ruins. Toward the hill of Pillucho is an extensive group of ruins of *pirca* construction arranged in a row that could well have been the *qollqa* of the administrative

97. Willka Waman. Plan of modern Vilcashuamán: 1. Church of
San Juan Bautista 2. The *usnu* 3. Building called the "house of
Thupa Inca" 4. South doorway to the enclosure 5. Remains of
the platform 6. The plaza 7. Line of modern constructions.

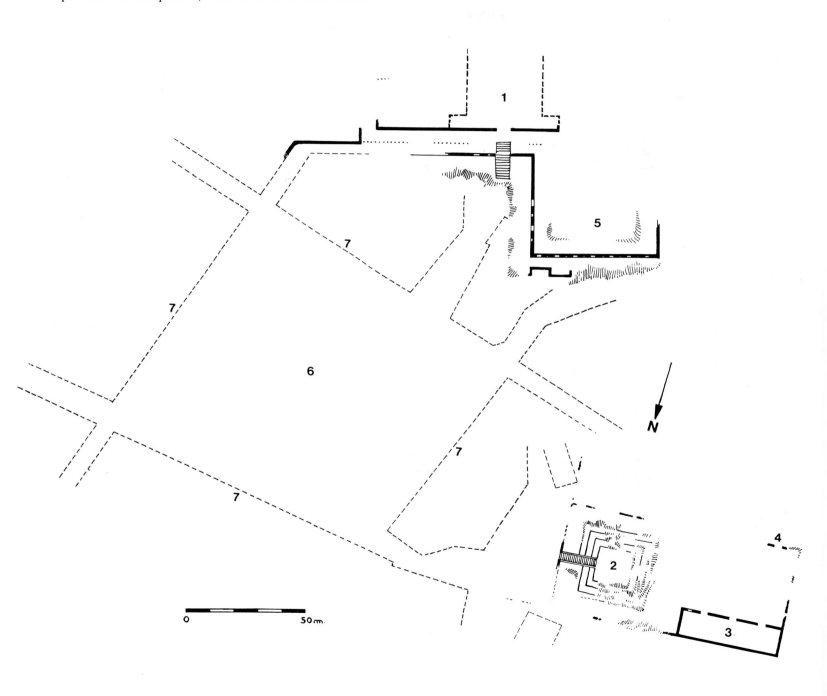

98. Willka Waman. Hypothetical plan: 1. Temple of the Sun
2. *Usnu* 3. Building inside the enclosure 4. South doorway to
the enclosure 5. Platform with niches and a base with
salients and recesses.

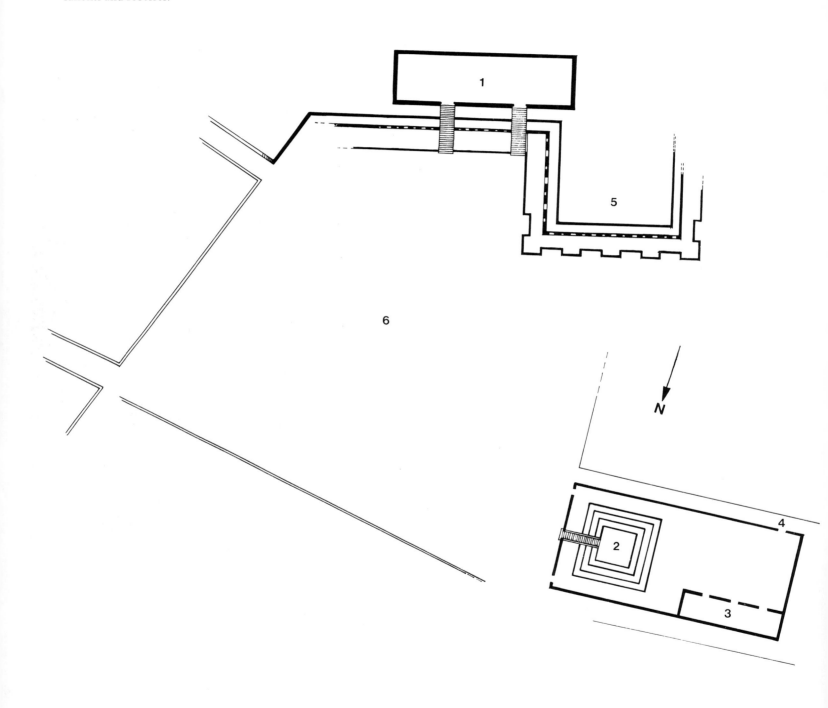

99. Willka Waman. Inca doorway of the Temple of the Sun with
    the recent rustic additions.
100. Willka Waman. The Catholic church, according to Angrand's
    1847 drawing, was parallel to the terrace system. The side
    door that appears in the drawing is today the main entrance.

center. Cieza says, "Next to a small hill there were and still are
more than seven hundred chambers where they accumulated
maize and provisions for the men of war who traveled throughout
the kingdom."[71] The seven hundred storehouses attest to the importance that Willka Waman must have had, since, if Cieza's
report is correct, this center had two hundred more *qollqa* than
Huánuco Pampa.

On the great plaza are the remains of two important monuments: the *usnu* (discussed in chapter 4) and the so-called Temple
of the Sun. This temple is located on the south side of the plaza
on the top platform of a system of three stepped terraces, where
today we find the church of San Juan Bautista built by the Spaniards. Until the end of the last century or the beginning of the
present one, the Catholic church was oriented parallel to the
stepped terraces so that one of its sides faced on the plaza, indicating that the church building availed itself of almost all of the
rectangular enclosure of the Inca structure. At the beginning of
this century, because of the poor state of the church, it was decided to rebuild it with the principal façade on the plaza. In this
rebuilding the Inca walls were again used, but what had been the
side door of the church and, in ancient times, one of the two doors
of the Temple of the Sun, was converted into the main door of
the renovated Catholic church. To give it greater decorative
importance, two crude fluted columns and a triangular pediment
were added (*fig. 99*). Angrand's drawing of 1847 (*fig. 100*) provides clear evidence of the change in orientation of the church.[72]
At that time the church still used the rectangular enclosure of the

101. Willka Waman. Hypothetical reconstruction of the Temple of the Sun made on a transparency over Angrand's drawing.

Temple of the Sun set lengthwise, parallel to the stepped platform. Today, however, the long axis of the church is perpendicular to that line.

Cieza says of the "temple" that "it was made of stone, very finely set, had two large doorways; to reach them there were two stone stairways that had, by my count, thirty steps each."[73] On the basis of Cieza's statement, Angrand's drawing, Wiener's plan,[74] and on-site observations, we have made a hypothetical reconstruction, drawing on a transparency over Angrand's drawing (*fig. 101*). The result, even if it does not rest entirely on trustworthy data, at least offers a suggestion of the main outlines. The location of the Temple of the Sun, on platforms decorated with sequences of large trapezoidal niches (*fig. 102*), recalls the similar arrangement at Chinchero.

Another interesting aspect of the same unit is the salient of the stepped platform that projects toward the north side of the plaza. Of the three terraces, the uppermost, at the level of the temple, preserves the smooth vertical face, the middle one repeats the sequence of trapezoidal niches (*fig. 103*), and the basal one is formed of alternating salients and recesses. We know of no similar examples in Inca architecture. The only possible comparison is with the saw-toothed terraces of Saqsaywaman, but it is not very close. The plan Wiener published in 1880 shows seven salients on the lowest platform. In our drawing we have put five on the basis of the proportions that Angrand's photographic pencil gave them. At the moment we need not know whether the exact number is five or seven. What is important is the architectural feature and its uniqueness. Archaeological research will take care of supplying the precise data.

Settlements in Qollasuyu and on the coast

The policy of founding large administrative centers was concentrated principally to the north of Cuzco along the *qhapaq-*

102. Willka Waman. Hypothetical reconstruction of the Temple of the Sun complex and the terrace system.

103. Willka Waman. Remains of the niched retaining wall belonging to the second terrace.

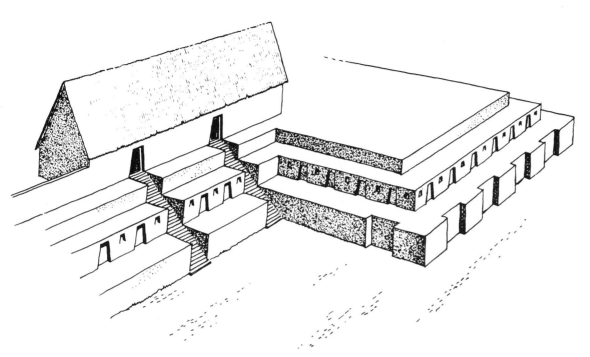

104. Inca road in Qollasuyu near Copacabana
105. Inkallaqta. Plan of the complex in which the great *kallanka*
fronting on the plaza is prominent.

ñan that reached to present-day Ecuador. Different criteria of territorial and administrative control must have been applied in Qolla territory to the south of Cuzco beyond Sicuani and Ayaviri, where Qollasuyu begins. "The Colla begin at Ayavire . . ." says Cieza, "the largest region, in my opinion, of all Peru and the most populous. . . ."[75] It was inhabited by large Aymara-speaking ethnic groups, true highland kingdoms with centers in the Titicaca basin and peripheral colonies controlling a number of ecological zones as far as the Pacific. They had large areas of pasture land and in 1532 were considered "wealthy Indians" by the first conquerors.[76]

In this region of high population density and high productivity, the Incas opted for occupying existing settlements rather than building administrative centers *ex novo* like those of the *qhapaq-ñan*. Possibly the presence of representatives of the Inca state in existing settlements, like the Lupaqas' Chucuito, was intended not only to facilitate administrative control but also to manifest the physical presence of power. Although administrative centers comparable to Huánuco Pampa were not founded, building activity related to territorial control and the storage of goods was intensive as in few other parts of Tawantinsuyu. One need only look at the department of Cochabamba southeast of La Paz to realize the proliferation of strategically located centers for the control of the valleys—not large settlements, although Inkallaqta (*fig. 105*) occupies a respectable area, but a great number of small complexes, *pukara*, garrisons, centers for controls that were more administrative than military, and a surprising number of storehouses. In the department of Cochabamba alone a hundred such centers are known. One of them, Cotapachi, with its 2,400 perfectly aligned *qollqa* (*fig. 106*) with a capacity of some 4,800 tons, suggests the importance the fertile valleys of this department had for the Inca economy.

On the coast the Incas found great urban settlements, some active, others abandoned. A planned city like Chanchan and structures of imposing dimensions like the Pyramid of the Sun at Moche (*fig. 107*) must have impressed the invaders, who came from the highlands and had never experienced spatial sensations and dimensional effects such as those encountered on the coast. Chanchan is impressive because of the scale of the complex formed

N

0   50   100 M

106. The 2,400 *qollqa* of Cotapachi, all perfectly aligned, are divided into two groups of 1,200 each.

107. Moche. The Pyramid of the Sun. For the Incas, architecture of striking dimensions.

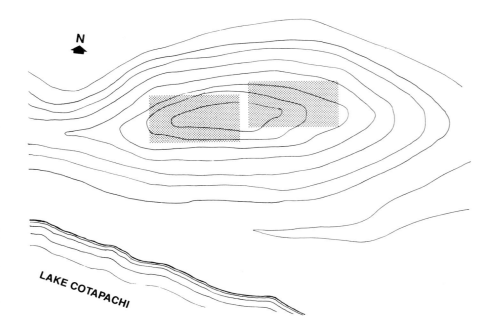

N

LAKE COTAPACHI

by eleven sectors enclosed by high walls with trapezoidal sections and built of millions of adobes (*fig. 108*). Even today, walking among the "streets" formed by the open spaces between one enclosure and the next, one experiences the sensation of monumental size that this singular urban and architectural concept emanates, in spite of the advanced state of deterioration. It is difficult to imagine the reaction of the Incas in the face of the highly developed urban and architectural manifestations of the coast. Probably they considered the control and administration of the settlements of first priority, using the existing structures. The presence of the Inca occupation in some coastal centers is more noticeable in the pottery than in the architecture.

On the central coast the largest establishment was surely Cajamarquilla, located in the Rimac Valley (*fig. 109*). Its urban character lacks the criteria of order used in the planning of Chanchan. The "sanctuary" of Pachacamac was respected by the Incas, a fact that did not, however, prevent them from adding temples related to their religion. At first sight one is struck by the formal and technical characteristics typical of the Incas.

108. Chanchan. Remains of the high adobe walls that formed the *barrio* compounds.

109. Cajamarquilla. Two views of the great urban settlement established in the Rimac Valley.

110. Valley of Lunahuaná. Sector of the ruins of Inkawasi.

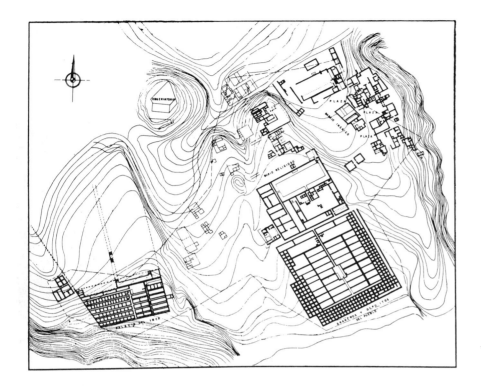

Besides settling into centers already established by local coastal cultures, the Incas built centers for administration and the control of strategic locations. In the valley of Lunahuaná, for example, the building of Inkawasi is related to the conquest of that region and to the resistance of Chuquimanco and his people to Inca domination.[77] Thus we have an installation that arose as the consequence of a prolonged siege. The ruins of the site (fig. 110) have been studied only superficially, and we still lack research that would clarify the uses of the many structures built on such rough and broken terrain.

Tambo Colorado (fig. 111) is surely the best preserved Inca center on the coast. It is located in the Pisco Valley in an easily controlled pass. The great trapezoidal plaza, the road that crosses it, the usnu on the west side of the plaza, the series of buildings around courtyards, and the trapezoidal niches testify to the application of repetitive patterns adapted to a different environment (figs. 112, 113).

111. Valley of the Pisco River. Panoramic view of Tambo Colorado
with the great trapezoidal plaza and, on the right, the *usnu*
structure.

112. Tambo Colorado. Plan of the Inca settlement in the Pisco
     Valley.
113. Tambo Colorado. The trapezoidal form and the coastal adobe.

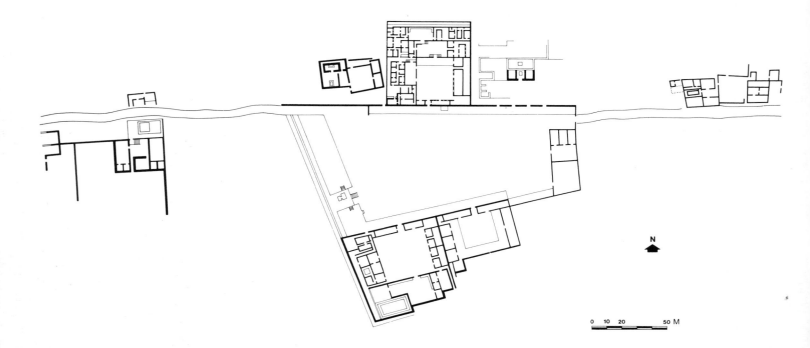

In the Acarí Valley, on the ruins of Tambo Viejo, a walled city of the Early Intermediate Period, the Incas built another administrative center adopting local techniques.[78] There are no substantial differences between the highlands and the coast in the use of adobe. *Tapia*, or tamped earth, which is found in so many coastal sites, is generally pre-Inca: Cajamarquilla is a good example. The adobe walls were covered with a fine mud plaster, then painted with bright colors. At Tambo Colorado there remain traces of paint, and one can imagine the striking appearance these architectural complexes must have had.

3

Domestic Architecture

The modern Quechua and Aymara rural dwellings with rectangular plans must not be very different from those built in Inca times.[1] Although in many areas the rectangular plan has replaced the circular one, which was used by many ethnic groups before they were conquered by the Incas, we should note that the present spread of the rectangular form is due more to the building systems introduced by the Europeans than to Inca influence. The circular plan continues in use among various Aymara-speaking groups and, to a lesser extent, in other regions of the central and northeastern Peruvian Andes. Just as in Inca times, the rectangular peasant house of today has a single room with quite limited interior space. When a family has other rooms for additional sleeping quarters, storage, or kitchen use, these are almost always separate buildings without internal communication between the rooms (*fig. 114*) To go from one to the other one must go outside into the open. Even in two-story houses the stairway leading to the upper story is always outside.

The nuclear-family houses of the Inca peasants, called *wasi*,[2] were clustered in groups, freely arranged but maintaining a certain order with respect to the space used for circulation. Referring to the houses of the Yunga *mitimaes* located in Ninamarka, Abancay, Waldemar Espinoza Soriano notes that "they were not isolated, but rather formed groups. . . . The houses of this village were independent from one another. They were almost scattered, depending on individual convenience; there was not, thus, a planned concentration. . . . Each dwelling, as we can see from the ruins, was small, sufficient for a nuclear family, built of stone and mud, covered with thatch."[3] The same characteristics are seen today in innumerable highland peasant villages, and are also found in Cieza de León's description written more than four centuries ago: "The houses of the Cañare natives, of whom I am speaking, are small, made of stone, with a thatch roof."[4]

Although the tendency to build houses of adobe with corrugated iron roofs is becoming more and more widespread, houses repeating traditional construction systems going back to pre-Inca times are still very numerous in rural areas. The use of adobe and corrugated iron implies economic resources that are always very scarce among peasants living in remote areas. On the other hand,

114. The peasant houses of the Quechua and Aymara always comprise a single room. Additional rooms are separate structures.

115. Present-day stone house with thatched roof, anywhere in the highlands

116. Near Yunguyo. Workers making adobes.

stones for the walls, branches for framing, and *totora* reeds, Spanish broom, or *ichu* grass for roofing the house are easily gathered and require no monetary investment. The resultant work is very rough in all respects (*fig. 115*).

Besides stone, the Incas made considerable use of adobe, both in modest houses and in palaces and temples. Important structures frequently combine the two materials in their walls, with stone to a height of two to four meters and adobe up to the top. Although walls of stone are especially striking because of their exquisite finish and the perfection of the joining of the blocks, adobe was surely the building material most commonly employed by Incas. Garcilaso notes that

they built walls of adobes which they made in molds as bricks are made here [in Spain]: they were of mud trod together with straw: they made the adobes as long as the wall was to be thick, and the shortest ones measured a *vara;* they were more or less a sixth wide and almost the same thick; they dried them in the sun and piled them up in order and left them to the sun and the water under a roof for two or three years so that they might dry out completely. They laid them in the building as bricks are laid: using as mortar the same mud as the adobes, trod together with straw.[5]

Adobe construction is still very popular and is surely the type most commonly used. Traveling through the highlands, one frequently sees workers preparing the mixture of earth and straw, and great quantities of adobes drying in the sun. Adobes were used in all the buildings of the colonial period and, up to the present, the method of making them has not changed at all.

Another technique used to build houses, storehouses, and fences is to cut the soil directly into sod blocks, which are laid without mortar. In the Cuzco area this technique is called *ch'ampa* (*fig. 118*). All the houses of the Chipaya in the department of Oruro, Bolivia, are built in this way.

It should be noted that Inca rural houses were always much better built and finished when they were part of the state building programs than when they were the houses of peasants who lived in remote areas and participated in the Inca system primarily by supplying *mit'a* labor. Nevertheless, rural dwellings of the modern

131

117. Cuzco. Manufacture of adobes using a wooden mold.

118. Junín. Detail of a house with walls of sod blocks cut directly
from the ground. In the Cuzco area this technique is called
ch'ampa.

Quechua and Aymara may have suffered a slow spatial and technical decline since the end of Inca rule. The village of Suriqui, on
the island of the same name in Lake Titicaca, provides an eloquent
example. Suriqui is in territory that was occupied by the Incas
around the middle of the fifteenth century. Every one of the 290
houses in the village has a rectagular plan and a single room. Of
these, 258 have *totora* reed roofs and the rest are corrugated iron.[6]
The roof frame "is filled in with an auxiliary structure of
branches, slender timbers and laths. All this is tied together with
string and cords twisted or braided of stiff grass."[7] Thus we see
that even in the construction of modern roofs, the traditional
methods observed and reported by the sixteenth-century chroniclers are still employed. The outside dimensions of the rectangular houses of the village of Suriqui vary between 4 and 5 meters
long and 2 to 2.80 meters wide. One single-family dwelling, with
outside dimensions of 4.30 by 2.20, has, allowing for the thickness
of the walls, an inside living space of 3.70 by 1.60 meters. That
is, within an area of only 5.92 square meters the family members
live, sleep, cook, and pass their time when bad weather prevents
going outside. Almost half of the interior is occupied by an elevated earthen platform some 30 centimeters high on which the
entire family sleeps, called *puñuna-pata* in Quechua and *p'atjati*
in Aymara. Untanned sheep or llama skins serve as a mattress, and
the family members, who do not remove their clothing to sleep,
are protected from the cold by woolen blankets called *k'añeri,*
which are woven by the women. Windows are still a foreign
element in Suriqui houses. The doorway is the only traditional
opening in the wall and is very small: 45 to 60 centimeters wide
and 120 centimeters high. More modern houses have larger doorways, but the maximum height is 160 centimeters (*fig. 119*). On
the inside walls there are always one or two niches, called *phutu,*
where the lamp and other items are kept, and wooden pegs from
which clothing is hung. Except for minor differences, the 290
houses of Suriqui, those of the villages on the neighboring islands,
and those on the lake shore all have the same characteristics.
Wealthier families have more than one sleeping room, a kitchen,
and a storeroom. Each room is a separate and independent building and the units are set around a courtyard and enclosed by a

133

The doorways of many peasant houses near Lake Titicaca
have a maximum height of 160 centimeters.

wall. The study of these dwellings permits us to suggest that, if indeed traditional structural and formal systems are preserved, they do not demonstrate—after four and a half centuries—any improvements in the concept of living space; quite the contrary, there is an obvious deterioration in comparison to the houses built by the Inca state in planned settlements.

The rectangular plan dominates almost all Inca building. From humble rural houses to the halls of the most sacred temple, the Qorikancha, Inca architecture showed no special interest in seeking a variety of alternative shapes. Likewise, in both peasant houses and temples and "palaces," the rectangular plan was the basis of a single chamber. One of the most identifiable features of Inca architecture is the number of single-chambered elements. Garcilaso says that "they did not connect rooms together, but made them all separate each one by itself . . . the four walls of stone or adobe, of any house or building, large or small, were made completely finished inside because they did not know how to connect one room with another nor to extend crossbeams from one wall to another, nor did they use nails."[8] Internal communication between one room and another was effectively unknown, or at least not used. If a single roof covered a structure with two or more rooms, access to each of these was independent and from the outside. The number of doorways was related to the size and function of the interior space. A humble dwelling always had a single doorway; other types of houses had two or three, and a *kallanka* some 70 meters long, up to fourteen. All doorways were on one of the long walls of the rectangle. In very large buildings, however, there were also side doors. The number of doorways on a façade had nothing to do with the number of rooms; were there one or fourteen entrances, the interior was almost always a single space. Houses with a central dividing wall on the long axis of the rectangle had two independent rooms that were entered from opposite sides.

Rectangular plans, lack of internal communication between rooms, and groups of separate unconnected chambers are the most frequent characteristics of Inca houses. These features, manifest in so many complexes, probably belong to formal patterns established, standardized, and diffused during and after the reign

120. Puno. Single-room houses roofed with *totora* reed.

121. Machu Picchu. Example of a single-room building with two doorways. It is difficult to determine what activities may have taken place inside it.

of Pachakuti. In fact, what do we know of Inca architecture before the "ninth Inca"? Was there an identifiable architectural style belonging to the Cuzco region before Pachakuti? Possibly there was, since there is evidence of pre-Inca occupation. It is difficult to arrive at a conclusion on this point, however, since archaeology has yet to clarify many questions. Meanwhile, the hypothesis that the so-called Inca architecture, associated with the Cuzco style, acquired its unified, planned, and repetitive characteristics almost entirely after Pachakuti's rise to power is becoming increasingly accepted. Moreover, it was his descendants, first Thupa Inca and then Wayna Qhapaq, who ordered the construction of the greatest number of the works, since it was during the government of these two sovereigns that the conquered territory reached its maximum expansion. Thus it is likely that the formal and spatial characteristics found in so many monumental complexes like Cuzco, Machu Picchu, Ollantaytambo, Vilcashuamán, Huánuco Pampa, and so many others belong to a standardized expression conceived during Pachakuti's reorganization.

The repetition of the rectangular plan and other formal elements in Inca structures may be due to the need to establish standardized and simplified patterns that could be applied to all the works the Incas were building in conquered territories. Since all activities within the Inca system were regulated, we must suppose that governmental buildings also had specific guidelines. These rules were applied equally to buildings erected in what is now Bolivian territory and to those in regions now belonging to Ecuador. The manpower that built the structures was acquired largely from groups of people obliged to abandon their homelands and be transferred to places that were sometimes located at the other extreme of the realm in order to provide their share of the *mit'a* labor.

Those charged with directing the works and giving instructions to these heterogeneous ethnic groups were expert builders employed by the state, who gave the orders they had learned: standardized patterns applicable anywhere. Accepting this hypothesis, one can better understand the repetitive nature of Inca architecture. Variations were dictated more by the requirements

122. Sacred rock and circular building near Calca, Urubamba
Valley, after Squier

of different environments and topography, as well as by the building materials available in a given region, than by inventive personnel. The coastal buildings are a good example of this situation.

The circular plan

Clearly the rectangular plan is typical of Inca construction.
It predominates in dwellings and in buildings destined for other
purposes. This does not mean that the rectangular plan was re-
stricted to the Incas or that they did not use other forms, such as
the circle. The circular plan was widespread in the Andes and
is still used in several regions, principally in Bolivian territory. In
various sites in the central and northeastern highlands, and even
in Quechua territory in the department of Apurimac, we find
archaeological remains with circular house plans,[9] and probably
such structures existed in the Cuzco area before the introduction
of the official architecture. The Incas made use of the circular plan
in buildings that were not to be used as dwellings. Many storehouses were circular, as were a number of funerary structures or
chullpa. The tower called Muyucmarka in the "fortress" of Saqsaywaman and a building at Runku Raqay on the road to Machu
Picchu also have circular plans. Still more numerous are structures
with curved walls that do not form a circle, of which there are
well-known examples at Pisaq, Machu Picchu, Cuzco, and Cusichaca. There are pre-Inca fortifications, such as Chankillo in the
Casma Valley, comprising several concentric circular or oval
enclosures. Garcilaso remembers a round tower in the plaza of
Cuzco opposite Amarukancha: "There also still existed for me to
see a most beautiful circular tower that was in the plaza in front
of the house. . . . because it was the first quarters the Spanish had
in the city (besides its great beauty) it were well that its conquerors maintain it. . . ."[10] Garcilaso clearly refers to the *sunturwasi*. Another *sunturwasi* was noted by Squier in Azángaro;
he also illustrates another circular building in Urco near Calca
(*fig. 122*)

It was, however, in pre-Inca dwellings that the circular form
was most often applied; it was frequently and widely used during
the Late Intermediate Period. In the course of the Inca territorial

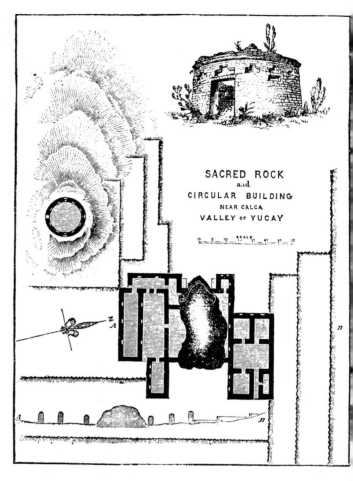

123. Two types of circular house: walls of the first are stone, of the second, sod blocks or *ch'ampa*.

expansion the subjugated ethnic groups who lived in circular houses did not abandon their customs. In the central Andes where the Vilcamayo River joins the Mantaro, there are remains of various hamlets of local ethnic groups. All these settlements have the same type of circular structure with stone walls that must have stood as high as a man and must have had a conical thatch roof on a framework of branches. The roof frame rested directly on the top of the wall and needed no central support. Among the various complexes studied, Danièle Lavallée notes that in Kuniare, Astomarka, Chuntamarka, Ollute, and Awkimarka she has not found a single rectangular or quadrangular structure.[11] Donald Thompson also comments on the great number of circular structures in the Upper Marañón area in the eastern Andes of northern Peru. At the site of Intikancha, for example, of 217 houses, 185 have a circular plan.[12] He also noted the presence of the circular form at other sites in the same region as well as in the villages located in the Huánuco Pampa area.[13] Duccio Bonavia indicates that all the houses he studied in the central highlands, department of Ayacucho, had a circular plan.[14] The circular shape of the dwellings of the peoples conquered by the Incas suffered no changes, even when they were near a *tampu* or an administrative center built in the Cuzco style. Inca domination was relatively brief in the conquered territories and not sufficiently influential to modify the traditional shapes in these regions. Thompson notes that "Architecturally, Inca rule seems to have had almost no effect on the peasant villages. All communities studied had a local peasant style of architecture; no Imperial Inca style architecture or house arrangement was observed. . . ."[15] What we wish to emphasize here is that, in the highlands, circular houses were more numerous than rectangular ones in the regions incorporated into the Inca system. The Incas, therefore, ignored or disdained the dwellings of the conquered ethnic groups and imposed their own standardized architecture whenever they built a large or small installation along the royal highway—an architecture that would be easily identified and would stand out when compared to the poor circular huts, thereby evoking and symbolizing the sovereign presence of the Incas.

The circular houses still being built in Aymara territory

139

124. Pre-Inca settlement of Ancasmarka, province of Calca. All the structures are circular.

125. Department of Oruro, Bolivia. Chipaya village with circular houses.

126. Cross section of a typical Chipaya house

relate directly to traditions established before Inca domination. The fact that there have been no substantial change-producing factors in some isolated regions explains the persistence and continuity of some unaltered customs. In this group fall the houses of the Chipaya in the department of Oruro, Bolivia (*figs. 125, 126*). These houses are of two types:

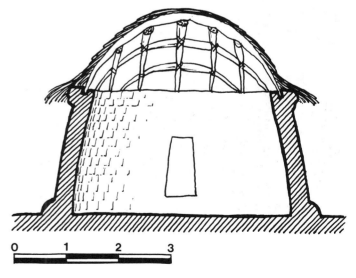

. . . one urban and the other rural. The urban house has a circular plan some 5 meters in diameter. Its walls are not vertical but are corbeled slightly toward the interior to a height of approximately 2.20 meters. These walls are of earth, not adobe but rather sod blocks cut directly from the ground, which are placed on top of one another without any kind of mortar. When the wall is completed, two courses of larger blocks are added, one on top of the other, where the roof is to be fastened. The roof construction is unusual. First a framework is made of bundles of dry grass, which the Aymara call *chipas*, whence probably comes the name Chipaya. These firmly tied grass bundles are placed on the wall and curved from one side to the other like arches. They form a very firm fabric onto which a mud paste is applied, and the whole thing is then covered with grass and fastened

141

down with a string net to keep the wind from carrying it off.

The house is built on a platform some 30 centimeters high. The door has a threshold about 40 centimeters above ground level and the total height of the doorway is not over 1.20 meters, so that one must stoop to enter. Inside the house, and built into it, is the stove which stands barely a span above the floor. About 1.5 meters up, a circular hole leading to the outside provides an outlet for smoke. Next to the stove there is a storage place for fuel, which is generally *tola* or dried animal dung. The Chipaya sleep on the ground and use neither chairs nor tables, so there is no furniture in their houses.

The rural house is similar to the urban one but instead of the grass roof, the walls extend in a false vault to form an oblong dome. These are also made of sod blocks cut directly from the ground.[16]

The corbeled vault

The rural Chipaya house, also called *putuku*, brings us to a technical structural problem of outstanding importance for the history of pre-Columbian architecture: the corbeled vault.

The lack of the arch and vault in pre-Columbian buildings has attracted the attention of various scholars and has been extensively discussed in studies devoted to the corbeled vaults of the Maya of Central America. It is unquestionable that, from the architectural and structural point of view, the Maya knew how to get more out of spaces covered with corbeled vaults than did any other pre-Columbian culture. Furthermore, in contrast to Andean usage, the Maya corbeled vault was also used as a formal element, visible in the façades. That is, it was not only a building device to cover interior space, but an aesthetic resource. In Copán, Tikal, Labná, and especially Uxmal (*figs. 127, 128*), the triangular form of the corbeled vault, visible on the exterior, identifies one of the most diagnostic formal characteristics of Maya architecture.

It should also be noted that the Maya corbeled vault almost always covers spaces arising from rectangular plans; the Andean corbeled vault, on the other hand, covers an interior space based on a circular plan.

In the Andean area, the corbeled vault was not part of the technical building repertory of the Incas. In fact, we cannot over-

127. Uxmal. Maya corbeled vault in the Pyramid of the Magician.

128. Uxmal. Maya corbeled vault as an important architectural element in interior-exterior integration.

look the contrast in Inca constructions between the perfect and enduring stone walls and the precarious and impermanent thatched roofs. In spite of the great number of vaulted structures that the Incas knew in their conquered territories, the corbeled vault must have presented a problem that, for whatever reason, did not attract their attention or interest sufficiently to merit perfecting the technique. Thus, the corbeled vault, although known, was not used in the official architectural plans. The Maya corbeled vault achieved a perfect finish on the surface of the inclined walls; the domination of this building technique permitted them to use the formula with security and aesthetic value. In contrast, the corbeled vaults of the Andean cultures (fig. 129) are rough, without the least attempt to smooth the finish. Stones were set in horizontal courses and the diameter was gradually reduced by corbeling until it could finally be closed with some larger sized slabs. The Andean corbeled vault is always used to cover small interior spaces and rarely does its form appear on the façade.[17] The most important conclusion is that the corbeled vault of the Andean area is much earlier than those of the Inca culture.

Hermann Trimborn has investigated and reported a great variety of structures with corbeled vaults on the coast and in the highlands of Peru.[18] He suggests the possibility of "considering the corbeled vault as an Aymara discovery, in which case its appearance in the coastal zone of Peru would have to be interpreted as evidence of an ancient penetration of the coast by the altiplano-dwelling Aymara."[19] That the Aymara made considerable use of the system of the corbeled vault is clearly true, but to consider them the discoverers of the building system is less convincing. There are a great many pre-Inca dwellings from the central and northern parts of the Peruvian highlands as well that display the same building technique. Might there have been Aymara influence through Tiwanaku-Wari cultural contacts? Such an idea is not improbable. These houses, clustered together in villages, are of stone with corbeled vaults and may be native to the area; they do differ from the Aymara houses in some details. For example, in the Yacha town of Wakan, department of Pasco, Ramiro Matos Mendieta notes that private dwellings consist of several rooms arranged around a courtyard (fig. 130). The wall

129. Department of Oruro. The two types of Chipaya house: the *putuku*, which is closed with corbeled vault, and the type with a thatched dome.

130. Plan of a dwelling in the Yacha settlement of Wakan. Rooms arranged around a courtyard. The structures close their corbeled vaults with long slabs. On top they have accessible flat roofs.

131. Cross section of one of the Wakan rooms

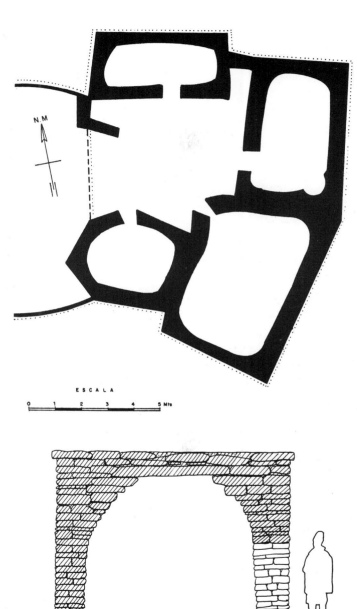

ESCALA

0 1 2 3 4 5 Mts

132. Typical interior of one of these dwellings. One of the long
 roof slabs is missing from the illustrated example. The light at
 the lower right is from the doorway, which opens onto the
 courtyard.

of the house "as it rises, gradually closes the dome until an oval opening is left which is closed with big long slabs that serve as ties. The ancient rural Andean architect was close to achieving the principle of the false arch. The stone framework is finished with a coating of mud and gravel, forming a flat roof which was probably also used for drying produce."[20] Although the corbeled vault was used, it should be noted that the accessible flat roof is not typical of the Aymara. According to Matos Mendieta, the Wakan complex probably dates to the Late Intermediate Period. In the departments of Junín, Pasco, and Huánuco, there are numerous localities with similar characteristics. If the inhabitants of these regions descend from the Wari occupation of the central highlands (even today a variety of Aymara, *kawki*, is spoken in Tupe), a possible and remote Aymara influence cannot be discarded. The houses that Ramiro Matos Mendieta studied are similar to those described by Villar Córdova for the Canta region, which extends toward the lower Marañón.[21] But probably it all began further south in the high regions above the valleys of Mala, Lurín, Rimac, Chillón, etc.[22]

The corbeled vault of the Chipaya rural sod house (*figs. 133, 134*) uses a very ancient building system recorded from prehistoric European buildings on the islands of Cyprus and Sardinia. The south Italian peasant houses called *trulli* have the same type of corbeled vault, and even so important a monument as the Treasure of Atreus in Mycenae has its great interior vault of the corbeled type, that is, horizontal courses of stone, each protruding further than the previous one, that gradually reduce the diameter at the same time as they rise in height until they achieve total closure.

The corbel-vaulted structures that have received the most attention are the *chullpa*, funerary edifices.[23] These occur in different types, sizes, shapes, and materials. Those with square or rectangular plan have the form of a parallelopiped; those with a circular plan are cylindrical or, as in Sillustani, have the shape of an inverted truncated cone; that is, their circumference increases with their height (*fig. 135*). They may be small and rustic of *pirca* construction; the majority are of adobe; but there is no lack of those that reach 12 meters in height and display a perfect

133. A group of Chipaya *putuku* type houses built of sod blocks
laid in horizontal courses and achieving complete closure by
corbeling.

134. Cross section of a Chipaya *putuku*

135. Sillustani. Circular *chullpa*.

136. Sillustani. The "lizard" *chullpa* displays the perfection of the curved faces of the stone blocks.

137. Molloko, Puno. One square and one circular *chullpa*.

138. *Chullpa* overlooking Lake Umayo

139. Sillustani. This *chullpa* was never completed. The ramp used to convey the stones to their final location is still preserved.

140. Sillustani. Chullpa group.

finish in the cutting, joining, and polishing of the stone blocks. The most impressive and best finished examples are found at Sillustani, a small peninsula in Lake Umayo near Hatuncolla. Rowe, referring to the *chullpa* of that site, states: "Although built in *Aymara* territory, the style of the masonry . . . is *Inca*."[24] This statement could imply that the Sillustani *chullpa* belong to the Late Horizon, or the height of Inca architecture, which is still doubtful. The similarity of the stonework with works of the Cuzco style is beyond question. Nevertheless, the walls at the base of the pyramid of Akapana at Tiwanaku, as noted in chapter 1, also appear to be of the same technique as a good Cuzco wall, in spite of being much earlier. The stoneworking technique of official Inca architecture appears suddenly during Pachakuti's reign. It is possible to suggest, therefore, that the ability of the ancient Qolla masons, evident at Tiwanaku in the high level of quality

141. Espinar, Cuzco. Circular *chullpa*. The convex hemisphere is a
   formal solution with no structural purpose, being solid inside.
   The corbeled vault is lower and of fieldstone.
142. Sillustani. Cross section of the "lizard" *chullpa*.

and perfection, may have served as a model for Inca architecture.
Once more it is convenient to recall that stonemasons from Aymara territory frequently worked on the constructions in Cuzco
in fulfillment of their *mit'a* labor obligation.

All *chullpa*, whether stone or adobe, rustic or with perfectly
finished masonry, have a corbeled vault in their interior. Bernabé
Cobo notes that "inside they are hollow to the height of slightly
more than an *estado*, like a vault, which is closed with some wide,
thin stones. From that point to the top they are solid. . . ."[25] In
fact, although the *chullpa* with fine stone masonry are finished
on the outside in the shape of a flattened hemisphere, this convex
top is purely formal and not at all structural (*fig. 141*). The
corbeled vault ends much lower down, as can be seen in the cross-
sectional drawing (*fig. 142*). *Chullpa* of well-finished stone,
whether rectangular or circular in plan, always have double walls:
the outer composed of fine masonry and the inner of fieldstone,
the latter being the one that closes to form the corbeled vault.
It is important to note that in *chullpa* with a rectangular plan, the
inner structure, that which closes the corbeled vault, maintains a
circular plan.

Squier noted an artifice used to keep the stones well bonded
to one another. In the "lizard" *chullpa* at Sillustani (*figs. 143,
144*),

The ends of the several stones were hollowed out like a bowl, so
that, when set together, there was a cavity in which a stone was
placed, and the space filled with tough clay. In this manner the
stones were neatly cemented together, without the means by which
it was effected showing on the exterior. . . . The builders of the
monuments of Sillustani did not extend this device to the upper and
lower sides of the stones, probably depending on the weight of the
superincumbent mass of the structure to retain them in position.[26]

There is an Inca building, Pilco Kayma, on the Island of the
Sun (also called the Island of Titicaca) in Lake Titicaca, which
supports a second story by means of a system of corbeled vaults.
Since this "palace" is in Qollasuyu territory and was surely built
by Aymara *mit'a* labor, its form may be interpreted as the persistence of regional building experience and not as the result of Inca

154

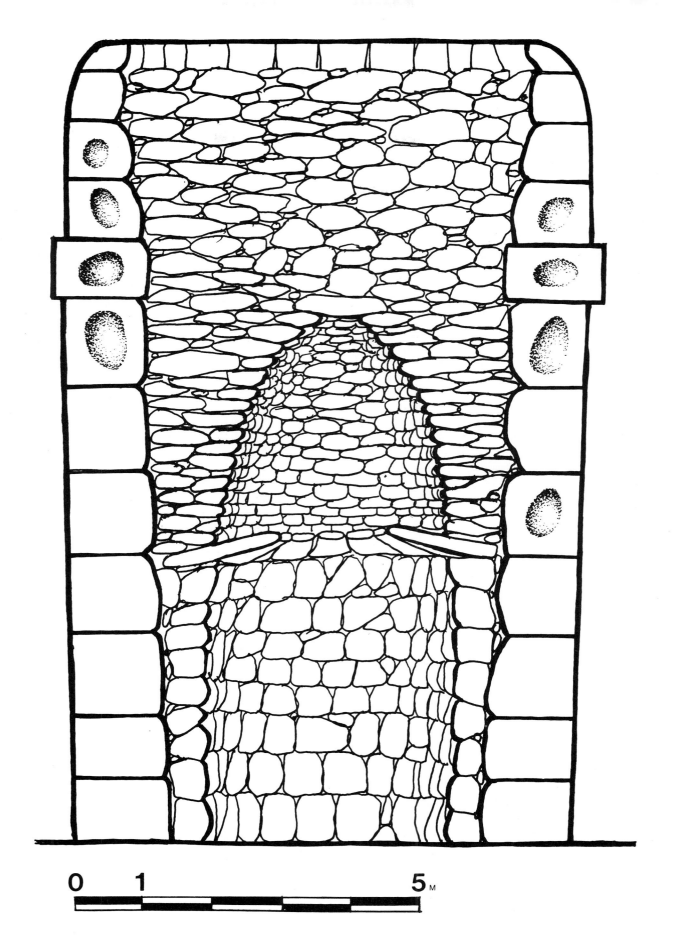

0   1   5 м

143. Sillustani. One of the hollow stones from the "lizard" *chullpa*. In the hole between two stones, another stone was placed in order to connect them and avoid possible movement.

144. Sillustani. Broken side of the "lizard" *chullpa*, in which the hollow stones are visible.

145. Paucartambo, Cuzco. These *chullpa* are of a different form and more modest construction.

146. Cutimbo, Puno. Zoomorphic decorations at the entrance of a *chullpa*.

147. Cuzco. Inca system for bridges and underground canalization.

government orders. We shall deal with this structure in the following chapter.

In Cuzco all the temples and "palaces" were roofed with thatch laid on wooden frameworks. No chronicler has mentioned the existence of vaulted buildings. Garcilaso, referring to the construction of underground passages (*fig. 147*) specifies: "They did not know how to build an arched vault; as they cut the walls, they left for the underground [passageways] some stone corbels on which they set, instead of beams, long stones, dressed on all

148. Chavín. The same structural system was used centuries earlier
in the underground galleries of the Chavín monuments.

six faces, very tightly fitted that reached from one wall to the
other."[27] On the basis of this description and recent evidence we
know that the bridges over the Huatanay and Tullumayo rivers
in Cuzco used the same solution indicated by Garcilaso, great
stone slabs set horizontally and supported on both sides on corbels. Exactly the same structural system was used in the subterranean galleries of Chavín (*fig. 148*).

House types

In the Inca planned settlements we cannot now determine with any certainty which buildings functioned as dwellings. The ruined state of many complexes and the similarity of the structures of the preserved sites prevent our determining the activities that were carried on inside of them. Only archaeology, by carefully examining the floors, can supply data that will help identify the original uses. In settlements like Huánuco Pampa and Machu Picchu it would be pretentious and dangerous to try to assign the original function to each of the structures; there are still many things we do not know about the spatial concept as it is related to family, collective, administrative, religious, and military activities. In spite of this fact, the special character of some buildings has allowed us to determine their function; on the basis of data from still limited archaeological investigations, the study of repetitive characteristics, and the persistence of traditional building customs, it has been possible to establish a typology of structures that could have served as dwellings. In this chapter we propose to analyze the forms and spaces of domestic architecture initiated by the state, that is, buildings that did not have a spontaneous origin. The technical structural problems will be studied in chapter 5.

A (*fig. 149*). The most simple single-family dwelling is always a single room with a rectangular plan. The least complex structure has no gables, so that the height of the walls forming the rectangular box is uniform. The hip roof rests directly on the top of the walls and is composed of a framework of small timbers interlaced with branches and then covered with *ichu* grass (*fig. 150*). The walls may be of stone or adobes. In the planned centers, fieldstone walls are always more carefully made than those built in areas not subject to state building controls. The interior area varies between 6 and 15 square meters. There is only one entrance and windows or other outlets for smoke are very rare.

There are rectangular buildings without gables of greater size and, sometimes, with more than one doorway. At Machu Picchu (*fig. 151*), Palkay, Patallaqta, Qhanabamba, and other centers of the Urubamba River area, there are various structures of this type. The interpretation of such structures as single-family dwellings is uncertain, however.

149. *A.* Type of one-room dwelling without gables. The roof frame
      rests directly on the walls. It is the simplest type of dwelling.

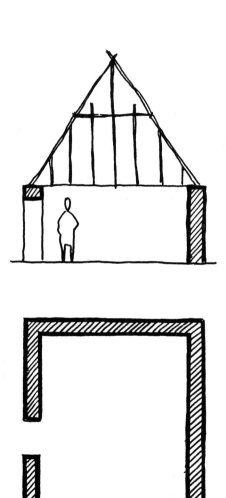

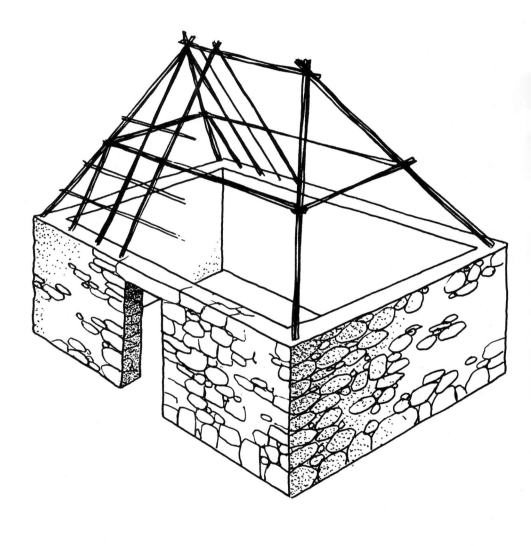

150. Modern peasant house with hip roof. Its state of disrepair
     reveals the structure of branches onto which the grass is tied.

151. Machu Picchu. Restored one-room house without gables in the agricultural sector.

B (*fig. 152*). The house with gables, which are always placed on the two shorter sides of the rectangular form, is also very common. The gables may be adobe or stone and are found equally on small buildings and on the great *kallanka*. Numerous well-finished stone and adobe examples are known from Machu Picchu, Wiñay Wayna, Raqchi, Pisaq, and many other sites. Some structures may have lost their adobe gables in the course of time; sometimes when adobe is unprotected and exposed for centuries to the eroding action of the rain, it is destroyed. In small houses both ends of the ridgepole rested on the apexes of the gables (*fig.*

152. *B*. Type of one-room dwelling with gables. It had a wooden ridgepole. The lower part of the frame rested directly on the walls.

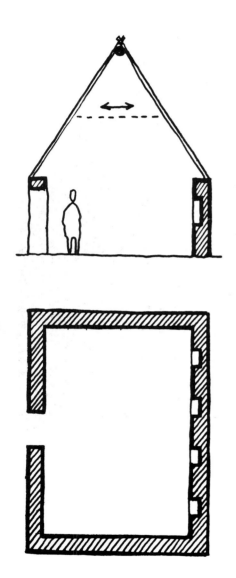

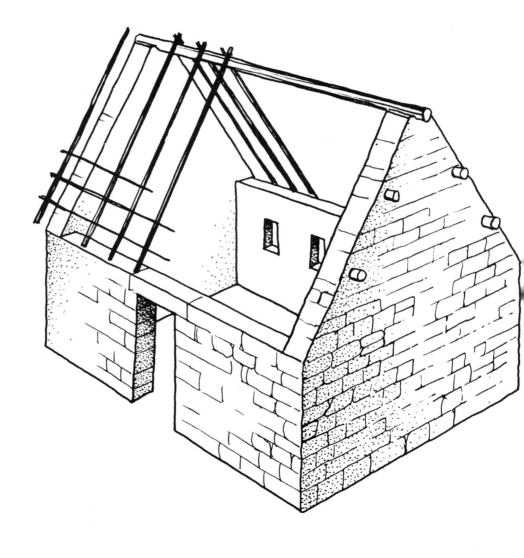

153. Machu Picchu. Example of one-room gabled dwelling. This type of house has a ridgepole resting on the apexes of the gables.

154. Machu Picchu. Exterior of the gable, with stone pegs to tie down the ends of the roof frame.

153). In longer chambers, where it was impossible to span the distance between one gable and the other with a single timber, wooden pillars were used to support the series of ridgepoles and the entire roof structure, a common practice in the *kallanka*. Cylindrical stone pegs, used to tie down and secure the roof, were often placed on the outside of the gables, parallel to the slope of the roof (*fig. 154*).

C (*fig. 155*). In another type of house the gabled roof lacks a ridgepole because the roof frame rests directly on a wall located on the long axis dividing the rectangular plan into two equal parts. In such cases the party wall established two separate and independent habitable spaces, since there was almost never any internal communication. The buildings adjacent to the Temple of Wiraqocha in Raqchi (*fig. 156*) illustrate this type of double chamber.

D (*fig. 157*). In more temperate regions, like the Urubamba River area, one of the long walls of the rectangular chamber disappears. Consequently, one of the roof slopes rests on a wooden

155. *C.* In this type of house the peak of the roof lies directly on the central wall that establishes two independent spaces. The drawing shows an example with one door on each side, but there are also some with two or more. Figure 166 shows one of the houses adjacent to the Temple of Wiraqocha at Raqchi that have two doors on each side.

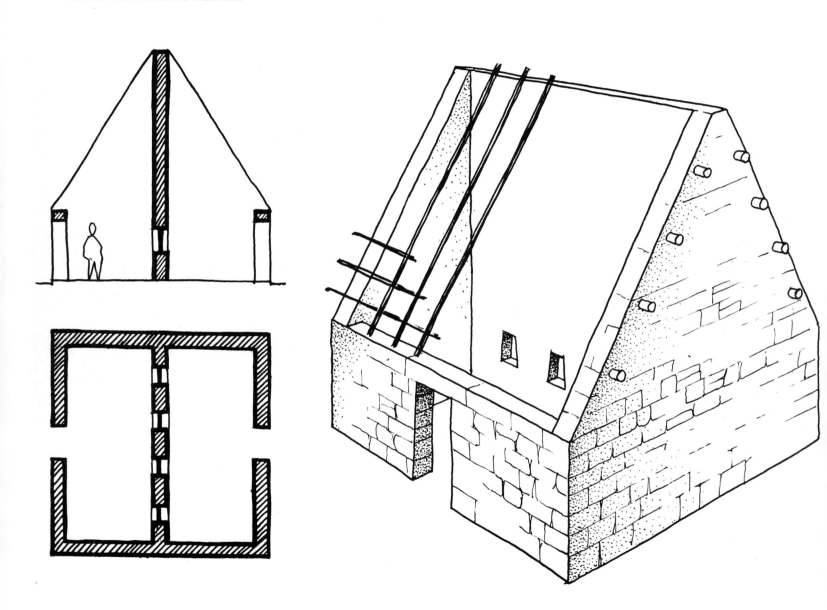

157. *D.* The house type called *masma*, possibly for temporary
occupancy. One of the long sides of the rectangle is open;
therefore, one of the roof slopes rests on a wooden beam.

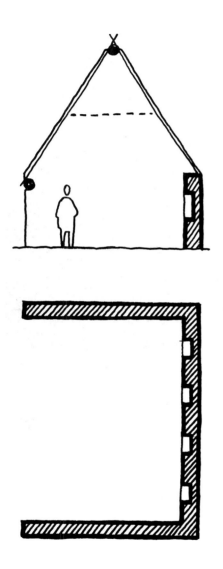

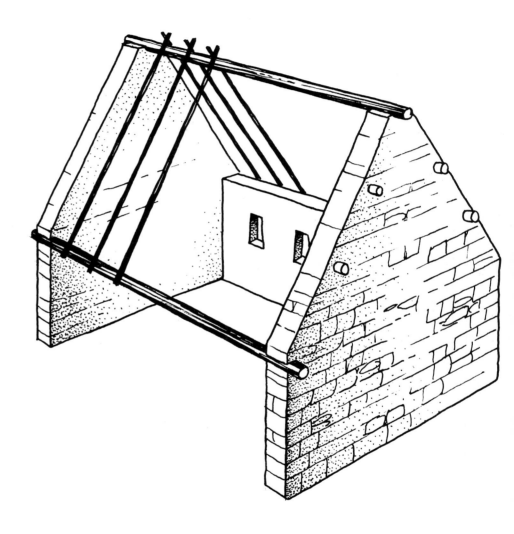

158. Machu Picchu. Two examples of *masma*-type houses with one
side completely open.

beam whose ends are set into the lateral walls at the height of the
angle of the gables. Luis Valcárcel calls this type of house
masma,[28] which means corridor, gallery, or enclosure open on one
of its sides (*fig. 158*). Although the large opening on one side
suggests a connection between this house and warm zones, similar
structures also exist in very cold places like Qollpa, at an altitude
of 3,800 meters. Possibly the *masma*-type structure had other
functions such as providing daytime work space.

E (*figs. 159, 160*). In the case of a very long *masma*, a pillar
was placed in the middle of the open side to help support the roof
and, also, to prevent the wooden beam from bending under an
excessive load.

159. *E*. When the open side of the *masma* reached a certain length,
a pillar was placed in the middle to prevent inflection of the
wooden beam.

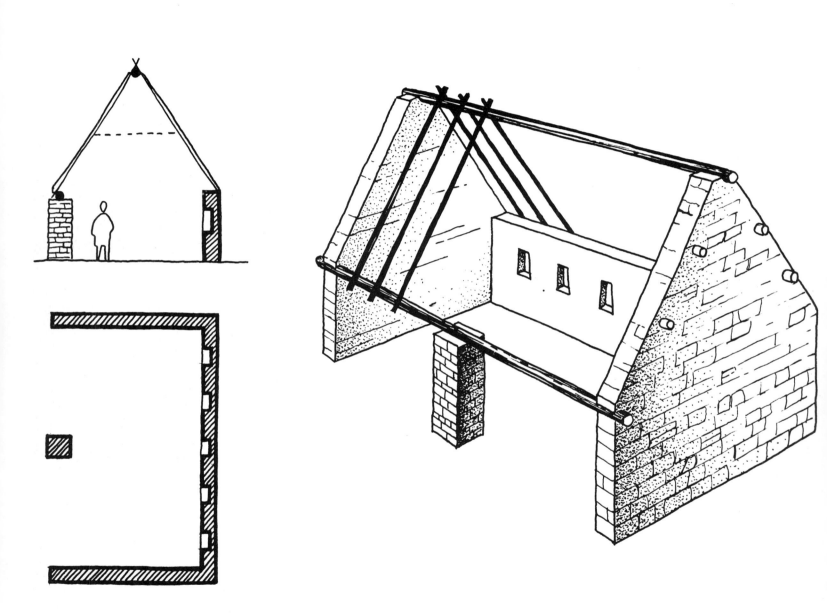

160. Machu Picchu. The famous "Temple of the Three Windows" was also a *masma*-type structure with a monolithic pillar in the middle of the open side.

F (*fig. 161*). There were also double *masma*. In these buildings the top of the roof frame rested on the central wall and the lower edge of each roof slope was fastened to a wooden beam set into the end walls as in type D. One of the best examples of this type is at Machu Picchu (*fig. 162*).

G (*fig. 163*). The two roof slopes of a dwelling or of a *masma* are not always equal. Often the front slope, where the entrance is, is much longer than the one resting on the back wall. In areas of frequent rain, the pitch is much greater to provide better water runoff.

H (*fig. 164*). There are various examples of two-story houses. When the building is on level ground the upper story has the same area as the lower, and the usable space is between the roof slopes. In such cases the long walls are the same height as those of one-story houses and the upper loft is used only as a granary or for storage. When a party wall divides the house in two equal parts, on each of the sides the ends of the beams bearing the upper story rest on a step built into the party wall; the other ends rest on the long outside wall. The upper story is reached from outside. In Ollantaytambo, near the plaza of Maniaraki, there is a well-preserved example of this type. In the planned section of the same town, the houses that have a central wall dividing and separating the two *kancha*-type living units have an upper story with the same characteristics. A similar arrangement probably existed at Patallaqta as well.

I (*fig. 165*). Most two-story houses are entered directly from the outside on each of the two stories because they take advantage of irregularities in the terrain. At Machu Picchu, Wiñay Wayna, and elsewhere we find ingenious solutions in the accommodation of buildings to steep slopes. At Machu Picchu the so-called House of the Ñusta provides an interesting solution for direct access to each of the two stories. On the other hand, the stepped house group called Pincuylluna at Ollantaytambo (*fig. 166*) and other similar buildings on the hill on the opposite side of the valley have a feature that prevents the determination of the level of the second floor as well as the discovery of their original functions. The doors providing access to the presumed upper floor, and the supporting step on which the upper floor beams must have rested,

161. *F*. The double *masma* also has a central wall on the long axis,
     repeating the two separate spaces.

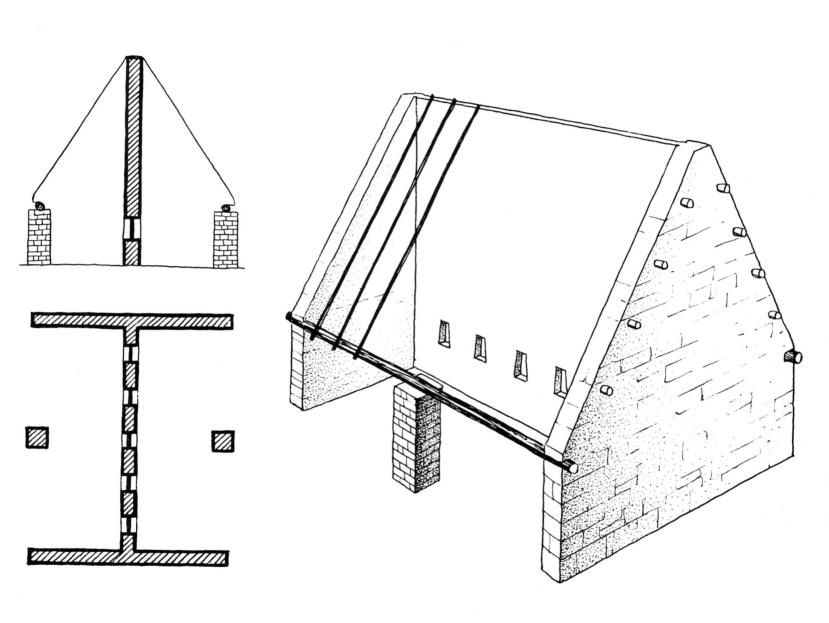

162. Machu Picchu. A good example of a double *masma*.

163. *G*. Machu Picchu. The two roof slopes are frequently of different lengths.

164. *H*. Ollantaytambo. Two-story house on level ground. Note the step where the joists of the upper floor were supported on the central wall.

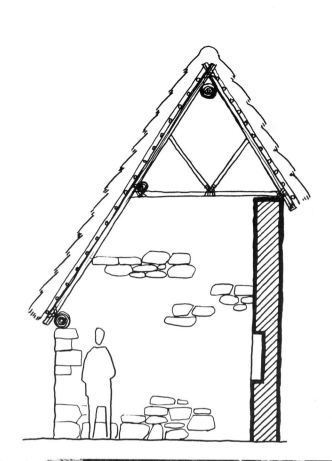

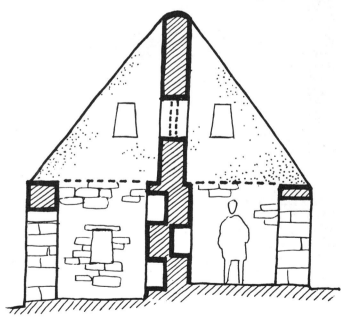

165. *I.* Machu Picchu. Two-story house. Using the uneven terrain, each story had direct communication with the outside. The supporting step for the second-floor joists is clearly visible.

166. Ollantaytambo. Stepped house group called Pincuylluna. 1930 photograph.

are completely unrelated to the level of the front wall, which ordinarily supported the opposite end of the beams. The accompanying drawing shows the difference in level and the difficulty of devising a convincing hypothesis (*fig. 167*). These buildings may not even have had a second floor, but then why have doors on the upper level? High on the lofty cliffs of the hills that overlook Ollantaytambo, these buildings have been subject to many interpretations. They have been called jails, workshops, houses of knowledge, schools, and storehouses—all suppositions lacking any solid basis. There are too many doors for a jail and the structures are too large to be *qollqa*, although they may have served to store products that needed a lot of ventilation. Since there is no certainty, however, it is better not to speculate on possible uses and to limit ourselves to pointing out the problem and indicating its structural characteristics.

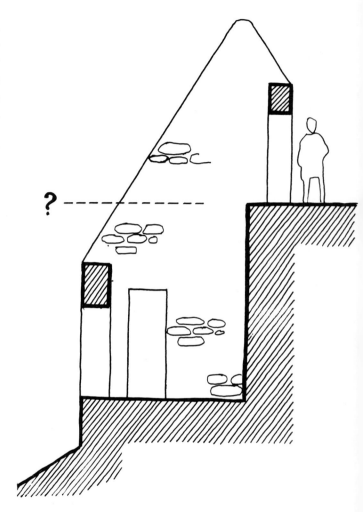

The coast

On the coast the Incas adopted the building systems characteristic of the region. There are no gables and no pitched roofs. Possibly the most identifiable Inca element is the trapezoidal shape, evident in many niches and doorways. Everything else —walls of adobe or tamped earth, flat roofs, a more complex distribution of interior space, and solutions provided by living complexes enclosed by walls—belongs to building experiences developed by coastal cultures before the Incas arrived. Tambo Colorado is a good example of an Inca establishment built with coastal techniques (*fig. 168*). Probably local *mit'a* labor worked on building the complex that the Inca ordered constructed. The result is an integration of Inca principles of organization with the coastal technical tradition.

On the coast the circular form and the curved line are practically nonexistent in dwellings. The very large urban settlements like Chanchan, Cajamarquilla, and Pachacamac solved their design problems within a rectangular system. Dwellings of the pre-Inca coastal cultures display more practical and functional distribution of internal space than do those of the Incas. This tradition developed over a long time and permitted the accumulation of experiences that gradually improved the *modus vivendi* of the

167. Ollantaytambo. It is hard to determine whether or not the upper doors of the hillside houses opened onto an accessible floor. The step for the presumed support of the floor joists is not related to the support on the outside wall.

168. Tambo Colorado. The Inca buildings on the coast apply local experiences without abandoning the formal elements that define their identity.

inhabited spaces. Sequences of rooms alternating with open court-yards, and corridors facilitating the performance of family activities, are frequently found. The plan of the country house at Puruchuco, Lima (*figs. 169, 170*) demonstrates a skillful spatial distribution, a clear concept of family intimacy, and an adequate adaptation to climatic conditions. The Inca *kancha* of the high-lands, on the other hand, are always more rigid and frequently repeat the same scheme, ignoring the discomforts produced by harsh climates and lacking the distributive versatility of the coastal structures.

The kancha

The concept of a walled rectangular block enclosing groups of one-room buildings destined for dwelling and other uses (*fig. 171*) was widely used by the Incas and, as noted, may have originated in coastal architectural experiences, especially those of the Chimú culture. If the Incas did receive this cultural loan from the coast, they paid more attention to the formal characteristics than to the functional relation of the form to the environment. On the coast it does not rain and temperatures are never extreme. Under such conditions, a person going from one room to another, passing through courtyards and open corridors, does not have to suffer from foul weather. In contrast, the same distributive criteria applied in the highlands in the most elementary form must have caused constant discomfort to those who had to endure the cold and rain every time they crossed the open space from one out-building to another.

The Inca *kancha* unites, within its confines, buildings in-tended for a single function. This criterion was applied equally to the Temple of the Sun, the Qorikancha, and to the "palaces" and the planned structures of Ollantaytambo, Patallaqta, and other places. The golden enclosure, the Qorikancha, was doubt-less the *kancha* of highest symbolic rank and its arrangement, with six buildings around a quadrangular courtyard, served as a model for temples in other urban centers. This monument will be dis-cussed in more detail in the following chapter. The Cuzco "palaces" located in the sacred zone of the city, that is, between

169. Panoramic view of the estate of Puruchuco after its restoration

170. The plan of the estate of Puruchuco. The rooms with shading
are those that were roofed. The plan reveals an understanding
of spatial distribution that never reached the highlands.

N

0   5   10 m

171. *Kancha* model with five separate and independent rooms inside
the enclosure. The pronounced roof pitch is striking.
(Archaeological Museum of the University of Cuzco.)

172. Cuzco. Ancient *kancha* walls with new doorways. Inca base
     and upper story with Spanish flavor. An example of spatial and
     temporal historical stratification and continuity of life in the
     city.

the Huatanay and Tullumayo rivers, were also large *kancha* that
effectively occupied an entire block each. A single door provided
access to the *kancha*, and the enclosure wall was of fine masonry.
In Cuzco there are good examples of walls that originally enclosed
the *kancha*. After the Spanish conquest, these great spaces suffered
multiple divisions and distributions. As a result of the process of
parceling out the *kancha*, various doorways were opened in the
enclosure walls, often very roughly, and a second story was added
in the Spanish formal tradition. Today this colonial superposition
on Inca walls represents the most outstanding feature of his-
toric-architectural stratification in the cultural continuity of the
city (*fig. 172*).

173. Double *kancha* at Patallaqta according to measurements made
by Hiram Bingham in 1912.

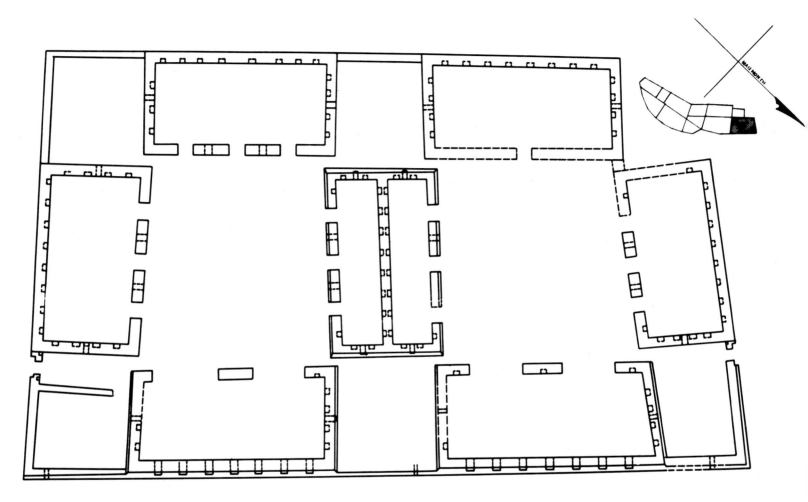

In various archaeological sites there are remains of groupings
than can be seen to have used the *kancha* distributive system.
Sometimes the *kancha* is well defined, with its enclosure wall and
a single entrance; in other instances there is no clear evidence of
the wall, but the remains of two, three, four, or more separate
rooms set around a courtyard are clearly visible. At Patallaqta, for
example (*fig. 173*), there are repeated groupings of two small
houses, facing each other across a courtyardlike open space; then
there are U-shaped groupings of three rectangular structures
around a courtyard; finally, the largest units consist of a quadrangular courtyard formed by four rooms, three of which have
three doors each while the fourth is a *masma*. This type of arrangement is very frequent in the Urubamba Valley centers, but

174. The *kancha* of Palkay have three rooms within the enclosure and a single entrance. The plan is by Hiram Bingham, made in 1912.

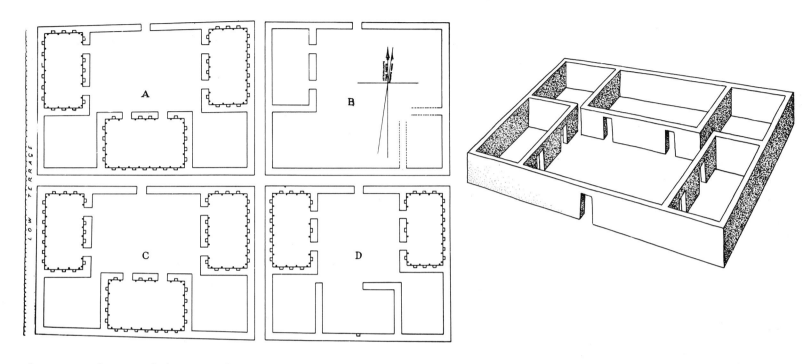

the same characteristics are also repeated in settlements quite distant from the capital. While it is possible to pass between one unit and another at Patallaqta, this cannot be done in the case of enclosed *kancha* with a single entrance. The *kancha* at Palkay have three independent rooms on three sides of the quadrangular enclosure; the fourth side consists of the wall with the entrance doorway (*fig. 174*).

Surely the best preserved example of *kancha* is found in the planned settlement of Ollantaytambo (*fig. 175*). The town plan has already been discussed in chapter 2, and here we will briefly describe the type of *kancha*. Each rectangular block, surrounded on all four sides by narrow streets, contains two completely independent living compounds with a single entrance to each compound opening onto opposite streets. The two units duplicate the same design, comprising four rooms set around a quadrangular courtyard (*fig. 176*). The only doorway opened into a structure, probably of the *masma* type, that is now the most deteriorated in all the compounds. In the courtyard two identical rooms face each other. At the back is the main house, which shares a party

175. Ollantaytambo. Repetitive design in the plan of three blocks of
the residential sector. This plan was made by Hiram Bingham
in 1913 and shows details no longer visible.

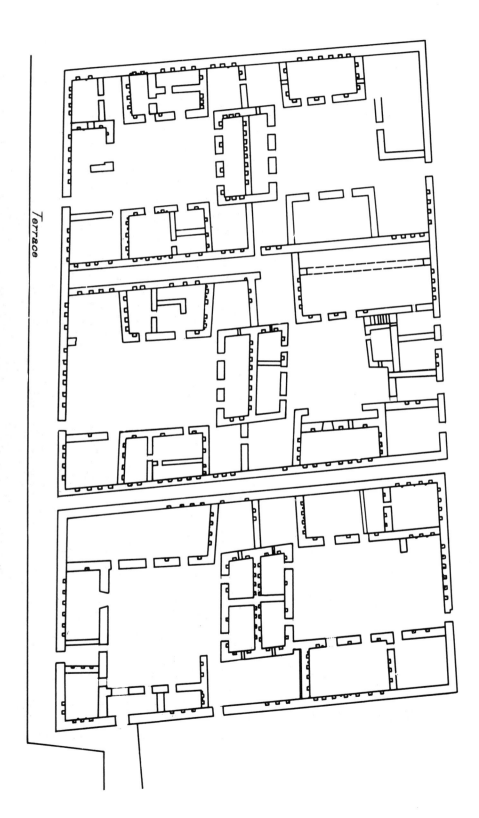

176. Ollantaytambo. Hypothetical reconstruction of one of the enclosures with double *kancha*. There is no communication between the two.

177. Ollantaytambo. Present condition of one of the entrances.

178. Ollantaytambo. In the inner courtyards many elements remain, permitting one to imagine the original shapes and spaces.

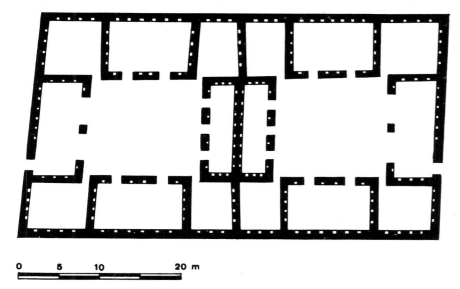

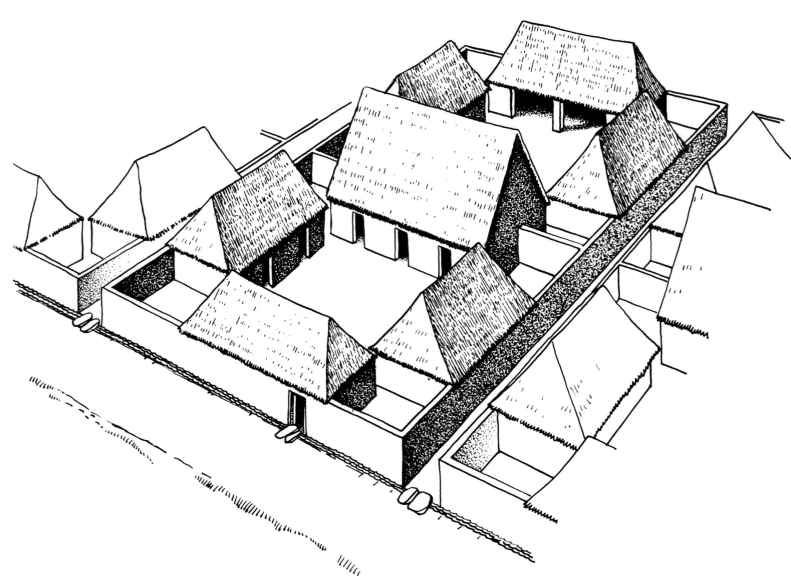

wall with the opposite compound so that only one of the two
roof slopes belongs to each compound. The structure at the back
is the largest house, with three doorways in the front and a loft.
Each of the rooms occupies one side of the quadrangular *kancha*,
and, since the corners do not meet, there is space for four corner
courts, possibly used for storage or as corrals for livestock (*fig.
179*). The doorways into the *kancha*, with double jambs, and

those into the rooms around the courtyard, with monolithic lintels, are very large, averaging 2.70 meters in height. These measurements, combined with the quality of the stonework, prevent the classification of these structures as rural houses, although we know nothing of the rank of their occupants. Luis Pardo calls these *kancha* "palaces."[29] Today, although modified and dilapidated, they are occupied by peasant families of Ollantaytambo. Kubler observes that they may be "the oldest continuously-occupied dwellings in South America."[30]

To summarize, it is clear that as far as Inca residences are concerned, the circular form was practically eliminated from state construction, and the rectangular plan prevailed. In Inca settlements the dwellings were single rooms of limited size, arranged within the distributive concept of the *kancha*, a solution that functioned equally for the nuclear family and for the requirements of religious ritual and of "courtly" life.

As a final observation we must reemphasize the insistence on building structurally separate chambers. In other words, in architecture built under state auspices, we do not find the type of house formed by the linked repetition of living cells separated only by a sequence of gabled walls. As noted, the only division applied was established by central walls on the long axis of the rectangular shape. But why did they not use sequences of gabled walls to form a continuous row of independent rooms? In known Inca examples, the gabled walls only close and delimit the extremes of a single rectangular unit, unconnected to any other.

The question is still open because there exists the precedent of Iskanwaya (*figs. 180–82*), in the canton of Aukapata, department of La Paz, Bolivia.[31] This is an archaeological site of more than 10 hectares, in which various groups of row houses form three sides of an unwalled quadrangular courtyard. The principal row of continuously connected rooms has seven compartments, each comprising an open corridor in front of a room. The party wall separates the two chambers. The Iskanwaya complex appears to be pre-Inca, but that is not certain. It is mentioned here to point out a system of continuous dwellings that is inexplicably lacking in the patterns of Inca official architecture.

180. Iskanwaya. View of a sector of the archaeological center.
181. Iskanwaya. Hypothetical reconstruction of the sequence of linked rooms.

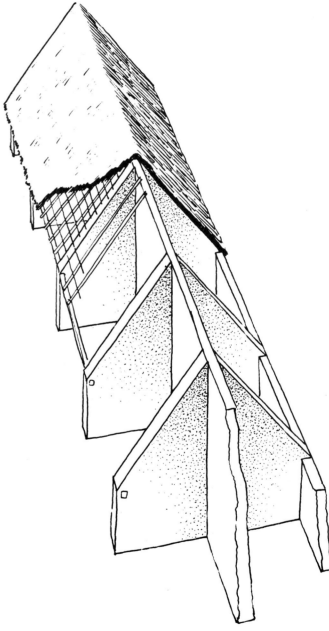

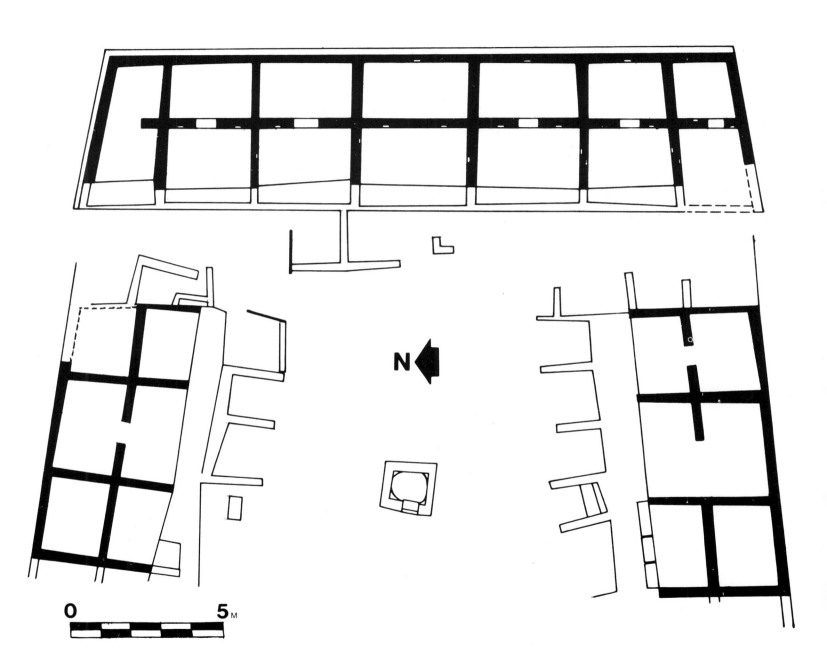

182. Iskanwaya. Plan of a sector of the settlement. The structure on the east (above) has seven rooms in a row. The system of using dividing walls in the form of a gable was not used by the Incas.

N

0   5 M

4

The Architecture of Power

This chapter deals with the edifices constructed by the Inca government for collective, administrative, religious, and military purposes. In a certain sense it refers to what we would call public works, in spite of the fact that there were many limitations to public participation. The Qorikancha, for example, and other temples and sanctuaries were places of very limited access, and the *inkawasi* and *aqllawasi* were privileged precincts to which very few were admitted. If by "public works" we are to understand those built by the state for various civil, religious, and military uses—independent of collective participation—we find that domestic architecture in the planned settlements, analyzed in the preceding chapter, also qualifies. In other words, everything built within the planned programs of the government, be it dwellings, temples, or cities, must be considered to have been regulated by the state. All Inca structures, without exception, belong to an activity planned and directed by government technicians and carried out by the participants in the *mit'a*. It is possible that almost all the structures that are today identified as "Inca architecture" may belong to an activity realized after 1440.

One of our most difficult problems is still that of identifying the functions of the buildings that we see today as ruins. In the case of some edifices of great importance and significance, like the Qorikancha in Cuzco or the Temple of Wiraqocha in Raqchi at San Pedro de Cacha, the functions are known, thanks to the fame that they enjoyed and to detailed chroniclers' descriptions. There are, however, other important and well-known structures that arouse doubt concerning the use attributed to them. The so-called fortress of Saqsaywaman, for example, was another "royal house of the sun . . . which the Spanish commonly call the Fortress," according to Cieza.[1] It is also hard to determine the function of the buildings at Machu Picchu, in spite of their better state of preservation and notwithstanding the literature for tourists by the "interpreters of ruins." Craig Morris discusses the same problem with relation to the great administrative center of Huánuco Pampa.[2] Of the thousands of structures of that settlement, which ones were actually related to administration? We really have very little chance of finding out. And the similarity among Inca structures, already noted, increases the difficulty of identifying functions. Nevertheless, when form and arrangement are repeated, it is precisely this similarity which sometimes permits the construction of a hypothesis that may explain the function of the inner space of the buildings. In this case, by similarity we mean the repetition of the same forms and building systems. Now repetition almost always results from a conscious intention to duplicate the model considered to be representative for a given function. This intent is strengthened when it is supported and imposed by the state, because in the repetition of the model one of the features of the dominant culture is identified in conquered territories. The symbolic model was Cuzco. Its plan, architecture, and surrounding topography were considered in founding new settlements. Its palaces and temples influenced the form and character of the buildings that were constructed along the highways of Tawantinsuyu.

One type of edifice that is found in Cuzco and is repeated from Cajamarca to Inkallaqta in Boliva is the so-called *kallanka*.

The kallanka

The general characteristics of this building are similar in all known examples, and only the dimensions vary. It consists of a great rectangular hall, very long, with a gabled roof supported by a series of pillars set the entire length of the long axis. One of the longer sides, with various doorways, always opens onto the main plaza. More rarely, as at Huánuco Pampa, there is also a doorway in one of the short sides of the rectangular shape. The interior is undivided: a single very large space covered by a thatched roof over a wooden framework. On the wall opposite the doors that face the plaza, there is no communication, but rather a continuous sequence of niches or windows. The short sides of this rectangular great hall always have stone gables, which sometimes terminate in adobe. Frequently two *kallanka* are lined up on one side of the plaza with little separation between them. Since there are also cases in which there is a single *kallanka* on one side of the plaza, we may interpret this difference as a hierarchical distinction between administrative centers of regional importance and the local *tampu* that the Inca government built all along the *qhapaq-ñan* at specified intervals. In Cajamarca, an important center, there were surely at least two *kallanka* on one side of the "immense" plaza. Jerez and Pizarro refer to these great halls, in which they quartered when they arrived in the city on November 15, 1532. Prescott, referring to Hernando Pizarro's letter, says that in Cajamarca "there was a square . . . which was almost triangular in form—of an immense size, surrounded by low buildings. These consisted of capacious halls, with wide doors or openings communicating with the square. They were probably intended as a sort of barracks for the Inca's soldiers."[3] Cieza de León, on passing through Huamachuco, another important center, observed the great plaza "wherein were built the *tambos* or royal palaces, among which are two [that are] twenty-two feet wide and as long as a race course, made all of stone, and embellished with long thick beams [and] placed on the very top the dry grass which they use very neatly."[4] In the administrative center of Huánuco Pampa there are also two quite well-preserved *kallanka* lined up on the plaza; each is about 70 meters long. In contrast, in the nearby *tampu* of Tunsukancha, a single *kallanka* occupies one side of the plaza. There are other similar structures, but they are on the other sides of the plaza. At Inkallaqta in Bolivia there is also a single *kallanka*, and the same is true of Huchuy Cuzco in the Urubamba Valley. There are evidences of *kallanka* at Pumpu, Tarmatambo, and other places.

In Cuzco there were also two great halls lined up on one side of the plaza of Haucaypata: the Cassana and Coracora. Similar structures occupied the other sides. Garcilaso deals with these edifices in great detail and notes:

In many of the Incas' houses there were very large great halls, two hundred paces long and fifty to sixty wide, one single chamber, which served as a plaza, where they held their festivals and dances when the rainy weather did not permit them to be outside in the plaza. In the city of Cozco I managed to see four of these great halls that were still standing in my childhood. One was in Amarucancha, houses that were Hernando Piçarro's, where the school of the Holy Society of Jesus is today, and another was in Cassana, where my schoolmate Juan de Cillorico's stores are now, and another was in Collcampata, in the houses that belonged to the Inca Paullu and his son Don Carlos, who was also my schoolmate. This great hall was the smallest of the four, and the largest was that of Cassana, which had a capacity of three thousand people. It seems incredible that there would have been timbers capable of spanning such large chambers. The fourth great hall now serves as the Cathedral.[5]

Much further along in his *Comentarios* he adds:

Then there is the Cathedral, which opens onto the plaza. That building, in Inca times, was a beautiful great hall which served them as a plaza for their festivals on rainy days. They were houses of the Inca Viracocha, eighth King; the only one of them still standing in my time was the great hall; when the Spaniards entered that city they all quartered in it that they might be all together whatever might happen. I knew it thatched and saw it roofed with tiles.[6]
    . . . there were two royal houses that opened onto the main plaza. They took up the entire side of the plaza; the one to the east of the other was called Coracora: which means meadows because that place was a large meadow and the plaza in front of it was a quagmire or swamp, and the Incas ordered it fixed up as it is. . . . The other royal house, to the west of Coracora, was called Cassana, which means that which freezes. They gave it this name in admiration, meaning that it had such large and beautiful buildings that they would freeze and stun those who looked at them attentively. They were houses of the great Inca Pachacútec, great-grandson of the Inca Roca, who, to favor the schools that his great-grandfather had founded, ordered his house built near them. Those two royal houses had the schools behind them. . . . of the [royal house] called Cassana there were still standing in my time a great part of the walls, which were of finely cut stone masonry, demonstrating that they had been royal seats, and a very beautiful great hall, which in Inca times, served on rainy days as a plaza for their festivals and dances. It was so large that sixty horsemen could very easily play *cañas* inside it. I saw the monastery of San Francisco in that great hall. . . . In the great hall they had set off a large portion for the church, with room for many people; then there were the cells, dormitory and refectory and the rest of the monastery offices, and, if it had been open, inside they could have made a cloister. . . .
    In front of those houses, which were royal houses, is the principal plaza of the city, called Haucaipata, that is terrace or plaza of festivals and delights. . . . At the end of the plaza, to the south of it,

there were two other royal houses; the one near the river, separated from it by a street, was called Amarucancha, which is *barrio* of the great snakes; it was facing Cassana; they were the houses of Huaina Cápac; now they belong to the Holy Society of Jesus. There remained of them in my time a great hall, although not as large as the one of Cassana. . . . To the east of Amarucancha, on the other side of the street of the sun, is the *barrio* called Acllahuaci, that is house of the chosen women. . . .

. . . the Incas had those three great halls on the sides and front of the plaza, in order to hold their principal festivals in them even though it might be raining, the days on which such festivals fell, which were on the new moons of certain months and on the solstices.[7]

The great halls of the Cuzco plaza were probably not formally and spatially different from the ones we know better, like those at Huánuco Pampa and Inkallaqta, because they were preserved with their gables. Although all cases indicate collective use, this use must have been adapted to different situations and purposes related to the location and rank of the settlement within the geography of Tawantinsuyu. For example, in Cuzco, a sacred city with many ceremonies, the functional attribution of Garcilaso may be correct: that of providing covered spaces for festivals in case of rain. Nevertheless, Pachakuti Yamqui Salcamaygua, referring to the great hall called Cuyusmanco (the same one Garcilaso indicates as the first cathedral), says that it was an "audience and council house," while Gonçález Holguín defines it as "The house of the Council, or of justice with three walls and one open."[8] Despite the brevity of this description it still marks the characteristics of the *kallanka*: three walls without access and the "open" one, which would be the side with the sequence of doorways.

In conquered and administered territory we may suggest other uses for these buildings. In relatively important administrative centers the *kallanka* that face on the plaza probably had more than one function. From time to time they may have served as covered space to celebrate festivals on rainy days during the visit of a high functionary, the celebration of some religious ceremony, or the passage of a triumphant army. It is more probable, however, as Morris has suggested,[9] that they served as tempo-

183. Huánuco Pampa. The remains of the two *kallanka* facing the plaza stand out among the ruins.

rary lodging, more for individuals than for families: transient human groups, soldiers or people fulfilling their *mit'a*. The archaeological excavations that Morris carried out in one of the *kallanka* at Huánuco Pampa demonstrated that there was no continuous occupation in that space.

Cristóbal de Molina, referring to the movement of transient human masses like armies, attributes a perfectly clear and definite function to the *kallanka* when he notes: "they were quartered . . . in the town they reached, in some great halls and large houses that they had made for the purpose, [the largest of which] were one hundred fifty paces long, very wide and spacious, with room for a great quantity of people in each, very well roofed, clean and neat, with many doors, so that they might be very light and pleasant. . . ."[10] Surely this attribution defines the functions of the *kallanka* very precisely.

The *kallanka* of the *tampu* of Tunsukancha may also have served as quarters for the garrison charged with the control and care of the site, or as occasional sleeping space for a passing army.[11] We still lack data, and only intensive archaeological research, as indispensable as it is rare, will provide further information. Nevertheless, it is very probable that outside of Cuzco these

184. Huánuco Pampa. Clearing operations in the northern *kallanka* during the 1965 field season.

185. Huánuco Pampa. In the foreground, a circle of stones that held one of the wooden pillars upon which the ridgepole rested.

great halls served primarily as temporary lodging for the human groups compelled to move frequently for military or occupational reasons. In passing we may suggest that the *kallanka* represent one type of programmed edifice in the administrative centers and *tampu* that the Incas founded along the *qhapaq-ñan*. These buildings are notably absent in establishments like those of the Inca central region, which had a different character because they were not exposed to the transit of large masses of people.

In 1965, during the clearing and consolidation carried out at Huánuco Pampa by the Institute of Andean Research (*fig. 184*), the archaeologist Craig Morris investigated the "*kallanka* on the north side [which] was cleaned and exposed down to the original floor; in the one on the south side only the walls were cleaned and exposed. In the center of the building some circles of stones were found indicating what were possibly seven pillars that supported the roof."[12] The discovery of the seven circles in the floor (*fig. 185*) is of great importance in understanding the structure

186. Huánuco Pampa. Present condition of the northern *kallanka*.
The drawing, made on a transparency over the photo, offers a
hypothetical idea of the interior of the *kallanka*.

of the roof. On the long axis of this *kallanka*, which measures
more than 70 meters, there were seven wooden pillars, actually
seven very tall tree trunks, that supported the ridgepole of the
gabled roof (*fig. 186*). They must have been wooden, because the
size of the circular hole surrounded by the stones precludes the
suggestion of masonry columns with such a small diameter and
yet so high. The shape of the gables reveals the pitch of the roof
and the height of the gable end, approximately 8 meters (*fig.
187*). The internal measurements of the rectangular form are 72

187. Huánuco Pampa. Façade of the northern *kallanka* in its present state. The drawing, made on a transparency over the photo, gives an idea of the possible volume and how the exterior of this building might have appeared.

188. Huánuco Pampa. The interior of the northern *kallanka*, which is 72 meters long.

meters long by 11.85 wide (*fig. 188*). Besides the nine doorways that open onto the plaza, in one of the short sides there is another one that communicates with the "street of the doorways" (*fig. 189*). On the wall opposite the nine doorways are ten windows. The other *kallanka* (*fig. 190*), which has not been explored to the original floor level, is very similar but somewhat shorter. It is distinguished by having only four doorways onto the plaza, which alternate with five windows. We cannot tell whether the smaller number of doorways relates to a difference in function.

189. Huánuco Pampa. Plan of the two *kallanka* facing the plaza. The "street of the doorways" begins in the space that separates them. The floor of the northern *kallanka* was excavated by Craig Morris, who discovered the stone bases for seven wooden pillars.

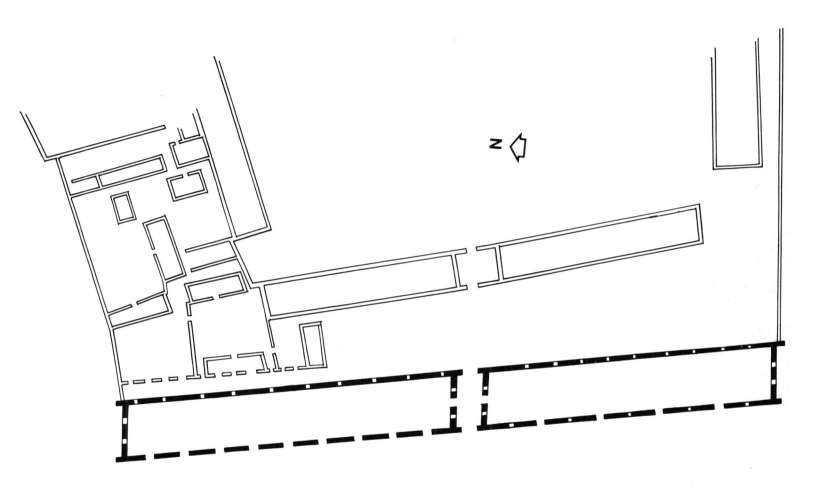

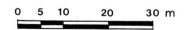

0   5   10   20   30 m

190. Huánuco Pampa. The south gable of the southern *kallanka* seen
     from inside.

191. Inkallaqta. Remains of the walls defining the enclosure. At the back is the large gable wall.

192. Inkallaqta. The *kallanka* enclosure seen from a nearby hill. See figure 105 for the plan of the Inkallaqta complex.

Another *kallanka* with remains that suggest its original form (*figs. 191, 192*) is located at Inkallaqta, a considerable distance from Huánuco Pampa and to the east of Cochabamba, in the area of the ancient Pocona. In chapter 1 we noted that, in the data gathered by Garci Diez de San Miguel on his inspection trip of 1567, the principal men of the Urinsaya division of Chucuito declared that they gave Indians to the Inca for *mitimaes* in Pocona, among other places.[13] The name of Inkallaqta, meaning Inca

193. Inkallaqta. The rectangular plan of the *kallanka*.

194. Inkallaqta. The retaining wall of the *kallanka* with its forty-four niches.

195. Inkallaqta. Present state of the only preserved gable wall. It has ten niches in the lower part and four windows in the upper part.

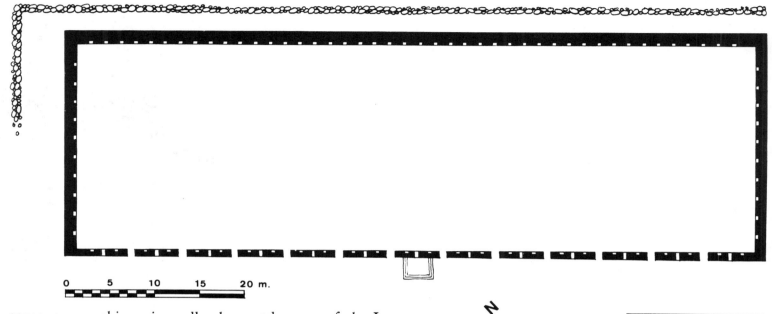

0   5   10   15   20 m.

N

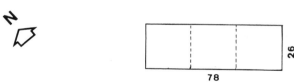

78

26

town, says nothing, since all urban settlements of the Incas are, by definition, Inkallaqta. It is a conventional name, probably accepted and popularized since the site was first seen with scientific eyes by the Swedish ethnologist Erland Nordenskiöld in 1914.[14] The rectangular building measures 78 meters long by 26 wide, an area of 2,028 square meters (*fig. 193*). Since the dimensions of the enormous great hall of Cassana in Cuzco are unknown, the covered area of the Inkallaqta *kallanka* is surpassed only by the Temple of Wiraqocha in Raqchi, which has 2,323 square meters. The façade fronting on the plaza has twelve narrow doorways only 78 centimeters wide. Between one doorway and the next there is a 40-centimeter wide window, for a total of thirteen windows. Between the sixth and seventh door are the remains of a small stepped platform that could well be the *usnu*. The back wall is a retaining wall and is much higher than the façade. It is enriched on the inside by a long sequence of forty-four niches (*fig. 194*). The doorways, windows, and niches are not trapezoidal but rectangular. Only one of the short sides of the rectangular shape preserves remains of the gable. This wall has ten niches in the lower part and four large windows further up (*fig. 195*). The triangular top portion of the gables was adobe, and

196. Inkallaqta. Detail of a gable wall. On the upper part are the
remains of adobe.

there are still remains of this material on the preserved gable (*fig. 196*). The reconstructive study of the roof does not allow us to propose that this *kallanka* had a single row of wooden pillars on the long axis like the one in Huánuco Pampa. A calculation of the length of each of the two slopes of the roof (*fig. 197*) yields a figure of more than 16 meters, a very long distance to span with single timbers. Given the example of the Temple of Wiraqocha in Raqchi, it is quite possible that this *kallanka* also had four naves (*fig. 198*). If not, the roof must have had a series of complicated frames to span such large spaces and avoid the inevitable sag. The reconstruction drawing (*fig. 199*) is not based on data; it is purely hypothetical, based on structural logic.

Jesús Lara uses the term *aranwa* instead of *kallanka* to identify this type of great hall in Aymara territory.[15] Roberto Terán suggests that the settlement of Inkallaqta was built by Thupa Inca between 1463 and 1472. He also indicates that the settlement was attacked and partially destroyed in 1525 in the course of an invasion by Guaraní Indians guided by the Portuguese adventurer Alejo García. The invaders were repulsed and from that incursion remained the nickname of *chiriguaná, chiriwanaj,* or *chiriwano,* meaning men who could not stand the cold of the Andean highlands.[16] It is highly unlikely, however, that that name derives from the Inca language.

There was great variation in the dimensions of the *kallanka*. The one on the plaza of Huchuy Cuzco measures approximately 40 by 12 meters and has adobe walls on a stone base more than a meter high. It has five double-jamb doors.

In Vitcos-Rosaspata, the *kallanka* may have been composed of four separate chambers with a single continuous façade having

197. Inkallaqta. The calculation of the length of the two slopes of
the roof.

198. Inkallaqta. Possible structural system for sustaining the roof
of the *kallanka*. Because of its width, it must have had four
naves.

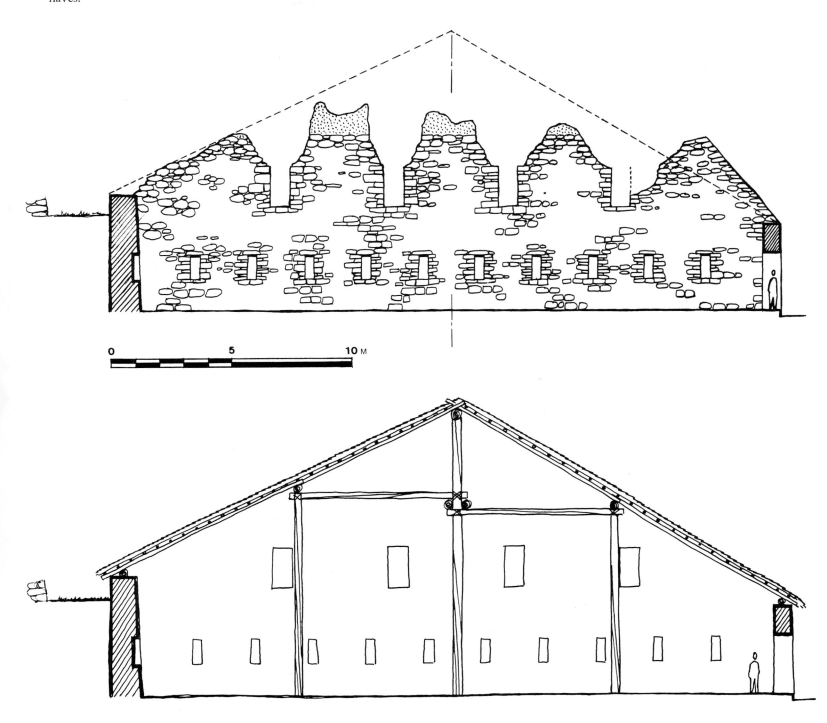

199. Inkallaqta. Hypothetical reconstruction of the *kallanka* with the four possible naves.

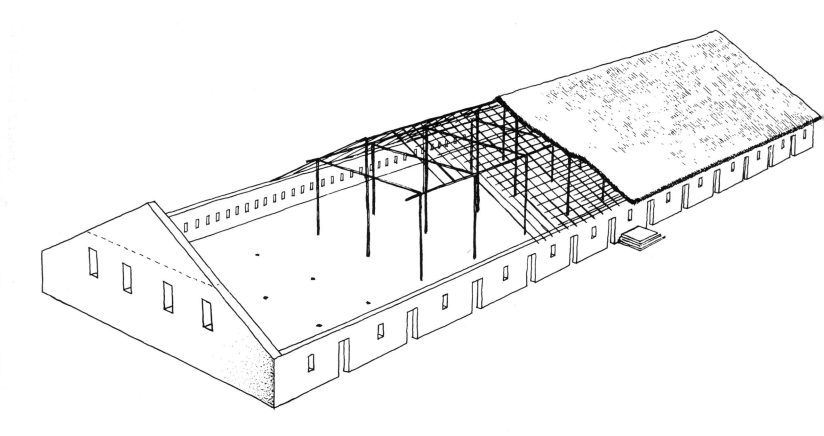

fifteen doorways opening onto the plaza (*fig. 200*). The doorways that correspond to the passages formed by the separation between the chambers have double jambs. This sort of *kallanka* may be a variant of the standard type and may also, because of its different form, have had other functions. Other cases of separate chambers with a single continuous façade are known. In the Qorikancha itself, in Cuzco, the two halls on the west side of the courtyard are separated by a passage but connected by a single façade. There, also, the doorway corresponding to the passage has a double jamb. The acquisition of better data from the Vitcos-Rosaspata complex is hindered by its present state of advanced deterioration. Hiram Bingham's 1911 plan (*fig. 201*) offers a clearer idea of the layout and served as a basis for our hypothetical reconstruction (*fig. 202*).

200. The structure with four chambers and one continuous façade is more than 73 meters long.

201. Plan of Vitcos-Rosaspata made by Hiram Bingham in 1911. Today the complex is badly deteriorated and very little remains of the long façade on the plaza.

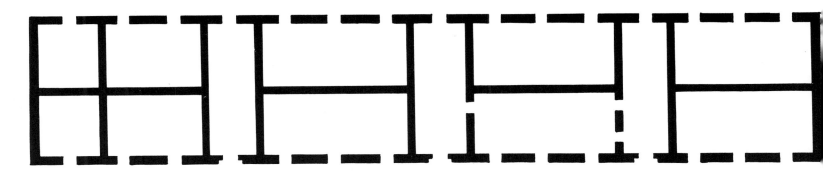

0   5   10   20 M

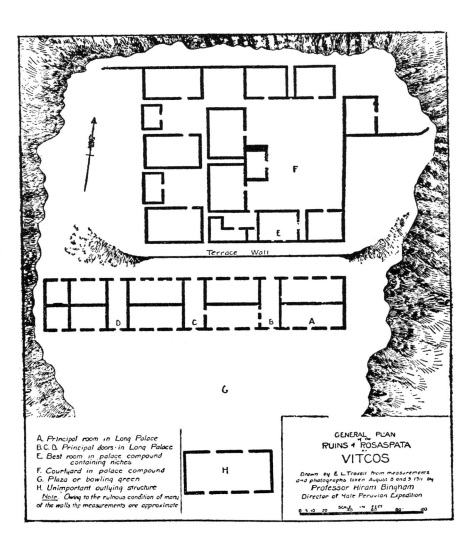

Terrace Wall

A. Principal room in Long Palace
B.C.D. Principal doors in Long Palace
E. Best room in palace compound containing niches
F. Courtyard in palace compound
G. Plaza or bowling green
H. Unimportant outlying structure
Note. Owing to the ruinous condition of many of the walls the measurements are approximate

GENERAL PLAN
of the
RUINS of ROSASPATA
VITCOS

Drawn by E.L.Troxell from measurements
and photographs taken August 8 and 9 1911 by
Professor Hiram Bingham
Director of Yale Peruvian Expedition

SCALE IN FEET

202. Hypothetical reconstruction of the Vitcos-Rosaspata structure. The double-jamb doorways coincide with the passageways (as in the Qorikancha) and do not break the continuity of the façade.

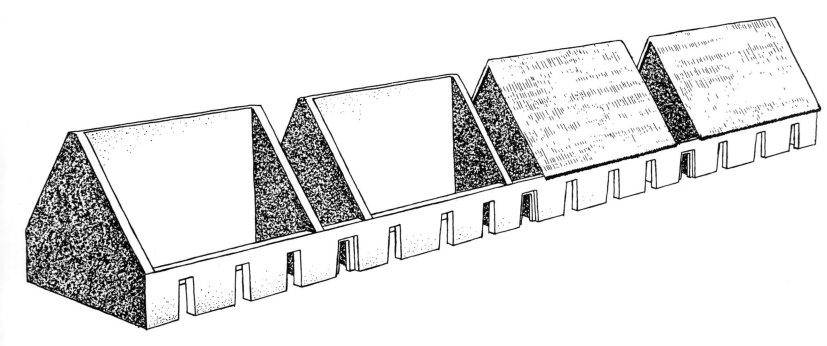

It is more difficult to attribute functions to the edifices in Chinchero that face on the great plaza of Capellanpampa. José Alcina Franch notes that the Chinchero complex may have been founded by Thupa Inca for the purpose of providing himself and his court a place for rest and recreation.[17] The Spanish archaeological mission used the key CH. 1, CH. 2, and CH. 3 to designate the three buildings aligned on the south side of the plaza (*figs. 203–205*). The first building, CH. 1, is 48 meters long by 6.60 wide. CH. 2 measures 17.80 by 12.10, and CH. 3 is 42 meters long by 10.25 wide. Unlike the *kallanka* discussed thus far, these three buildings have no direct access to the plaza. Because they are built on a terrace, their floor level is considerably higher than that of the plaza, so the openings on the plaza side seem to have been windows rather than doorways. Access to the three buildings from the plaza is accomplished via a short stepped street permitting lateral access. CH. 1 has six double-jamb windows on the plaza side, and on each end of the rectangular shape is an atrium with an off-center doorway. The structure probably had wooden supports on the long axis to support the roof. Building CH. 2 has

203. Chinchero. The three buildings, CH. 1, CH. 2, and CH. 3,
face the great plaza of Capellanpampa. A. Another important
Inca structure, upon which the Catholic church was built
B. Retaining wall with large niches that separates the atrium
of the church and the marketplace (see figure 82) C. Plaza
of Capellanpampa.

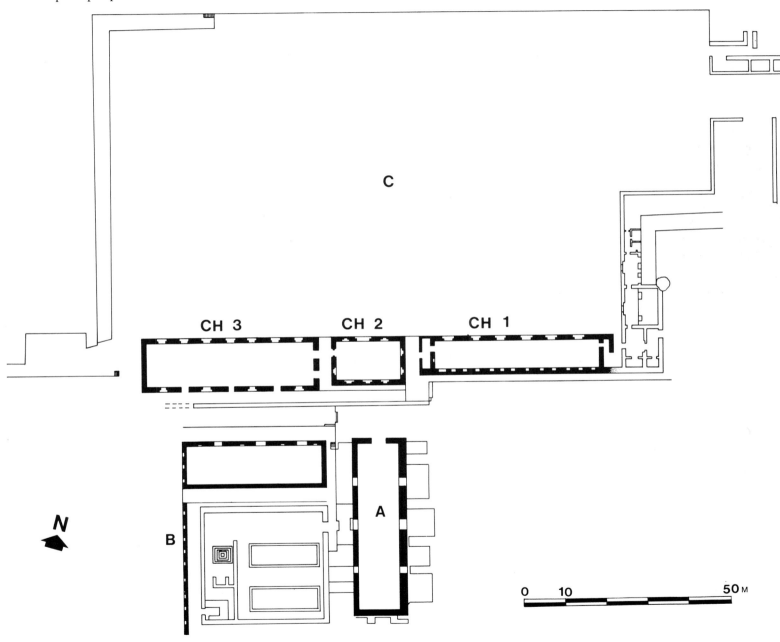

CH 3   CH 2   CH 1

C

A

B

N

0   10   50 M

204. Chinchero. Structures CH. 2 and CH 3. At the bottom of the
photograph is the stepped ramp between CH. 1 and CH. 2.

205. Chinchero. Access ramp between CH. 1 and CH. 2. In the
background is the Catholic church built above the Inca structure
marked *A* on the plan (figure 203).

206. Chinchero. Side entrance of structure CH. 2.
207. Chinchero. Base of a double-jamb niche in CH. 2.

a single double-jamb window opening onto the plaza, and on its inside walls are eight great niches (*figs. 206, 207*). This is the structure which least resembles a *kallanka*. Finally, the rectangular space of CH. 3, 42 meters long, also has great double-jamb openings onto the plaza, two doorways on the little street to the east, and other openings communicating with the southern passageway. Because of their shape and location on the plaza, these structures, especially CH. 1 and CH. 3, remind one of *kallanka*. The data are insufficient, however, to attempt to ascertain their uses. Behind the three aligned buildings and on a higher platform, where the church is, there are other groups of buildings. This distribution is similar to the Vitcos-Rosaspata complex, which also has a group of buildings on a higher level behind the four-chambered *kallanka*.

A certain similarity to the Chinchero structures is also found in some buildings at Mawk'allaqta in the province of Paruro, department of Cuzco (*fig. 208*). Here there are also enclosures with great double-jamb niches, one of which was made into a doorway. As in CH. 2 at Chinchero, the "shrine" of Mawk'allaqta has a total of eight niches, with the ninth serving as a doorway. The back passageways, the off-center doorways, and the same masonry technique are also repeated.

208. Mawk'allaqta, Paruro. Off-center entrance to a chamber.

The temples

The sacred and hallowed places where religious rites and ceremonies were carried out were of the most varied forms. Certainly the naturally shaped *wak'a* and the open-air *usnu* shrines or altars were much more numerous than enclosed and covered temples. Father Cobo says, "not all shrines were temples and dwellings; because those that were hills, ravines, rocks, springs and other things of this sort had no house or building but at most a hut or shelter in which the ministers and guards of the *guacas* stayed."[18] However, on various occasions chroniclers referred to the existence of "temples of the Sun" in the provincial centers founded in the course of territorial expansion. In Ecuador there were temples in Quito, Latacunga, Cañaripampa, Hatuncañari, and Tumipampa. In Tumbes and Wankapampa they are also mentioned. On the coast the temples of Pachacamac and Chincha enjoyed considerable fame. In the highlands there were temples in Cajamarca, Chachapoyas, Huánuco Pampa, Jauja, Warivilca, Pukara, Vitcos, Willka Waman, Ayaviri, Copacabana, some islands in Lake Titicaca, the area of the Urubamba River, and who knows how many other sites. Having already seen that all the installations founded along the *qhapaq-ñan* repeated the urban and architectural characteristics of Cuzco, it is logical to suggest the presence of temples in all these centers.

The Qorikancha—Cuzco

The most important temple of the Inca religion, called the Temple of the Sun since the conquest, was the Qorikancha, which means "golden enclosure." No other structure in all of Tawantinsuyu achieved such a reputation for its sanctity or as much fame for the wealth it contained. "The marvels of that house were so incredible that I would not dare to write of them if all the Spanish historians of Peru had not already done so,"[19] says Garcilaso. In fact there is no chronicler who has failed to be inspired by the golden myth of Inca treasures, and, as a consequence, to exaggerate the riches of Cuzco and the Qorikancha. Cieza reached the point of asking himself why "the buildings of the city of Cuzco and its temples were not made of pure gold."[20]

So much has been written and fantasized about the Qorikancha that it does not behoove us to repeat all the complex, as well as hypothetical, interpretations related to the cult of the Sun, Moon, Stars, Thunder, Lightning, Rainbow, and other deities who were sheltered in the "sanctuaries" located around the courtyard.

Following the earlier descriptive works of Squier, Father Zárate, Max Uhle, and Lehmann-Nitsche, in 1944 John H. Rowe published the most complete scientific study of this complex, accompanied by an exact plan (*fig. 209*).[21] For its analysis of the chroniclers' accounts and its discussion of the modifications imposed by the construction of the church of Santo Domingo, as well as for a number of personal observations, Rowe's work constitutes the obligatory source for anyone wanting to understand the evolution and function of this temple.

On May 21, 1950, six years after the publication of Rowe's study, a violent earthquake caused serious damage to the monumental complex Qorikancha–Santo Domingo. Only in 1956 did restoration work begin seriously, first with the reconstruction of the colonial tower and then moving on to the parts that joined the Inca Qorikancha to the colonial monastery and church of Santo Domingo. The criteria of restoration became somewhat confused regarding the procedures to be followed because the intention of emphasizing the Inca remains prevailed, to the detriment of the colonial contribution, which, after all, establishes the value of the historical stratification of the monument in time. It was not realized that restoration seeks neither stylistic unity nor the elimination of contributions of later periods. It was felt that what was Inca had preference. Surely this impulse was based on nationalistic partiality, which, although understandable, is not necessarily justifiable. On the basis of such convictions, the Inca-colonial monument was subject to a series of interventions that have not yet solved the problem of reconciling the different architectural expressions. The preoccupation with exposing the Inca evidence led to the use of a dubious anastylosis in the completion of parts that were lacking in the "Cuzco style." The Qorikancha–Santo Domingo monument has been waiting over twenty-six years, since the 1950 earthquake, for a definitive restoration that, slighting neither the Inca nor the colonial elements, may unify the complex in an expression of cultural continuity.

To understand the modifications suffered by the monument and to explain some details that Rowe could not have been aware of before the 1950 earthquake, it is interesting to compare Rowe's 1944 plan with the one we made in 1974 (*fig. 210*). The letters refer to specific locations on both plans.

A. *1944 Plan*. Sala Capitular. It has buttresses with arch ribs and cross vaults. To enlarge the Sala Capitular, the Inca wall that formed the passage between halls A and B was demolished during the colonial period. Part of the niche ("tabernacle" according to Garcilaso) was invaded by the colonial doorway (*fig. 211*).

A. *1974 Plan*. The buttresses, arches, and vaults were eliminated. Today the Sala Capitular has no roof or upper story. The Inca wall, demolished in colonial times, was reconstructed in its original position to reestablish the passage between halls A and B. The colonial doorway was removed to complete part of the niche-tabernacle with pieces found in explorations after 1950 (*figs. 212–14*).

B. *1944 Plan*. Part of the Inca walls of this chamber were demolished during the colonial period to open direct communication between the entrance to the monastery, the cloister, and the sacristy (I). There is also the colonial stairway leading to the upper story and a small room under the stairs.

B. *1974 Plan*. The passage between the cloister and the sacristy (I) was closed by reconstructing the "Inca wall." The stairway and small room were demolished. Investigations carried out on the floor of the church revealed that the dimensions of hall B were the same as those of A.

C. *1944 Plan*. In Rowe's plan there are no Cuzco-style doorways on the courtyard side.

C. *1974 Plan*. The front of this chamber was reconstructed with "Inca" doorways. The room has neither roof nor second story. Investigations in the Salón de Recibo revealed that the dimensions of this hall were the same as those of E.

D. *1944 Plan*. Surely this was orginally a small court between halls C and E. The face was walled up in the colonial period to provide a room.

209. Cuzco. The Qorikancha. 1944 plan by John H. Rowe.

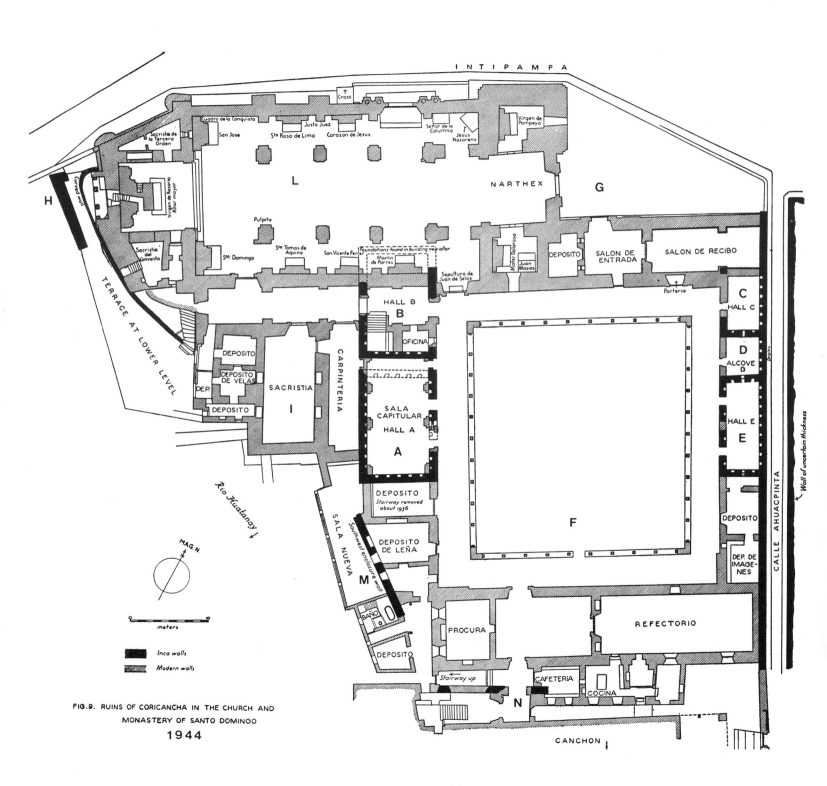

FIG.9. RUINS OF CORICANCHA IN THE CHURCH AND
MONASTERY OF SANTO DOMINGO
1944

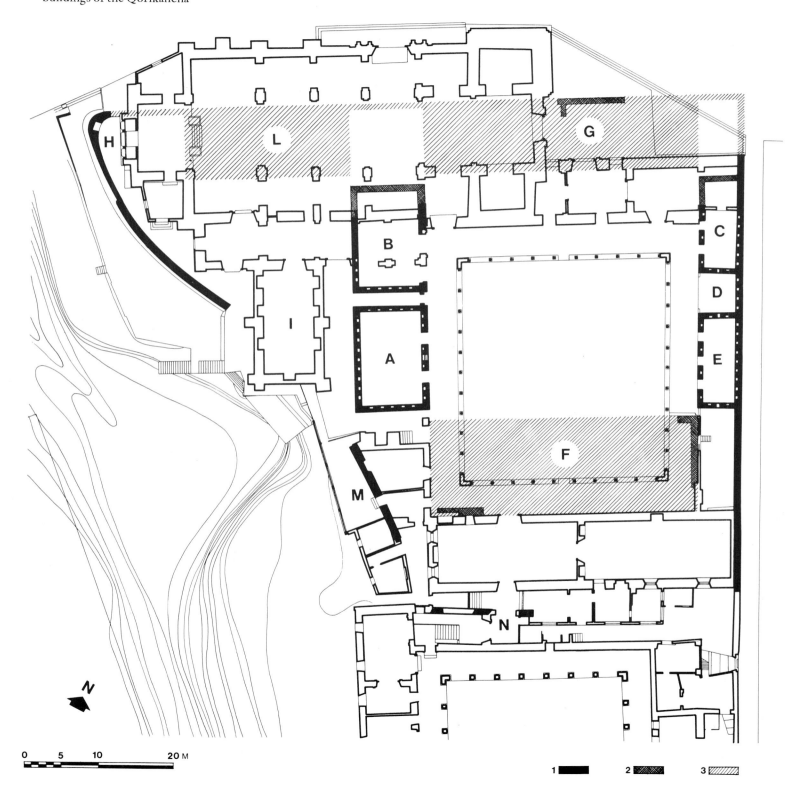

210. Cuzco. The Qorikancha. 1974 plan by the authors.
1. Inca walls   2. Inca foundations   3. Possible location of other
buildings of the Qorikancha

N

0   5   10   20 M

1 ■■■   2 ▨▨▨   3 ▨▨▨

211. Cuzco. The Qorikancha. The "tabernacle" when it had the colonial doorway beside it.

212. Cuzco. The Qorikancha. Present state of the inside of Hall A.

213. Cuzco. The Qorikancha. Back corner of Hall A.
214. Cuzco. The Qorikancha. The "tabernacle" in its present reconstruction.

215. Cuzco. The Qorikancha. Hall C, courtyard D, and Hall E. Present state.

D. *1974 Plan*. In the restoration work the colonial wall was removed to reestablish the space of the Inca court (*fig. 215*).

E. *1944 Plan*. Of the three Inca doorways, the center one is walled up.

E. *1974 Plan*. The walled-up door was reopened. The upper story over the entire sector C/D/E, which was previously supported on the Inca walls, has been removed.

F. *1944 Plan*. Nothing shown.

F. *1974 Plan*. The discovery of corner foundations near hall E and in the southern part of the cloister could indicate the location and dimensions of the Inca structure that closed the enclosure on the south.

G. *1944 Plan*. Nothing shown.

G. *1974 Plan*. In 1957, during work on the foundation of the tower facing the present entrance to the monastery, an 8-meter long fragment of Inca wall was found.[22] This find is very important since it may define the possible northern limit of the Qorikancha. In drawing our plan we observed that a projection of the line of this fragment of Inca foundation connects with surprising exactitude with the famous curved wall (H). Max Uhle said that in 1905 he saw the remains of Inca foundations some 12 meters long inside the church in front of the altar of Santa Rosa de Lima.[23] Uhle also noted that he saw remains of corners and doorways. In view of these observations, and since the projection of the hypothetical wall to the curved wall passes exactly in front of the altar of Santa Rosa de Lima, we have suggested the possibility of another chamber (L) in that location, with the same width as G. Chamber G may well be what Garcilaso called the "abode of the Sun." The entrance to this "abode" from Intipampa coincides with the axis of the present entrance to the monastery. Possibly the Dominicans used the southern door of chamber G. Garcilaso says: "Beyond the temple there was a cloister with four walls; one of them was the wall of the temple [G]. . . . Surrounding the cloister there were five squares or large squared chambers [A, B, C, E, and F], each one separate, not connected to another, roofed in the shape of a pyramid, of which the other three walls of the cloister were formed."[24] The existence of four of these chambers (A, B, C, and E) and the

discovery of foundations for F and G allow us to establish the possible dimensions of the six chambers that defined the enclosure. The proposed location of the six unconnected chambers coincides with Garcilaso's description and, at the same time, displays the typical *kancha* arrangement with corner courts (*fig. 216*).

H. *1944 Plan*. The apse of the Dominican church is built over the curved wall and prevents determination of its interior characteristics.

H. *1974 Plan*. To emphasize the curved Inca wall and explore its interior, the colonial church was subjected to drastic modifications. The entire body of the apse was removed and reconstructed, reducing the size of the presbytery and the thickness of the walls. Other rooms were removed, mainly those on the west side of the sacristy (I). On the inside of the curved wall there is a large niche that is now accessible.

L. *1944 Plan*. Nothing shown.

L. *1974 Plan*. Possible location of a structure based on data from Max Uhle and the projection of the line of the foundations of G to the curved wall. This chamber may have served as the first church of Santo Domingo. The doubts concerning this sector of the temple suggest the need to carry out a complete exploration of the floor of the present church.

M. *1944 and 1974 Plans*. The remains of Inca wall existing in this location suggest the possibility of connection with the curved wall (H.)

N. *1944 and 1974 Plans*. Other wall fragments. Probable "quarters" on the south side of the enclosure related to the needs of the temple and occupied by the numerous personnel who served there.

The work done since the 1950 earthquake has revealed additional information that tells us more about the size and dimensions of the Qorikancha. Nevertheless, there are still many questions related to structural details and ceremonial functions. In spite of the many superlatives that have been used to describe this temple—its riches, its walls covered with gold and silver plates—it is difficult to imagine it as an architecturally exceptional monument once its forms, spaces, and dimensions have been examined. Leaving aside the riches and the mythical and sacred

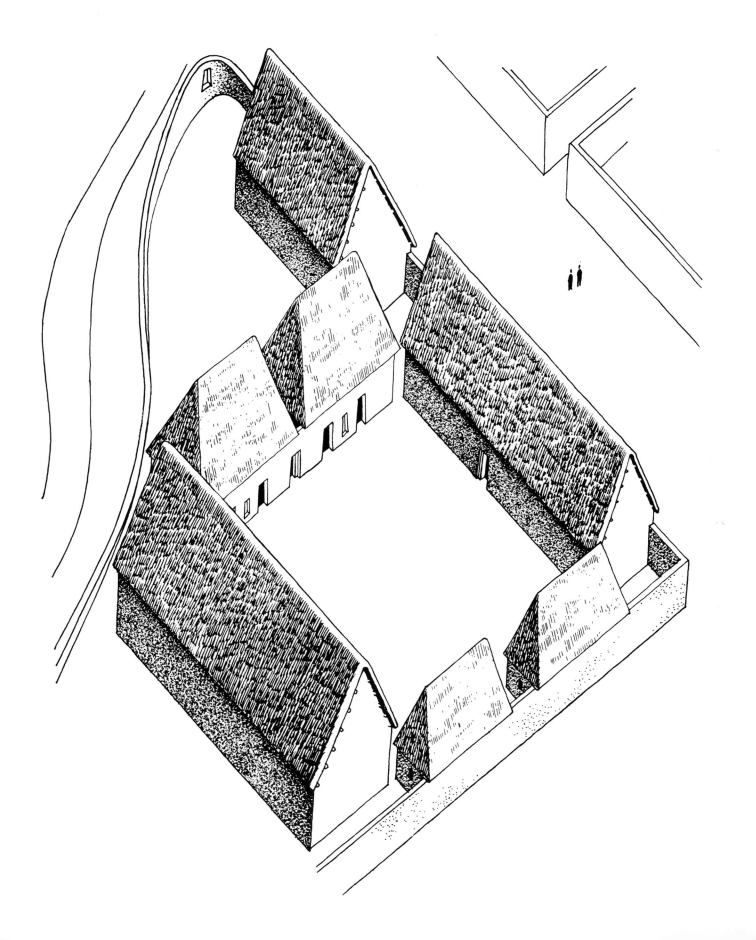

217. Cuzco. The Qorikancha. Detail of the outside wall facing on Ahuacpinta Street.
218. Cuzco. The Qorikancha. Curved wall corresponding to the apse of the church of Santo Domingo.

significance of the building, the Qorikancha is basically analogous to other *kancha*-type structures. Its outside appearance must not have been very different from that of the Cuzco "palaces" with well-finished walls and thatched roofs. Considering the status of the edifice, it is superfluous to ask why its walls show fine finish. If the quality of the stonework is associated with the importance of the building, we may assume that the Qorikancha received the finest treatment (*fig. 217*). "In all Spain I have seen nothing that could be compared to these walls and [the] fitting of the stones . . . ,"[25] says Cieza. Nevertheless, the entire height of these walls was not stone. The stone reached to the point where we see it today. From there on up adobes were used. At the line marking the juncture of the different materials was fastened a band of gold about a span in width.

The roofs were thatched over wooden frames, and it appears that the four chambers whose remains are known did not have gables. Garcilaso says that they were "roofed in the shape of a pyramid," which could be interpreted as referring to hip roofs; therefore, gables would not have been present. The longest and

219. Cuzco. The Qorikancha. Detail of the curved wall.

220. Cuzco. The Qorikancha. The curved wall at the base of the apse of Santo Domingo has a delicate entasis in its profile, as if the wall felt the weight of the stones and the outward thrust of the fill.

largest chambers were to the north and south of the courtyard and are now gone, but they surely had gables like the *kallanka*.

Rowe notes that he did not find a single reference to the shape of the curved wall (*figs. 218–20*) in historical accounts from the colonial period. The only reference is related to the list of *wak'a* that Cobo copied from the information gathered by Polo de Ondegardo. According to this list the first *wak'a* of the first *ceque* of Cuntisuyu was a stone called Subaraura, located where "the balcony of Santo Domingo is now."[26] If the curved wall enclosed a sacred stone in its concavity, we might suggest a formal similarity to the stone enclosed by the curved wall of the "Watchtower" at Machu Picchu. The reconstruction work in the apse of the church of Santo Domingo has revealed only the large niche already mentioned.

From the point of view of the stonework, the *kancha* system, roofing and spatial arrangement, the Qorikancha may be considered a Late Horizon building. If, as many chroniclers state, the temple was rebuilt by Pachakuti on the site where a more modest earlier one had stood, this fact would corroborate the relationship of the Qorikancha to the characteristics of Inca architecture evident in all works built by the state after 1440. Cieza observes "this temple is as old as the very city of Cuzco, but Inca Yupanqui, son of Viracocha Inca, increased its riches until it reached the state in which the Christians found it when they entered Peru. . . ."[27]

Also of interest is the suggestion that the Qorikancha served as a model for the building of temples of the Sun in various regional settlements throughout Tawantinsuyu. Garcilaso says: "Similar to this temple of the city of Cozco were the rest that were in many provinces of that kingdom. . . ."[28] The Cuzco Temple of the Sun, Qorikancha, was in the *hurin* division of the city and, as we have noted, was composed of six "quarters" (two large, two medium-sized, two small) enclosing a courtyard. Probably the characteristics of the Temple of the Sun were repeated in various Inca settlements, just as were other characteristics. It seems logical, therefore, to seek such temples in the *hurin* sector of those settlements. The repetitive elements that are so typical of Inca architecture permit an attempt to identify build-

233

ings showing certain formal and functional similarities to those of Cuzco. Applying this comparative method, Zuidema feels he has localized the six "quarters" surrounding a courtyard that form the Temple of the Sun at Huánuco Pampa, at Tambo Colorado, and at Machu Picchu.[29] Although these identifications are dubious, a knowledge of the characteristics of Cuzco buildings may help in the identification of those with similar functions in those centers far removed from the central region. It is worth noting, however, that the "similarity" is related more to the functional and ritual aspects of the sanctuary than to the physical appearance of the Cuzco edifice.

The Temple of Wiraqocha—Raqchi

The Temple of Wiraqocha in Raqchi, district of San Pedro de Cacha on the road from Cuzco to Sicuani, is completely different in form from the Qorikancha, rather reminding one of a great four-naved *kallanka*. This is a building that enjoyed considerable fame and high repute and was described by a number of chroniclers; Garcilaso says that Wiraqocha Inca ordered it built, while Cieza de León attributes the work to Thupa Inca.[30] The reasons for building this temple in a place so far from Cuzco are not clear. All the reports are based on legendary accounts with very conflicting interpretations.

The ruins of the temple and adjacent structures suggest the importance that this complex must have had.

The site of Raqchi (*fig. 221*) is located on the right bank of the Vilcanota River at an altitude of 3,460 meters above sea level and a distance of 118 kilometers from Cuzco. It occupies a natural depression surrounded by black volcanic rock from an ancient eruption of the volcano Quimsa Chata. The entire area of the complex, about 80 hectares, was enclosed by a wall of which some 3,500 meters are still preserved.

To the southeast of the temple is a sequence of houses and courtyards adopting the *kancha* system (*figs. 222, 223*). There are six perfectly aligned courtyards that are almost square, measuring about 27 by 31 meters each. Except for the first one, nearest to the entrance to the temple, they are all surrounded on three

221. Raqchi. Plan of the area enclosed by the wall that defines the
zone devoted to the Temple of Wiraqocha.

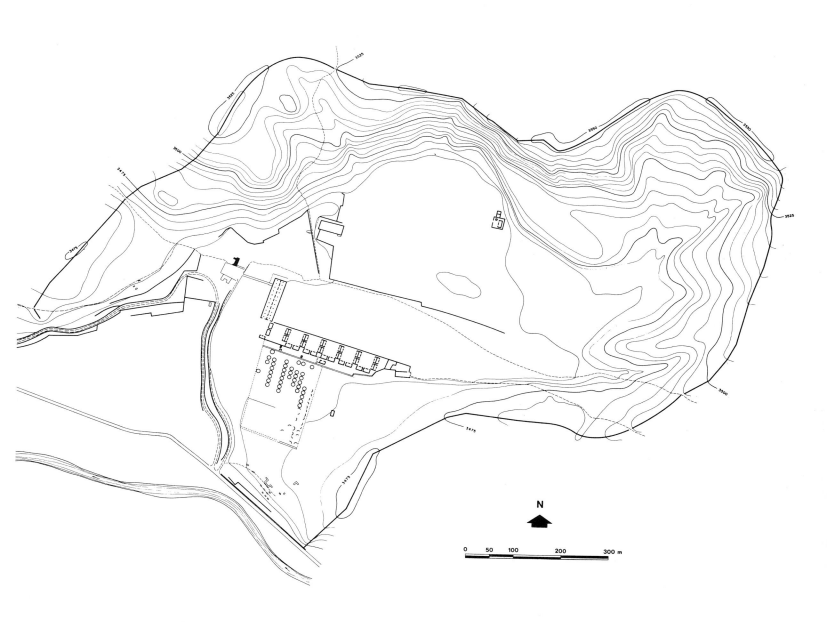

N

0   50   100   200   300 m

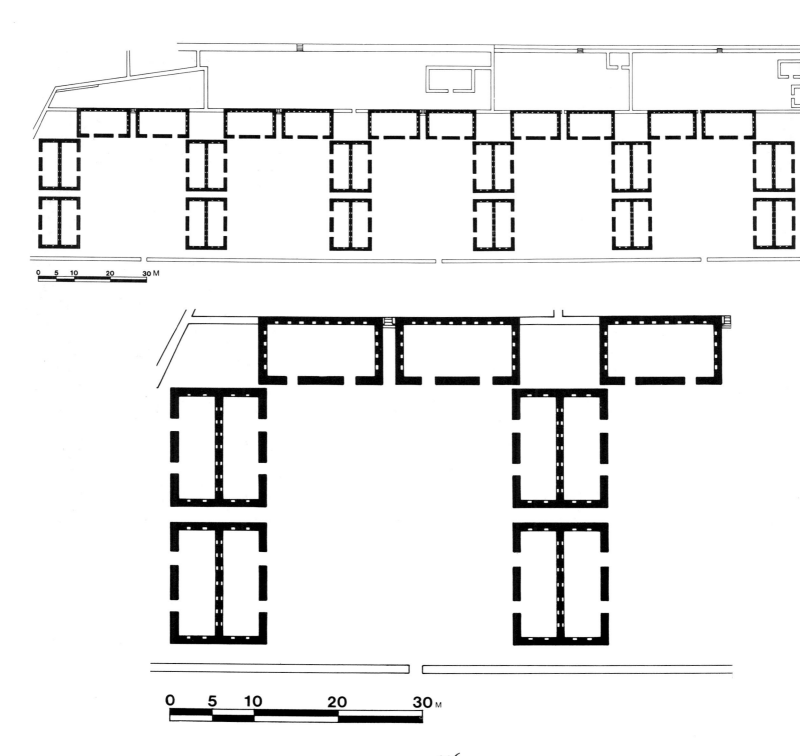

222. Raqchi. Plan of the sequences of houses and courtyards to the south of the temple. On a larger scale, one of the modules with a central courtyard.

0 5 10 20 30 M

0 5 10 20 30 M

223. Raqchi. Panoramic view of the ruins of the temple and the
group of houses and courtyards.

sides by the same number of structures. Two houses, each with a central dividing wall, are situated between one courtyard and the next, so that each half of a house opens onto a different courtyard. The two houses that separate the courtyards are themselves separated from each other by a passage 2.20 meters wide, which, because of the perfect alignment of the buildings, provides an interesting perspective (fig. 224). There is a total of twelve houses with central walls (fig. 225), all with one room on each side, for a total of twenty-four rooms. Each room is 12 meters long by 4.50 wide, and all have seven niches in the back wall and two on the inside of each of the gable walls. Each room has two doorways to the courtyard. The walls are stone terminating unevenly at a height of about 2.50 meters. From there to the top, both the dividing walls and the gable walls are adobe. On the south side of each courtyard there are two separate one-room chambers without gables. They have eight niches on the back wall and four on each of the side walls.

This complex shows such precision in the rectangularity of the plan, in the repetition of measurements, in the sequence of the spaces, and in the alignment of the structures (almost 250 meters from one extreme to the other), that it suggests a complete mastery of units of measurement to achieve perfectly duplicated contours and to form 90° angles. As far as the functions of these houses are concerned, it is hard to make a convincing suggestion. Well-planned archaeological research has still not been carried out in the Raqchi zone. It has been suggested that these houses were priests' residences or temporary dormitories for pilgrims, or that they fulfilled other needs related to the service of the temple. They may also have had some administrative functions, since to the south of the complex there are many circular buildings, measuring as much as 8 meters in diameter, that may well have been storehouses (fig. 226). There are remains of some forty of these structures in good condition and evidence of many more.

The Temple of Wiraqocha was a great rectangular hall, 92 meters long by 25.25 meters wide (fig. 227); the roofed area of 2,323 square meters is the largest yet known. Its architectural characteristics differ from other Inca structures, and, surely, this

224. Raqchi. Central passage separating the houses located to the
south of the temple.

225. Raqchi. One of the twelve houses with a dividing wall and two entrances opening onto the courtyard.

226. Raqchi. Various circular structures similar to the one illustrated suggest that there was a zone devoted to storehouses at the site.

227. Raqchi. Plan of the temple.

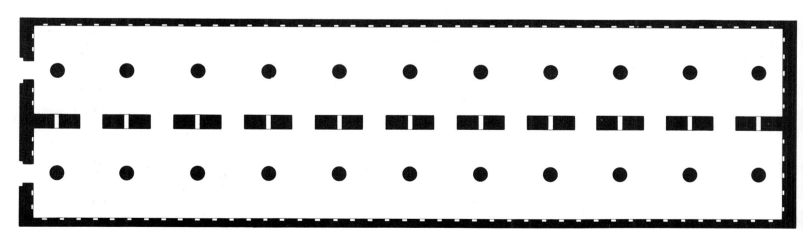

0   5   10   20

is one of the reasons explaining the attention it has received from chroniclers, travelers, and investigators. Nevertheless, since we have not found a satisfactory reconstructive hypothesis, we propose our own interpretation below. First, however, we must present Garcilaso's description, which is both detailed and disconcerting. Although long, it is worth quoting extensively:

. . . in a town called Cacha, which is sixteen leagues to the south of the city of Cozco, Inca Viracocha ordered built a temple to honor and revere his uncle, the spirit who had appeared to him. He ordered that the structure of the temple imitate, as much as possible, the place where it had appeared to him; that it be open (like the countryside), without a roof; that they build him a small chapel, covered with stone that it might resemble the hollow in the rock where he was lying; that it have a loft, raised above the ground: a different kind of plan and structure from any those Indians made, before or after, because never did they build house or room with a loft. The inside of the temple was one hundred and twenty feet long inside, and eighty wide. It was of polished stone masonry, with beautifully worked stone, as is all that those Indians do. It had four doors, at the four cardinal points; three of them were closed up, being only doorways to adorn the walls. The eastern door served as entrance and exit for the temple; it was in the middle of the gable wall, and because those Indians did not know how to make a vault to put a loft on top of it, they made walls of the same stone masonry, to serve as beams, because they would last longer than wood. They put them at intervals, leaving a seven foot space between one wall and the next, and the walls were three feet thick; these walls formed twelve lanes. They were closed above, not with planks but with [stone] slabs ten feet long and half a *vara* thick, dressed on all six faces. Entering the door of the temple, they turned right through the first lane until they reached the right-hand wall of the temple; then they turned left through the second lane, to the other wall. From there they again turned right through the third lane, and thus (as the spaces of the lines of this plan go) they progressed through the interior of the temple, from lane to lane, until the last, which was the twelfth, where there was a stairway leading to the loft of the temple.
At each end of each lane were windows like narrow slit-shaped openings, that gave abundant light to the lanes; beneath each window was a hollow cut into the wall, where an attendant was seated, with-

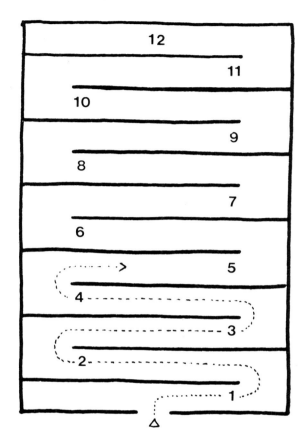

out obstructing the passage of the lane. The stairway consisted of two
opposing flights, so that they could go up and down by one side or
the other; the top of it came out facing the main altar. The floor of
the loft was paved with some very lustrous black slabs, that looked
like jet, brought from far-off lands. Instead of a main altar there was
a chapel twelve feet square inside, roofed with the same black slabs,
fitting into one another, raised in the shape of a pyramidal spire: it
was the most admirable [part] of the entire work. Inside the chapel,
in the thickness of the temple wall, there was a tabernacle, where they
had placed the image of the phantom Viracocha; on each side of the
chapel there were two other tabernacles, but they contained nothing;
they served only as adornment and to accompany the principal chapel.
The walls of the temple, above the loft, rose three *varas* high, without any windows; they had a stone cornice, finished inside and out,
on all four sides. In the tabernacle that was inside the chapel there
was a great pedestal; on it they put a stone statue that the Inca Viracocha ordered made, of the same figure as the spirit he said appeared
to him.

* * *

What motive Inca Viracocha may have had and to what end he
may have ordered that temple built in Cacha and not in Chita, where
the spirit appeared to him, or in Yahuarpampa, where the victory over
the Chancas took place, either of those two places being more appropriate than Cacha, the Indians cannot say, more than that it was the
will of the Inca; and one can only believe that it had some hidden
motive. The temple being such a strange work, as has been said, the
Spanish have destroyed it, as they did so many other famous works
that they found in Peru, although they would have done better to
maintain them themselves, at their cost, so that in the centuries to
come people might see the great things that they had won with their
arms and good fortune. But it seems that knowingly, as if envious
of themselves, they have torn these things down, so that today scarcely
the foundations remain of this work, and of other similar ones that
there were, a fact that has greatly sorrowed prudent men. The main
reason that has moved them to destroy this work, and all those that
they have thrown down, was saying that it was impossible that there
not be much treasure underneath it. The first thing to be torn down
was the statue, because they said that under its feet much gold was
buried. The temple was excavated bit by bit, first here, then there,
down to the foundations, and thus they have demolished everything.

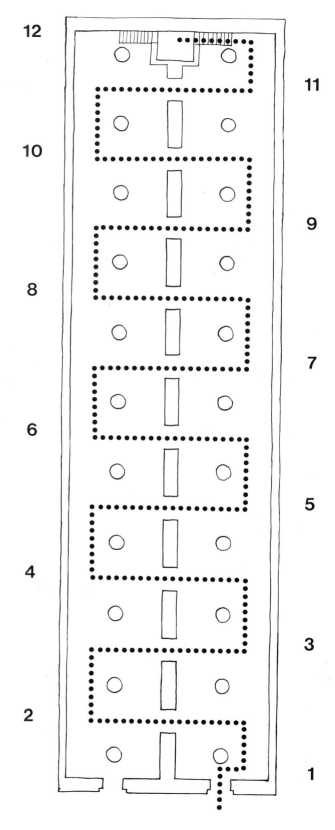

229. Raqchi. The twelve symbolic "lanes," or twelve turns of the course to reach the "chapel," can be adapted to the present plan of the temple and, incidentally, justify the existence of ten openings in the central wall.

The stone statue was alive a few years ago, although completely disfigured, from having stones thrown at it.[31]

Almost none of Garcilaso's description coincides with the remains of the temple. We should not discard the possibility that Garcilaso may never have seen the site and used secondhand accounts. The proportions he assigns to it of 120 by 80 feet correspond to a rectangular form composed of one and a half squares. The real form, however, is of three and three-quarters squares. The temple does not have four doors (three walled up) to the four cardinal points. The two doors known today are located in the south gable wall and seem to have been the only ones. We have no information on the north wall, which has disappeared. Nor is it known whether the east façade, on the plaza, had a series of doorways like the *kallanka*. Of the complicated arrangement of twelve lanes with stone walls, there remains not a trace—neither foundations nor any sign on the stone portions of the central wall. In an attempt to interpret Garcilaso's description we arrived at the scheme shown in figure 228. It is easy to see the difference between his version and the existing plan.

We can, however, adapt a course through twelve lanes to the real plan if these "lanes" are considered as symbolic rather than architectural. In fact, if one enters the temple and crosses to the right through the first "lane," the twelfth can be reached via a course that would justify the existence of the ten great doorways in the central wall (*fig. 229*). What is difficult to believe is that they might have been covered by monolithic slabs. If there was a "chapel" in a "loft," it must have been located in the limited space of the twelfth lane, where the double stairway was also supposed to be. Garcilaso says that the chapel was twelve feet square, that is, a room of only 3.35 by 3.35 meters. The part of the temple corresponding to the location of the chapel is totally destroyed (*fig. 230*), thus preventing the fashioning of any reconstructive hypothesis. Nevertheless, the presence of that small elevated room would not change the form of the temple and the structural system that we are going to suggest.

It is not true, as Garcilaso states, that scarcely the founda-

230. Raqchi. The end of the temple corresponding to the twelfth
     lane is the most completely destroyed segment. Only fragments
     of foundations remain, thus preventing a formal hypothesis.

tions remain and that the Spanish "demolished everything." In Garcilaso's time much more must have existed, since today, four centuries later, enough remains to permit an attempt at hypothetical reconstruction.

The great interior space is divided by a wall approximately 12 meters high following the long axis (*fig. 231*). To facilitate passage from one side to the other, ten doorways, which may be related to Garcilaso's lanes, were opened in the base. Between one doorway and the next there is a niche some 70 centimeters high that completely penetrates the 1.65 meters of wall thickness. The entire base of this wall is finely cut stone terminating unevenly at a height of about 2.80 meters. Beyond this height, up to the top formed by the ridgepole, the wall was of adobe. In this adobe portion, above each of the ten doorways that unite the two halves of the temple, there are two openings, one above the other. Today, looking at this long high wall with three rows of holes, one has the impression of contemplating the remains of a building with more than one story. All modern investigators have made the mistake of considering the upper openings to be doorways belonging to vanished upper stories and assumed that the Temple of Wiraqocha had two or three stories. The upper openings in the adobe part of the central wall, located over the vertical axis of those on the "ground floor," are neither doorways or any other kind of passageway, but rather relieving openings

232. Raqchi. Hypothetical reconstruction of the structural system of the Temple of Wiraqocha made on a transparency over the photograph. The upper openings serve to reduce the weight load on the weak lintels of the "ground floor" doorways. In no case do they indicate assumed upper floors.

that eliminate, by their presence, a considerable weight from the lintels, which were formed by a series of slender timbers tied together with plant fibers. The system of relieving openings over lintels is very ancient, and numerous examples are known in Egyptian, Mesopotamian, and Greek architecture. Besides, on the adobe wall at the level where the supposed upper stories would be, there is no trace of beams set into the wall to support them (*fig. 232*).

246

233. Raqchi. Another hypothetical reconstruction emphasizing the
     sequence of cylindrical columns.

This temple has other important characteristics. Each of the
two halves formed by the longitudinal dividing wall had a series
of eleven columns on the long axis; thus the temple is divided
into four naves. Although roof supports in the form of pillars
with a quadrangular section are known, the cylindrical columns
of the Temple of Wiraqocha are unique in the repertoire of Inca
buildings. In discussing the *kallanka* of Inkallaqta we suggested
the possibility that that structure might have had four naves
formed by three series of wooden roof supports. If it did not have
that arrangement it would be difficult to explain how the roof
was framed. The same is true of the Temple of Wiraqocha. The
columns functioned to bear wooden beams upon which the
smaller beams that formed the framework of the two slopes of
the roof were supported in two sections. The first section went
from the top of the dividing wall to the beams that rested on
the columns, the second, from the beams on the columns to the
side walls (*figs. 233, 234*).

234. Raqchi. Hypothetical reconstruction of the structural system of
     the Temple of Wiraqocha. The structure has four naves.

235. Raqchi. The only cylindrical column of the Temple of
     Wiraqocha that has survived to our time.

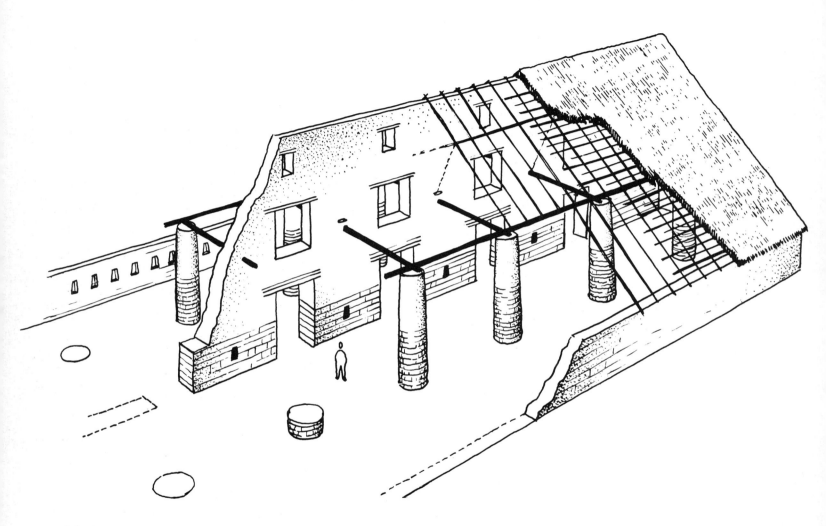

Of the twenty-two original columns, only one remains; it
is stone up to a height of 3.30 meters, then adobe (fig. 235). The
total height is about 6 meters. At that same height, in the central
wall, are very clear traces of a pair of embedded timbers corresponding to each column. These timbers were tied to the beams
that ran lengthwise on each row of eleven columns and formed an
equal number of crossbeams. This prevented the tangential
thrust produced by the inclined beams from displacing the horizontal beams on which they were supported (fig. 236). We
should note that the crossbeams were embedded in the central

248

wall at a level that does not coincide with that of any supposed upper story, because the marks where they were fixed are at a height almost coinciding with the middle of the upper opening. Thus, an upper story would be impossible at this second level (*figs. 237, 238*). Suggesting that the "loft" was on a level with the highest openings brings with it structural problems in the height of the columns, the inclination of the roof slopes, and the height of the lateral walls. If we add to these observations the difficulty of finding wood in the region strong enough to support a floor, we reach the conclusion that the Temple of Wiraqocha displays a structural system similar to that of so many great halls that never had an upper story.

The two rows of eleven columns are on the same axes as the

237. Raqchi. In almost all the sections of the temple the sawed-off butts of the crossbeams are still visible. These timber crossbeams establish the height of the columns. As can be seen, the remains of the wood are on a level almost in the middle of the opening, so it would be impossible to have a "second floor" at that level.

238. Raqchi. In each adobe section the mark can be seen where the crossbeam was embedded. In this photograph the bases of the columns are also shown.

239. Raqchi. The two rows of columns lie on the axes of the entrances.
240. Raqchi. Remains of the wooden lintel in one of the upper openings.

entrance doorways (*fig. 239*), a solution that provides an un-expected experience since, instead of appreciating the great open space when one reaches the entrance, one comes up against the mass of the support. It is also likely that the eleven columns of each side mark the place where one turned in completing the twelve-lane course.

On the stone bases of the dividing wall are traces of a finely ground mud plaster covered with red paint. The plaster had a stepped shape and it is still possible to discern the remains (*fig. 241*).

Based on the characteristics of the shape and structural technique of the temple and the adjacent annex with the six courtyards, the complex belongs to the Late Horizon. Therefore Cieza's report that we owe the work to Thupa Inca seems the most probable.

241. Raqchi. One of the fragments of the central wall and the base of a column.

The Temple of Huaytará

In the department of Huancavelica, province of Castrovir-reyna, lies the town of Huaytará. The Catholic church, dedicated to San Juan Bautista, used the entire space and structure of an elaborate Inca building. We cannot state positively that this structure was an Inca "temple," and some prefer to consider it a "palace" or an *inkawasi*. Nevertheless, we may suggest that it was a temple because, following the conquest, the religious orders and priests customarily built a church on the same site where an "idolatrous" temple had stood. In the fanatical activity of rooting out idolatries, the total destruction of not only idols but also temples was ordered (Royal Cedula of 1538, Instruction of 1545, Constitution 3 of the Council of 1551), and it was recommended that a church be built on the remains of the latter.[32] Partial destruction was also permitted if the foundations and walls could be used for the Catholic church. The case of Qorikancha–Santo Domingo is prototypical. This sort of superposition was also practiced at Chinchero, Vilcashuamán, and Huaytará as well as other places. In the case of Huaytará, the Inca structure suffered very little, permitting us to observe new architectural characteristics.

The Inca temple has a rectangular plan approximately 26.50 meters by 10.50 (*fig. 242*). The wall on the south side was demolished with the object of lengthening the single nave of the Catholic church. It was probably in that wall that the door (or doors) opening into the Inca building were located. The northern wall preserves the adobe gable intact, permitting a clear appreciation of the pitch of the ancient gabled roof (*fig. 243*). To support this roof there may have been a series of tree trunks set into the floor on the long axis of the rectangle as in the *kallanka* of Huánuco Pampa. The different spatial concept of the Catholic church, and a more advanced technique of roof framing, resulted in the elimination of the central supports and the raising of the side walls (*fig. 244*). This entire process of adaptation and superposition is clearly visible, since the walls have no plaster on the outside. What is most striking in this building is the richness and variety of niches in the stone walls;

242. Huaytará. Plan of the Catholic church, which used the Inca structure (shown in black). The exceptional niches with a triangular plan stand out.

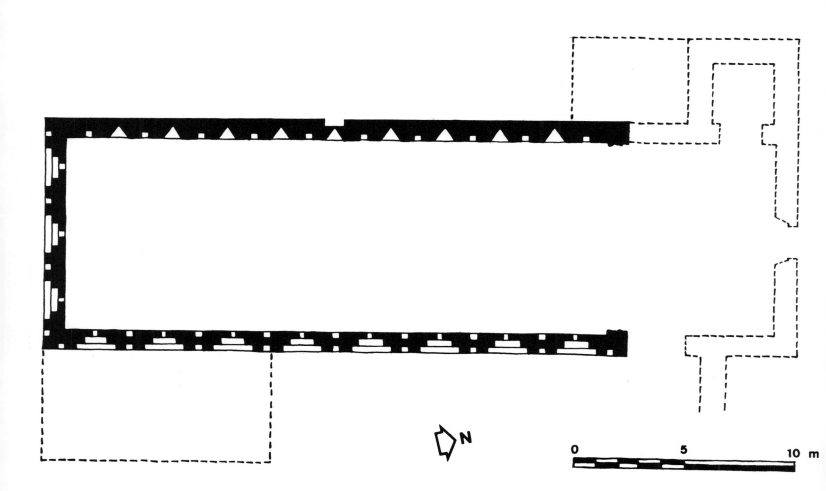

243. Huaytará. Hypothetical reconstruction of the Temple of
Huaytará made on a transparency over the photo. The shape of
the original gable is clearly visible, and it still preserves some of
the stone pegs.

257

244. Huaytará. Hypothetical reconstruction of the interior of the temple. Possibly there was a series of wooden pillars on the long axis of the rectangle.

245. Huaytará. The exceptional shape of the niche with the triangular plan.

246. Huaytará. Catholic images placed in the Inca niches.

it was entirely constructed with an excellent stonework in the Cuzco style.

Entering the temple, one sees on the right-hand wall a sequence of nine very large niches alternating with ten small trapezoidal ones. The special feature of the large niches is that they have a triangular plan (*fig. 245*). This is an exceptional case within the standardization of this formal element, which can be considered the *leitmotiv* of Inca architecture. The triangular base, set back from the face of the wall, today holds Catholic images (*fig. 246*). Both the back wall and the long wall on the left have a sequence of trapezoidal niches on two levels. Those on the lower level perforate the wall as small windows; those on the upper level have the usual form of backed niches. The outer face of the west wall is more simple, with only a single walled-up opening corresponding to the central triangular niche. The northern wall, which today is the apse of the church, has three great double-jamb trapezoidal niches, each the size of a doorway; above the stone wall rises the intact adobe gable with two windows. The east wall (*figs. 247, 248*) is the richest, with a sequence of eight double-jamb niches, the same as those on the north wall. In the central part of each of them is the window-niche, which provides light and ventilation to the interior. It is a façade with great movement, since the formal elements are developed on three different planes and are very close together, establishing a repetitive rhythm of chiaroscuro effect absent in other buildings. In front of this lateral façade there is an artificial esplanade achieved with fill and reinforced with a retaining wall of up to 5 meters in height.

The other structures that were probably near the temple have disappeared. There are remains of retaining walls and magnificent terracing.

Islands of Lake Titicaca

On the islands of the Sun and of Koati there are various groups of Inca ruins that have, as yet, not been the object of satisfactory research. In spite of the great religious significance of the place, legendary cradle of Wiraqocha, archaeology has

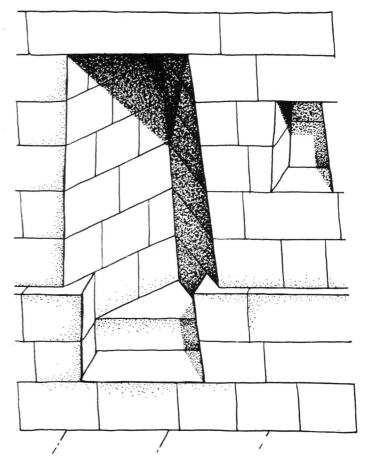

259

247. Huaytará. East façade of the temple with eight great double-jamb niches, nine small niches, and eight openings (in black) providing ventilation to the interior.

248. Huaytará. Present state of the niches on the east wall. At the extreme right is the side door of the church, on the point corresponding to the corner of the Inca structure.

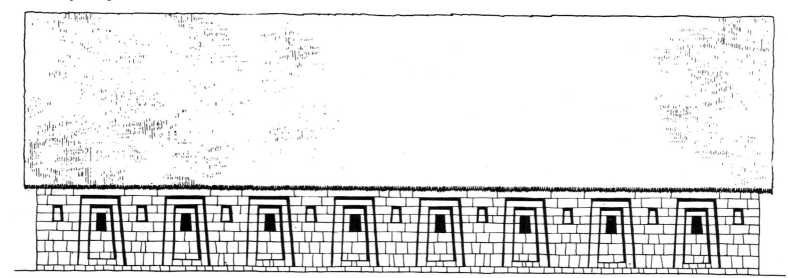

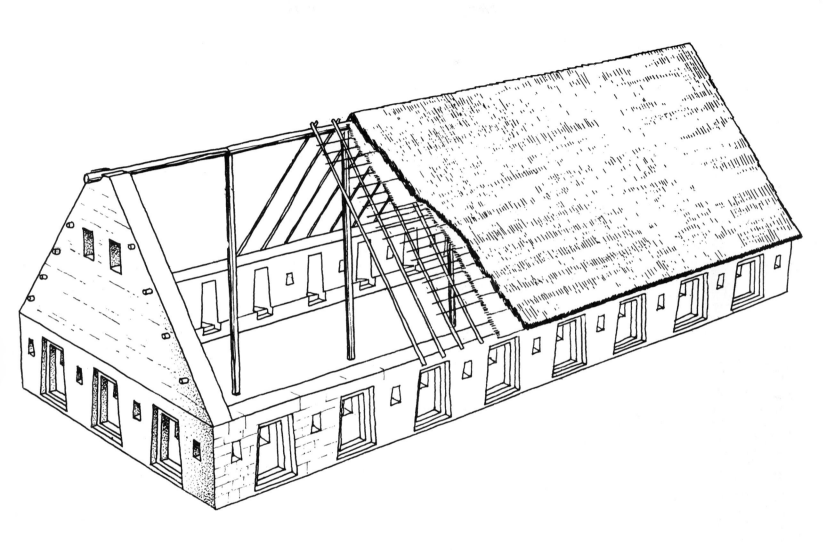

249. Huaytará. Possible architectural form and structural system of
the temple.

250. The "palace" of Pilco Kayma on the Island of the Sun in Lake Titicaca, after Squier

251. Lower floor of the "palace" of Pilco Kayma, after Squier

252. Present state of the lower floor of the "palace," according to a plan made by the students of the Faculty of Architecture, University of San Andrés, La Paz

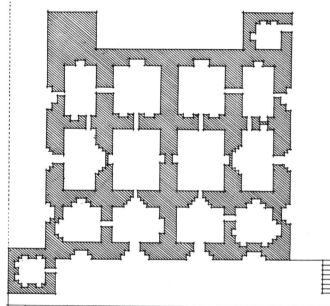

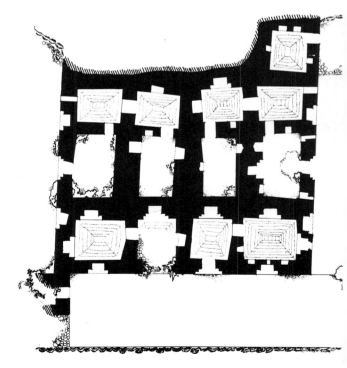

contributed little to the greater knowledge of the Inca presence in this part of Qollasuyu. The study of the monuments in this zone is of particular architectonic interest, since the influence of ancient Tiwanaku formal motives continues in the Inca structures. Without treating the ruins of Tikikala, Kasapata, and Pukara, the most important complex on the Island of the Sun is the "palace" of Pilco Kayma (*fig. 250*), mentioned in the previous chapter with reference to the corbeled vault. This exceptional two-story structure has a ground floor of various chambers (*figs. 251, 252*) with corbeled vaults and walls with great double- and triple-jamb niches that, by their depth, contribute to increasing the space of the smaller chambers. The façade has a rigidly symmetrical arrangement; where there were no doors they were simulated by blind ones like very large niches; all have a sunken lintel with the Tiwanaku "stepped sign." The trapezoidal form of the opening and the "stepped sign" are the formal symbols that most surely identify Inca and Tiwanaku. At Pilco Kayma they are integrated in the same work. As we commented in chapter 1, in view of the many examples present at Tiwanaku, it is not improbable that the double jamb so frequently found on Inca

253. Recent photograph of the ruins of Pilco Kayma

openings may derive from the Tiwanaku double jamb and that it, in turn, may have Pukara and Chiripa antecedents.

On the Island of Koati (*fig. 254*), Ramos Gavilán noted the existence of a "convent" or *aqllawasi*.[33] According to the Mesas, this is the most impressive of the Inca buildings at Lake Titicaca.[34] The complex is formed by a series of rooms occupying three sides of a rectangular courtyard approximately 53 by 25 meters. The north side has no buildings and opens to a view of the lake. The influence of Tiwanaku decorative elements is much more pronounced here than at Pilco Kayma. The walls facing into the courtyard display a series of large niches, each consisting of a sequence of progressively more deeply recessed frames with alternating stepped and level tops, ending in either an open or blind doorway (*fig. 255*). The geometric movement of these recessed planes produces a marked chiaroscuro effect. On the wall between the great niches there are sunken cruciform designs exactly like those found at Tiwanaku. The architectural design is unique as much for its plan (*fig. 256*) (which in some respects has a certain air of Puma Punku as reconstructed by Edmund Kiss in 1937) as for the persistence of Tiwanaku forms.

The usnu: throne and altar

The three temples (the Qorikancha in Cuzco, the Temple of Wiraqocha in Raqchi, and the Temple of Huaytará) and the structures at Lake Titicaca just analyzed (Pilco Kayma and the *aqllawasi*) were selected principally because they present architectural characteristics that, although differing from one another, all vary somewhat from the repetitive formulae typical of the Inca buildings. Other temples, sanctuaries, and supposedly religious buildings, but with more common and standardized forms, are found in various places. Some of them were mentioned in our discussion of urban centers in chapter 2. So at this point we will not return to the buildings of Limatambo, Huánuco Pampa, Chinchero, Machu Picchu, Pisaq, Ollantaytambo, Vilcashuamán, and so forth. Without slighting the importance of the religious structures in a settlement like Machu Picchu, for

255. Corbeled arches and stepped niches in the ruins of the Island of
Koati in Lake Titicaca (1914)

the purpose of this work, most buildings of the famous "citadel" present no noticeable differences in their formal and spatial characteristics.

It is worth remembering, also, that the buildings most easily identified as temples were the objects of a systematic destructive mania on the part of the Spaniards from the earliest years of the conquest. A careful observer like Cieza de León, who traveled Peru from north to south only fifteen years after Pizarro's arrival in Cajamarca, found the countryside completely devastated: "wherever Christians have passed conquering and discovering, nothing is to be seen but everything is burned up."[35] Of the great establishment at Tumipampa he says that "everything is now ravaged and devastated. . . ."[36] In Huamachuco he finds that everything is laid waste and the idols destroyed.[37] In the province of Tamboblanco, "The ancient temples, which they generally call *guacas*, are now all despoiled and profaned. . . ."[38] He encountered the same situation from Huamachuco to Ayaviri.

The few temples that survived the furious extirpation of idolatries are those that were partly used in building Catholic churches or those that remained remote and ignored. The latter, nonetheless, suffered the deterioration and destruction caused by the elements, lack of care, and indifference.

The "Anonymous Jesuit" says that the ancient Peruvians "had two kinds of temple, some natural and others artificial. The natural ones were skies, elements, sea, earth, mountains, ravines, rushing rivers, fountains or springs, ponds or deep lakes, caves, prominent rock outcrops, mountain peaks. . . ."[39] The artificial ones were the temples that had been built. Cobo, in his account of the *wak'a* of Cuzco, which were arranged in a precise plan along ideal lines, or *ceques*, notes a large number of these *wak'a* that were simply natural rocks or stones.[40] Today, in hundreds of places throughout what was Tawantinsuyu, one finds rocks in natural or modified states, some stepped, others with altars, shelves, niches, cuts, moldings, thrones or a "seat of the Inca"—a sample so varied that it merits a separate study. The rocky site of Kenko, with its monolith and altars in caves, and the "sacred" rocks of Machu Picchu, Ñusta Hispana, Chinchero, Ollantaytambo, and many other places are witness to the complex Inca symbolism

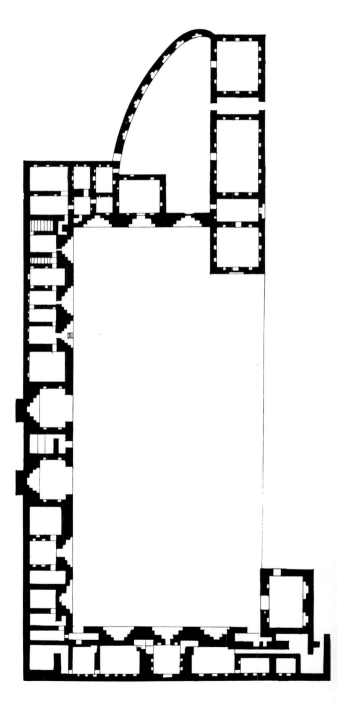

266

257. Month of February. Prayer and offering before an altar-*usnu*, after Guaman Poma de Ayala.

258. Month of March, after Guaman Poma de Ayala. The shape of the altar-*usnu* recalls the *intiwatana* at Machu Picchu.

related to rocks. The deeply rooted cult of the rock, whether the rock was natural or modified in multiple ways by the stone-carver, represents an area of investigation apart from architecture. It is mentioned here for two reasons: to emphasize the plastic value of these rocks; and to introduce the analysis of an element that can be a simple stone or a structure, an altar, or a throne: the *usnu*. There are diverse opinions among both the chroniclers and the modern interpreters with respect to this element. The Anonymous Jesuit, referring to "natural" altars, says that "at most they made in such places a stone altar, which they called *osno*, for their sacrifices."[41] This datum suggests the vast quantity of *usnu*-altars that there must have been everywhere. Cabello Valboa, referring to Wayna Qhapaq's trip to Tumipampa, says that the Inca "also built in the plaza a certain place called Usno (and for another name Chuqui pillaca) where they sacrificed chicha to the Sun on its times and occasions. . . ."[42] So we have another *usnu*-altar, this one related to the worship of the Sun. Moreover, Cobo says that on the fifth *ceque* of Antisuyu, "The first [*wak'a*] was a stone called *Usno*, which was in the plaza of *Hurinaucaypata*. . . ."[43]

Guaman Poma drew some of these altars, and the one in the drawing corresponding to the month of March (folio 240) closely resembles the so-called *intiwatana* at Machu Picchu (*figs. 258, 259*).[44] Very possibly many of the *intiwatana* were other *usnu*-altars rather than "places where the Sun is tied."

In other accounts the *usnu* is said to function as a throne. Cristóbal de Molina, discussing Inca settlements, says that "in each town [they had] a great royal plaza and in the middle of it a high square platform, with a very high stairway. . . ."[45] Although this description easily fits the type of *usnu* found at Huánuco Pampa, it does not specify any functions. Guaman Poma, on the other hand, is very specific when he represents Atawallpa (folio 384) "in the city of Caxamarca, on his throne, usno"[46] (*fig. 260*). In yet another drawing by the same author (folio 398), entitled "Mango Inga named himself King Inca," the base of the structure is labelled: "throne and seat of the Inca called usno" (*fig. 261*). These two drawings clearly indicate the *usnu* functioning as a throne on a stepped base. The drawing of folio 369 may also

267

259. Machu Picchu. The so-called *intiwatana* may well have been an altar-*usnu* similar to that of Guaman Poma's drawing.
260. Atawallpa on his throne-*usnu*, after Guaman Poma de Ayala.
261. On the steps the legend reads: "throne and seat of the Inca called—usno—in Cuzco," after Guaman Poma de Ayala.

represent a stepped *usnu* in the city of Cuzco. The information provided by the early writers thus allows us to interpret the *usnu* as an altar and as a throne; possibly, however, the two functions were combined. Referring to one of the most well-known *usnu*, the one at Willka Waman, Cieza says that Wayna Qhapaq "climbed, to pray, onto an elegant and finely made terrace built for that purpose; they sacrified, in conformity with their blindness, the customary things and killed many animals and birds. . . ."[47] That is, on top of the *usnu* of Willka Waman—on the "elegant and finely made terrace," which still exists and where the monolithic throne with two seats remains—the function of throne and prayer (altar) were united.

The famous "throne of the Inca," cut into the very rock facing the "fortress" of Saqsaywaman, could also have been an *usnu* while simultaneously serving as throne and altar (*fig. 262*).

Donald Thompson has observed that "The most important settlements, including all the administrative centers mentioned, have platforms or *ushnu cuna* in their plazas. The majority of the structures are of stone laid with clay mortar, *pirka*, but some of the most important centers like Vilcashuamán or Huánuco Viejo, display fine stone cutting and the architectural technique that characterizes the Cuzco area."[48] Thompson's observation coincides with that of Cristóbal de Molina, cited earlier (see note 45). Reiner Zuidema notes that "The best data that we have are from the Usñu of the Inca city of Vilcashuaman, which still exists in its entirety and was perhaps the most splendid of the Incas [*sic*]. The Usñu was a five-step pyramid or simply a rectangular elevation where the Inca—in other towns the governor—sat to govern and judge. It seems that the Usñu was the symbol of the power and government of the Incas in the conquered town."[49]

When the first Spaniards reached Cajamarca in 1532, they observed a "fortress" in the middle of the plaza that was ascended via a stone stairway. Jerez writes that Atawallpa invited Pizarro to "quarter himself wherever he wished so long as he not climb the fortress in the plaza. . . ."[50] Surely the "fortress" so venerated was an *usnu* reserved for the exclusive use of the Inca.

In 1562 the informants of Iñigo Ortiz de Zúñiga explained the uses of the plaza of Huánuco Pampa: "This governor named

269

262. Cuzco. The "throne" facing the "fortress" of Saqsaywaman could also be an *usnu*.

263. Willka Waman. Present state of the *usnu*.

Tucuyrico . . . had authority over all the *caciques*. . . . He gathered all the *caciques* and principal men of that land and many other Indians and in the plaza in the presence of all told them that they might see how that justice was done. . . ."[51] It is most probable that this governor imparted justice from the *usnu* that still stands in the middle of the plaza.

In conclusion, the *usnu* may have had various functions: altar, place of prayer, place of sacrifice, seat, throne, and place from which justice was imparted.[52] On the basis of this variety of uses, we may suggest that there was also a variety of design and form. Such, at least, is indicated by the drawings of Guaman Poma if one compares them with the *usnu* of Willka Waman and Huánuco Pampa, the two examples that have best survived to our time.

The Willka Waman *usnu* (*fig. 263*) is located in the town of Vilcashuamán.[53] The structure has the form of a stepped pyramid. Of its four sides, only the eastern one, which is embellished by the stairway (*fig. 264*), is reasonably well preserved. The three remaining sides have lost the greater part of the stepped taluses and are badly deteriorated. Comparing its present state of preservation to Angrand's drawing of 1847 and Wiener's engraving of 1880 (*figs. 265, 266*), the progressive destruction of the monument is easily observed.[54] It appears to have had five stepped platforms (at least so Angrand indicates on the left side of his

264. Willka Waman. The stepped platforms and the stairway
leading to the top recall similar Mesoamerican structures.

265. Willka Waman. The *usnu*, after Léonce Angrand (1847).
266. Willka Waman. The *usnu*, after Wiener (1880).

drawing). Today four are visible, but possibly the fifth was the base, defined by the precinct wall, which is at a higher level than the plaza. Our drawing offers a hypothetical reconstruction of its original form (*fig. 267*). The *usnu* was set in a large trapezoidal walled compound.[55] Of the enclosing wall the only remaining evidence is around the double-jamb doorway in front of the stairway that ascends to the upper platform (*fig. 268*), and the side doorway located at the end of the enclosure on the south side. All the stone blocks of the enclosure have been looted. That the two doorways have managed to survive is due to the greater difficulty of removing the stones. In fact, the weight of the lintels has compressed the stones of the jambs, rendering their dismemberment more difficult. Around the side doorway the stones have been removed to the point of its near collapse (*fig. 269*). The wall of the principal façade, on the plaza side, almost certainly had two doors or probably three. Today only the central one in front of the stairway remains (*fig. 270*). In the illustrations of Angrand and Wiener the presence of the second door to the left of the central one is clear. The possible third portal is suggested entirely on the basis of the principles of symmetry.

Cieza de León, who visited Willka Waman in 1548, described the *usnu* complex:

273

267. Willka Waman. Hypothetical reconstruction of the *usnu*.

268. Willka Waman. The principal entrance is in front of the stairway and has a double-jamb doorway.

269. Willka Waman. The side doorway, about to collapse if not consolidated immediately.

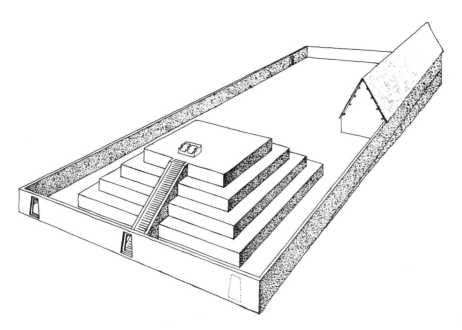

270. Willka Waman. The main doorway seen from the top platform.

271. Willka Wàman. The double throne on the top platform of
the *usnu*.

272. Huánuco Pampa. The *usnu* imposes its volume in the center of
the plaza.

On one part of this flat area [the plaza], toward the rising sun, was
a shrine of the rulers, made of stone, enclosed by a small wall, from
which projected a not very large terrace, six feet wide, with other
stone walls set upon it up to where the seat was on top where the
lord went to pray, made of a single block so large that it is eleven
feet long and seven wide, in which two seats are made for the purpose mentioned [*fig. 271*]. They say that this stone used to be full
of golden jewels and precious stones which adorned the place that
they so much venerated and esteemed. . . . Behind this shrine were
the palaces of Topainga Yupangue and other large buildings. . . . .[56]

In fact, behind the *usnu* and still within the walled precinct are
the remains of a great *kallanka*-type rectangular structure some
40 meters long. Cieza's description coincides perfectly with the
present remains, in spite of 427 years of abandonment and decay.
The other *usnu* is at Huánuco Pampa in the middle of the
enormous plaza of that administrative center.[57] It is less elaborate
than the Willka Waman *usnu* but more impressive because it has
an austere voluminal force that imposes itself on the great open
space (*fig. 272*). Its simple rectangular form, approximately 50
by 30 meters, rises some 4 meters above the great platform that
serves as its base. All four sides display fine stonework of the
Cuzco type. On the south side a monumental stairway provides

277

273. Huánuco Pampa. The *usnu* seen from the side with the stairway leading to the top platform.

access to the upper level of the *usnu* (fig. 273), whose floor is a meter below the upper edge of the wall, which is finished by a projecting cornice (fig. 274). This elevated enclosure has two small entrances, decorated with the same feline that appears on the portals of the "House of the Inca" in the same settlement (fig. 275). Apparently there were various seats on the inner side of the wall that encloses the upper platform; four are well defined on the north side. It is difficult to determine the exact number of the others because of vandalism. Both the Willka Waman and the Huánuco Pampa *usnu* belong to the Late Horizon.

274. Huánuco Pampa. North side of the *usnu*.

The Pumpu *usnu* recalls the placement of the one at
Huánuco Pampa, being located in the middle of the trapezoidal
plaza, but it is smaller and built of *pirca*-type fieldstone construction.

The *usnu* of the administrative centers, such as Cajamarca
mentioned by Jerez, Huánuco Pampa, Pumpu, and Willka
Waman, are of dimensions that impose their volume on the plaza.
This suggests that in the conquered and subjugated territories,
the *usnu* was supposed to produce a visual impact that would
evoke the power of the Incas. In fact, no *usnu* similar to those
mentioned is known from the Inca central region. In general,
usnu were placed in the center of the plaza, but the location of
those of Willka Waman and Tambo Colorado shows that there
were variations. Nothing is known today about what motives
might have produced such differences.

The fortresses

Besides mentioning the existence of temples, palaces, shrines,
and storehouses in various settlements of Tawantinsuyu, the
chroniclers frequently refer to the presence of fortresses. In
those border regions that most strongly resisted the expansion, the
Incas probably felt the need to build some defensive enclosures
for quartering the garrisons that were to maintain control over
the conquered area. Besides these forts, the chroniclers may have
considered some pre-Inca and Inca structures with high walls or
enclosures, the function of which we do not know, to be fortresses. Any building with stone enclosures and few entrances
that was situated in broken terrain could easily be interpreted as
a fortress by the sixteenth-century European mentality accus-
tomed to medieval structures. This interpretation was reinforced
by the aspect of the austere walls of huge stone blocks, a building
technique similar in some respects to medieval walls and the
works that the Romans left in Spain. The Spaniard was familiar
with those works and they are often cited in comparison with
Inca walls.

Although small strategically placed fortified centers, *pukara*,
are known, Inca urbanism did not develop on the basis of fortified

plans. Settlements like Huánuco Pampa, Tumipama, Willka Waman, Pumpu, and many more, founded along the *qhapaq-ñan*, present no militarily defensive aspect. On the contrary, they are open on all sides without a trace of walls. Cajamarca was not fortified, in spite of Jerez's calling the *usnu* in the middle of the plaza a fortress, nor was Cuzco. Ollantaytambo is no more a fortress than Machu Picchu is a citadel in the military sense.

Once the military conquest of new territories was carried out by force of large armies, battles, and massacres, the nature of the military occupation in the subjugated areas became weaker and weaker, giving way to an increasing control of manpower, which compelled people to leave their homes to be put to work in other places that were sometimes very far off. Without requiring great fortified constructions, the *mit'a* system was very effective in keeping under control those groups who most fiercely resisted the invader. In the many and varied chroniclers' accounts of the Inca expansion there is one detail that is common to them all: they agree that the armies left from and returned to Cuzco. The same was true whether the purpose was to conquer new territory or to put down rebellions of ethnic groups unhappy with the "pax incaica." Almost no mention is made of the need to maintain a great permanent contingent of troops on the spot to control a conquered region. The state sent another class of personnel to organize and regulate life in the subject territories, principally administrators, *khipu-kamayoq*, and colonists from Cuzco. Various cases are known in which a local rebellion easily eliminated the Inca government representatives. Then, once again, the implacable armies went out from Cuzco to punish the rebels. It is unlikely that a system of controlling conquered territories based on the regulation of manpower would consider the building of large-scale military works to be of first priority in securing the occupation. What we know is that the administrative centers and *tampu* founded the length of the *qhapaq-ñan* present no military characteristics. It must also be considered that, no matter how fortresslike its appearance, a walled structure, rather than having defensive ends, might have functioned to protect a space into which, because of its exclusive religious nature, very few were admitted.

Saqsaywaman—Cuzco

The Inca monument most impressive to everyone visiting Cuzco is the "fortress" of Saqsaywaman. All who have written about this structure have sought the most hyperbolic adjectives and most forceful comparisons. From the first description up to the present day the tone has changed very little. In 1534, Pedro Sancho, the first Western man to describe Cuzco, says that "neither the bridge of Segovia nor any of the buildings that Hercules or the Romans built are so worthy of being seen as this. The city of Tarragona has some works in its walls that are similar, but not as strong nor of such large stones. . . ."[58] Four hundred and thirty-six years later, Luis Pardo emphasizes:

I doubt there is in the world a similar construction; not even the pyramids of Egypt, great and colossal as they are, equal it; the very cyclopean ruins of ancient Greece cannot surpass it. The cities of Chaldea and Assyria are paltry. The epopee of stone, the marvelous buildings of Renaissance Rome, the architectural remains of Memphis and Thebes, the Mexican teocalli, all are insignificant in the face of the monstruous magnificance of the stones that are set one upon the other in this secular edifice that we call SACCSAYHUAMAN. . . .[59]

For more than four centuries numerous and varied analogies have been made, and not even the seven wonders of the world have escaped comparison; everything written reflects astonishment, stupor, admiration and wonder.

What most impressed the chroniclers was the immensity of the stones (*fig. 277*). "The marvelous thing about that edifice is the incredible size of the stones," says Garcilaso. Sancho notes that the walls "are of stones so large that no one seeing them would say that they were placed there by the hands of human beings, for they are as large as pieces of mountains and cliffs. . . ." Cieza states that some stones are "more than twenty [feet] long, and others thicker than an ox, and all set so delicately that between one and another they could not fit a *real* [small coin]." ". . . there are stones," affirms Polo de Ondegardo, "that would require the work of twenty people an entire year to dress a single one," while for Sarmiento de Gamboa it is "a most admirable thing to see."[60]

N

0   50   100 m

And according to Francisco de Toledo, "it was extremely beautiful stonework of such large stones that it seems impossible to have been made by the strength and industry of men."[61]

Many questions arise when one attempts to ascertain the intended functions of this complex edifice and to learn the reasons behind such an exhibition of titanic architecture. Was it really a fortress? Was the building of a fortress in Cuzco justified when none was built in the administrative centers far from the capital? Was there fear of attack? From within or without? Was it a display of the power of *hanan* Cuzco? Was it a structure with multiple uses? It seems that Garcilaso also had his doubts when he said, "it was built more to be admired than for any other reason."[62]

We indicated at the beginning of this chapter that Cieza attributed functions of a "royal house of the sun" to the edifice "which the Spanish commonly call the Fortress." Garcilaso, indicating that only the Incas could enter it, says, "those of other nations could not enter in that fortress, because it was the house of the Sun, of arms and war, as the temple was of prayer and sacrifices."[63] Antonio de Herrera also says that "The work was begun and it was called the House of the Sun, and today the Castilians call it the Fortress. . . ."[64] It is probable, as Garcilaso states, that the structure had various uses: temple, storage, residence, and also fortress. If some day it should be demonstrated that there were two kings reigning simultaneously in Cuzco, as some poorly based modern speculations suggest, the "fortress" of Saqsaywaman could be interpreted as a fortified temple and residence of the section corresponding to *hanan* Cuzco, the most powerful division after the reforms and rebuilding of the city by Pachakuti. And it is specifically to Pachakuti that the beginning of the construction of the "fortress" is attributed, a task in which, according to Cieza, twenty thousand men participated. Garcilaso says that "it took more than fifty years to finish it, until the time of Huaina Capac."[65] Francisco de Toledo reports having "found the fortress that Tupac Ynca, Huayna Capac and Huáscar his son made. . . ."[66] In the *Noticias cronológicas del Cuzco*, written by Diego de Esquivel y Navía in 1746, it is stated

278. Cuzco. Aerial view of Saqsaywaman with its saw-toothed walls. On the right the circular foundation of the tower of Muyucmarka.

279. Cuzco. Plan of Saqsaywaman: 1. Chuquipampa   2. Tower of
Muyucmarka   3. Tower of Sallacmarka   4. Tower of
Paucamarka   5. Principal doorway of Tiapunka   6. *Qollqa*.

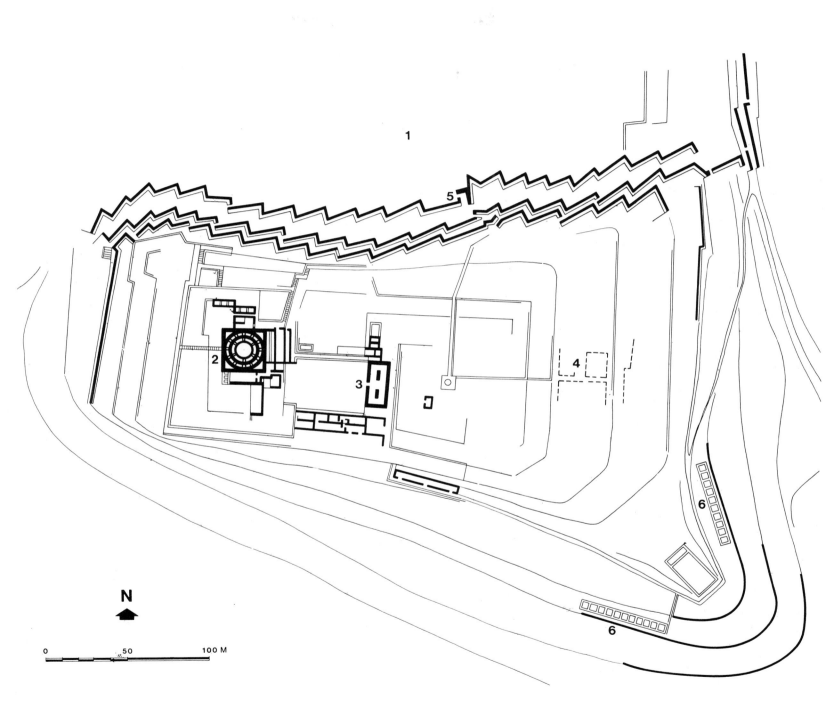

N

0   50   100 M

that "The construction lasted sixty-seven years. . . ." and was completed during the reign of Wayna Qhapaq.[67] The hypotheses that saw in Saqsaywaman a pre-Inca structure belonging to supposed megalithic periods have been discarded ever since Luis E. Valcárcel carried out the first scientific investigations in 1934.

After the conquest the Saqsaywaman complex was used as a quarry from which stones were removed to build the houses and churches of Cuzco. It would be difficult to find a more useful quarry, with all the stones already cut. According to Garcilaso, "they demolished all of the polished masonry that was built within the fortification walls, so that there is no house in the city that was not built with that stone. . . ."[68] It was also used to build the churches: "the Ecclesiastical Council by an accord of October 6, 1559, ordered that the stones of the fortress be brought for the building of the Cathedral. . . ."[69] What we know of the "fortress" today we owe to the size of the stones; they were too heavy to move and too much work to break up (fig. 280). It was not worth the effort since there were other structures to raze. Cieza realized the importance of the monument and, with the attitude of a conservationist, lamented its destruction: "It would be appropriate to order it preserved in memory of the greatness of the land. . . ."[70] Today the three saw-toothed stepped levels (fig. 281) testify to the grandeur of the monument and the great capacity for utilizing the manpower that built it.

There has been considerable speculation about the origin of the stone, which, to the end of exalting the superhuman effort, has been attributed to distant sources. The geologist Carlos Kalafatovich, who has studied the geological formation of the Saqsaywaman group, notes:

Regarding the quarries used for the construction of the walls of the Fortress it is evident that they used the limestone which crops out in more or less extensive masses a few hundred meters to the north and east of this archaeological group, but many blocks may also have been extracted from the site of the Fortress itself, since, as can be seen on the geological map, there are outcrops of limestone above the walls.[71]

This same geologist notes the presence of stone foreign to the site, and suggests that it may have been brought from the quarries of Rumicolca, a volcanic center some 30 kilometers to the southeast of Cuzco.[72] Rowe also refers to the use of limestone in the "great fortifications of Sacsahuaman," and indicates that andesite was available from Huaccoto as well as Rumicolca.[73]

Observing the zig-zag form of the walls, it is worth asking if that feature may be related to the "idea" of fortress. Near Ollantaytambo, toward the Lares Valley, is the complex of Puma Marka, a group of structures inside a large walled enclosure that has a saw-toothed arrangement on one side (figs. 282, 283). The wall appears to have been built to protect the buildings located within the enclosure. Nevertheless, nothing is known about the functions of this isolated complex. At this point we simply wish to note the similarity and the possible relationship between form and function.

The "fortress of Paramonga" on the coast, on the other hand, has every appearance of having been intended for defense and territorial control. This work may have been built by the Chimú in the southern extreme of their domains and then used by the Incas as a temple. It is a stepped structure built entirely of adobe. It is skillfully adapted to the terrain and its design is very appropriate for defense. It could almost be considered a precursor of the bastion system. The sequence of walls and stepped platforms gives a markedly horizontal aspect to the complex and a strong impression of mass to the landscape (fig. 284).

Another monument that is striking because of its exceptional form is called Ingapirca, built at 3,160 meters above sea level, near the city of Cañar in Ecuador. The name Ingapirca is generic and not significant; it implies nothing about function, and calling the complex a "castle" or "fortress" is no more satisfactory. This is a frequently visited monument that has merited attention from various travelers and scholars. As early as 1739 La Condamine drew a plan that was much more exact than the one made by Jorge Juan and Antonio Ulloa in 1748. Humboldt visited the site in 1803, and in 1904 the Second Geodesic Mission drew up another plan of the buildings. In 1967–68 the work of clearing

280. Cuzco. Stones of Saqsaywaman.

281. Cuzco. View of the three zig-zag platforms of the "fortress" of
Saqsaywaman.

282. Plan of Puma Marka in the heights above Ollantaytambo

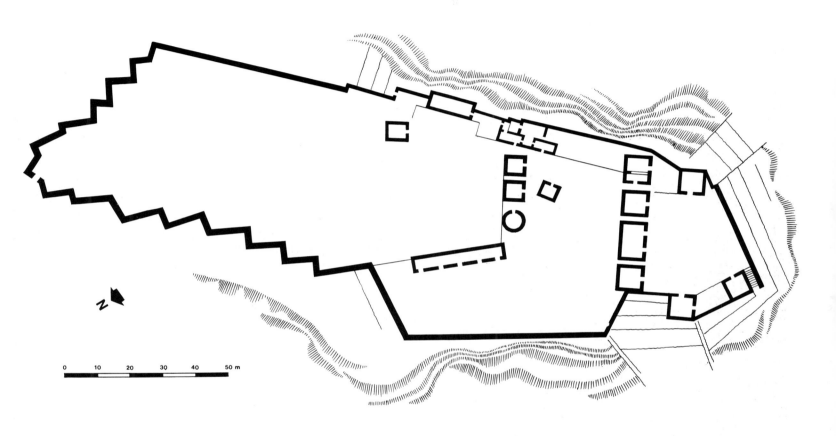

0   10   20   30   40   50 m

283. View of the Puma Marka complex

284. The so-called fortress of Paramonga on the coast, an adobe
      structure

285. Plan of the Ingapirca complex near the city of Cañar, Ecuador,
according to the archaeologist Gordon Hadden. The elongated
oval form of the main structure stands out.

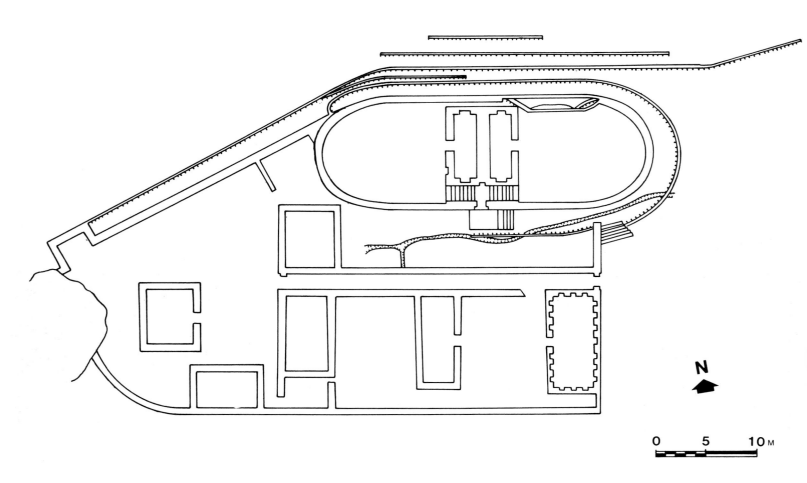

and consolidation was undertaken, directed by the archaeologist
Gordon Hadden (*fig. 285*).[74]

The most interesting structure of the Ingapirca complex is
the long oval platform (not elliptical as has so often been stated),
which is 37.10 meters long and 12.35 wide (*fig. 286*). The entire platform is supported by a wall of well-cut stones, which
varies from 3.15 to 4.10 meters in height. On the south face of
the wall is the entrance leading to the upper platform. The trapezoidal, double-jamb doorway is reached by a five-step stairway
parallel to the outside of the wall and adjoining it. Through the
doorway there is a landing from which two facing stairways
rise to the eastern and western parts of the platform (*fig. 287*).
Probably the outside stairway also had two opposing flights lead-

286. Ingapirca. The platform seen from the south; remains of the house are preserved on top.

287. Ingapirca. The niche facing the landing from which the two stairways rise in opposite directions.

ing to the entrance landing (*fig. 288*), as is indicated by the plan produced by the Second Geodesic Mission in 1904. The Incas frequently used the solution of two facing stairways. Garcilaso mentions them for the temple of Wiraqocha in Raqchi, and good examples are also known at Yucay (*fig. 289*) and Tambo Colorado. Possibly the formal antecedents of this type of opposed stairway derive from the temple of Chavin, since such arrangements are not known in Tiwanaku architecture.

On top of the platform is the poorly named "guardhouse"; it was a building with two rooms that did not communicate because they were separated by a party wall on the long axis. The characteristics of this building are the same as those noted for this type in the preceding chapter. The walls of the house were stone up to the beginning of the triangular gable. From there on up, adobe was used, including on the party wall.

297

288. Ingapirca. Hypothetical reconstruction of the access to the top of the oval platform.

289. Yucay. Stairway with two facing flights similar to that of Ingapirca.

290. Ingapirca. Three circles, each 12.35 meters in diameter, lined up on the same axis, establish the proportions of the elongated oval platform.

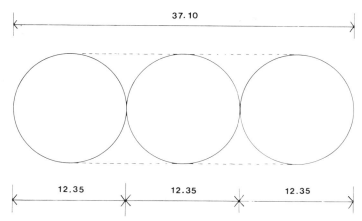

Any attempt to attribute definite functions to this structure is hazardous. "Castle," "fortress," and "guardhouse" are not persuasive, and, always within the realm of speculation, the building might also be interpreted as a sanctuary with its elongated oval *usnu*. We rather tend to relate this structure to religious functions, since the measurements of the oval form were achieved by combining three circles 12.35 meters in diameter for a total length of 37.10 meters, that is, the length of the oval platform (*fig. 290*). The number three was of great symbolic significance in religion, and it would not be surprising for this importance to be reflected in the architecture. Fernando Cabieses comments:

. . . the Sun in its three aspects of *Apu, Churi* and *Guauqui* was a trinity; also a trinity was the lightning (the lightning bolt, thunder, sheet lightning) personified as *Chuqui-illa, Catu-illa* and *Inti-illapa*. And when each divinity was presented individually, the ranking within the Inka pantheon was trinitarian also, with the first three posts occupied by *Viracocha, Inti* and *Huanacauri* . . . or by the Sun, the Moon and the Thunder . . . or by the elements of things existing: Water, Earth and Fire . . . or by the three kingdoms of Viracocha, *Hanan Pacha, Cay Pacha* and *Ukju Pacha* . . . or by the three windows of *Tampu Tocco* or by the three positions of the Sun: *Anti, Inti* and *Cunti*. . . .[75]

The fact that the Ingapirca platform is so exactly formed around a line of three contiguous circular modules increases the acceptability of hypothesizing that religious rather than military functions were more probable. We might note, in passing, that the great *kallanka* at Inkallaqta in Bolivia also adopted a triple module to establish the dimensions of its plan.[76]

291. Ingapirca. East side of the oval platform.

Other state works

The architectural examples analyzed in this chapter are related to representative structures that can be considered under the generic term of "monuments." They are equivalent to the temples, forts, and palaces of any other historical period analyzed in their architectural manifestations. The variety of architectural and urban expressions are identified with the cultural level reached by different human groups in time and in space. Architectural works that are classified as "monuments" almost always reflect the power attained by a given social organization. But that power, whether political, religious, or economic, is also revealed in other types of achievement that are sometimes more important than the "monuments" because they demonstrate the high organizational level attained by that society.

In the case of the Incas, it is somewhat difficult to classify such works as "public." Today when we refer to public transportation works, it is understood that they represent the entire transportation network of roads, highways, bridges, etc., which the state constructs to facilitate the communication and movement of great numbers of people who are engaged in the most varied activities. Inca roads, on the other hand, more than a communication network at the service of the community, may be interpreted as a means used by the state to maintain strict territorial control. In this respect Murra says:

Some aspects of the political organization of Tawantinsuyu, that is— the Inca State—have attracted attention for centuries, and their functioning is well understood; roads, for example. The enormous territory and the many cultures incorporated through conquest, spread over many ecological zones, in the mountains, the deserts and deep valleys, required some system that would keep the periphery in touch with the center and the coast with the highlands, the potential rebels within striking distance of the Cuzco garrisons; that would permit the *khipu kamayoq* to enter in their *khipu* the information needed to report to their superiors in the administrative bureaucracy. The Inca road network provided for all that and much more.[77]

Using the same criteria, based on territorial control, the bridges, *tampu*, and administrative centers were built along the *qhapaq-ñan*. The same is true for the construction on an immense scale of agricultural terraces and of *qollqa* for the storage of all kinds of products. These works, however, are related to the control exercised by the state over production and the redistribution of goods.

It is not the purpose of this book, devoted to architecture and urban settlements, to linger over the description of roads, bridges, storehouses, terraces, and other works pertaining to the state administrative system. They are mentioned only because we consider them to be intimately related to the building programs and because we cannot ignore the striking impact they still have on the Andean landscape.

The chroniclers were impressed by the extensive network of stone-paved roads, by their state of repair, and by the difficulties overcome in building them. From Ecuador to Chile there are still innumerable stretches of road, many even now in use. Some are wide, like the *qhapaq-ñan* and those on the coast; others are narrow, sometimes cut into the living rock or built with retaining walls to reinforce the outer edge, like the roads still traveled to visit the archaeological centers of the Urubamba zone.

The state bridges were built of long timbers resting on stone bases or, when there was a very great distance to span, were suspended. They had watchmen and a toll was even charged; like the roads, they were constantly repaired.[78]

The hundreds of *qollqa* built near the inhabited centers impressed the chroniclers more than did the roads. Cieza de León refers to "large storehouses full of necessary things, which were to supply the men of war, because in one of these storehouses there were lances and in another darts, and in others sandals, and in others the other arms that they had. Likewise some storehouses were supplied with rich clothing, and others with coarser stuff, and others with food and all kind of provisions."[79] Further on, referring to Tumipampa, he adds: "The woolen clothing that was in the storehouses was so much and so rich that if it were kept and not lost it would be worth a great treasure."[80] And in Jauja he observed "many storehouses full of all the things that there could be."[81] Besides Cieza, many other chroniclers left a

record of the great number of storehouses and the variety of the goods that they contained.

At Huánuco Pampa there are 497 *qollqa* situated on the lower slope of the hill south of the administrative center (see chapter 2). Cieza indicates that there were 700 at Willka Waman. Doubtless the largest Inca storage center known to date is at Cotapachi in the department of Cochabamba, Bolivia, where there are 2,400 *qollqa*. The system of state storage may have been related to various aspects of the Inca economy. For example, the storehouses at Huánuco Pampa, among other functions, certainly served to fill the needs of the settlement itself. On the other hand, the 2,400 storehouses of Cotapachi, where there was no important settlement nearby, were most likely related to functions of re-distribution.

The architecture of the *qollqa* is essentially functional; walls are fieldstone, the plan is circular or quadrangular, and the roofs were thatched on frames of branches and had a pyramidal or conical form. It seems that the circular *qollqa* were used to store maize. In spite of the simplicity of these structures, ingenious ventilation systems that permitted the preservation of quite perishable products have been found in many of them. In the Cotapachi *qollqa* an underground channel in the floor, open on the windward side, provided interior ventilation and constant air circulation through other openings located at roof level (*fig. 294*). The *qollqa* at Cotapachi have a fixed diameter of three meters and they are all exactly spaced with 5.15 meters on the east and west sides and 9.50 on the north and south. Geraldine Byrne de Caballero is quite correct in commenting that "the maintenance of these measurements without a single mistake in either the 2,400 circles or the alignment is a startling architectural feat."[82]

Finally, we must also point to the prodigious building activity represented by the agricultural terraces that have altered the natural topography in so many places, transforming it into a "monument" of agricultural architecture. The terraces of Pisaq, Machu Picchu, Chinchero, Ollantaytambo, Zurite, Tipón, and many more places continue as mute witnesses to the importance of agriculture in the Inca economy. They are stepped terraces that provide level surfaces on uncultivable slopes, following the contour of the topography. Communication between the different levels is provided by steps set into and extending from the retaining walls. And everywhere we see the remains of irrigation canals executed with a skill that overcame all natural obstacles to bring water, whatever the distance, to villages and cultivated areas. The works of river canalization, reservoirs, diversion of irrigation canals, fountains, aqueducts, and the supplying of water via distribution networks constitute an inexhaustible field of investigation for the entire area of the Andean cultures, from remotest times to the Incas.[83]

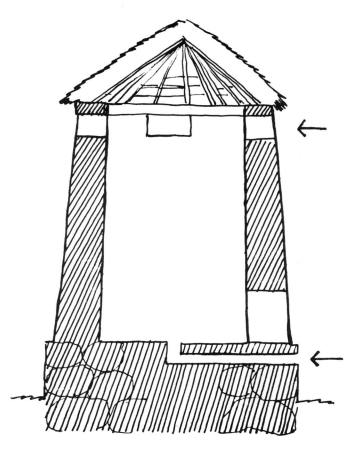

5

Technical and Aesthetic Problems

Technology

Dismissing, for the moment, the variety of walls and the stonemason's skill in fitting the stone blocks, let us consider the repetitive nature of structural solutions. We have already noted that the formal character of Inca architecture was eminently repetitive, a fact ascribable not only to the reduced repertoire of technical solutions, which inevitably necessitated their repeated application, but also to a possible intention not to seek new technical procedures so as not to create additional problems. In other words, it seems that the state advised or ordered the avoidance of new structural solutions, since those already known and used were backed by experience. Such a policy could explain the disinterest of the Incas in the vaulted system or in linked sequences of dwellings.

The simple one-room, rectangular design plans were accompanied by a limited variety of structural solutions to cover them. Although Garcilaso exalts the palaces of the Incas and says that "they surpassed all the houses of Kings and Emperors yet known in the world,"[1] he recognizes "the inability of the mechanics in their trades when it is seen with what poverty and lack of necessary things those people lived."[2] He then proceeds to enumerate, as he does in other passages of his *Comentarios*, that "they did not know how to make anvils of iron . . ." or "extract iron," or to "make hammers with wooden handles," or "files or burins" or "tongs for removing the metal from the fire. . . ."[3]

Regarding building materials and technology, he notes that "the Indians of Peru did not know how to make lime or plaster, tile or brick."[4] Nor did they "connect one room with another, nor [use] cross beams. . . ."[5] Carpenters' tools were also very crude and primitive:

They did not know how to make a saw nor a drill, nor a plane nor any other instrument for carpentry, and thus they knew not how to make chests or doors, but only to cut the wood and remove its bark for their buildings.[6] For axes and adzes and some few tools that they made, silversmiths served in place of blacksmiths, because all the tools that they worked were of copper and brass. They did not use nails, so that whatever wood they put into their buildings was all tied with grass ropes and not nailed.[7]

Regarding the masons, he indicates that:

. . . they had no other tools to work the stones than some black stones that they called *hihuana*, with which they dress [the stone] by pounding rather than cutting. To raise and lower the stones they had no machinery at all; they did it all by manpower. And with all that, they made such grand works, so skillful and polished that they are incredible, as the Spanish historians extol them and as is seen by the remains of many of them that have survived.[8]

Garcilaso reaches a rather unflattering conclusion when he comments, "they invented little or nothing of their own, and, on the contrary, are great imitators of what they see . . . done. . . ."[9]

Cieza de León also praises the ability and rapid learning of the artisans and states that:

. . . they lay foundations and build strong buildings very well; and thus they themselves build their dwellings and houses for the Spaniards, and make the brick and tile and fit the very large stones, one on top of the other, with such a nicety that the join can hardly be seen; they also make carvings in the round and other larger things, and in many places what they have made and make without any tools other than stones and their great ingenuity can be seen.[10]

Garcilaso and Cieza arrive at the same conclusion: the lack of implements did not prevent the execution of remarkable monuments that even today are most impressive. Today's interpreter may also consider that the most efficient tool, and the one that made the execution of these works possible, was the skillful use of human energy by the Inca state. Large contingents of people, coming from various parts of Tawantinsuyu, alternated in the *mit'a* cycles to cut stone, make adobes, braid ropes of plant fiber, gather and move materials, or simply contribute their manpower. In other words, the state would not have achieved the objectives of its building program if it had not had an efficient organization. And when this organization is based on the power of the state,

as has occurred in other historical periods, great works can be achieved.

Although the Inca builders attained an indisputable superiority in the building of cut stone walls, they nevertheless confronted various obstacles in resolving structural problems. The three most frequently encountered were: (1) retaining walls, (2) walls that supported roofs, and (3) roof frames.

1. Retaining walls are most commonly used in terrace construction—agricultural terraces with a flat surface that adapt themselves in steps to the mountainsides (*fig. 295*). The principal

296. Limatambo. Retaining wall of the platform at Tarawasi.

function of these walls is to contain the soil of the fill. Today, observing the vast quantity of terraces in a good state of preservation after uninterrupted use, we can suggest the accumulation of considerable experience in the construction of this type of wall. In most cases fieldstone construction was used, but there are also terrace walls of well-cut stones near centers that had some religious significance or other prestige. The retaining walls also support nonagricultural platforms in urban centers; sometimes they are enriched with large niches, as in the cases of Willka Waman and Tarawasi (*fig. 296*) already mentioned.

The retaining wall almost always slants inward, which helps to counteract the thrust of the fill and, at the same time, reduces the danger of collapse. When these walls are of well-cut stones, polygonal shapes are used, because they interlock better with one another, achieving a more rigid and stronger bond. Stone blocks with rectangular faces or isodomon were not used in terrace walls.

2. The walls that support roofs are the walls defining interior space that may be inhabited or may serve for any of the multiple needs and activities of man. Dwellings, temples, palaces, *kallanka*, storehouses, workshops, and barracks all have walls to sustain the roof that sheltered the interior space. In other words, we are dealing with the walls of all the covered architectural examples analyzed in the preceding chapters. The conformation of these walls includes all the techniques and materials known to the Incas, from the most rustic ones to those with unrivaled and perfect finish; they may be of stone or of adobe, or combine both materials in the same structure.

Adobe walls are set on stone foundations. Such foundations may extend to a considerable height above floor level. Garcilaso noted that adobes were made in molds,[11] essentially as they are today. Rowe, on the other hand, after observing and studying the shapes and dimensions of this building material in various kinds of works, has arrived at the conclusion that the adobes were hand-made without the aid of molds, a solution that would explain the great variety of sizes.[12] It must be emphasized that adobe is on no account to be considered a building material of "inferior" quality. For today's aesthetic taste, stone walls may be more

297. Huánuco Pampa. The center of the double walls is fill.
298. Pisaq. Stone blocks receive careful finish on the two visible
faces. In the middle of the wall, where the blocks meet, there is
no such care.

highly valued on the grounds that stone is "nobler." For the Inca builders, however, such a difference need not have existed, and, if it did, it must have had a significance difficult to interpret today. Adobe not only was a complementary building material but also was used in buildings of much more importance and rank than others in which only stone was used. In the Qorikancha itself, the building of greatest prestige among all those built by the Incas, adobe was used to complete the stone walls, which are of unequalled perfection in the fitting of the stones. We have already pointed out this structural characteristic in discussing the temple in the previous chapter. Here we mean to show that adobe was the top portion of many walls built of polished stone blocks and that it was never considered a material of inferior quality. Had it been, it would not have been used in the Qorikancha. It seems, rather, that this combination was the standard building system, as we gather from the information that Betanzos provides on the rebuilding of Cuzco. This historian notes that: "[Pachakuti] ordered adobes made of mud and sticky earth, into which . . . a large quantity of grass was thrown; which grass is like Spanish *esparto*; this earth and grass was mixed together so that the adobes were well made and dense, with which adobes they were to build from the stone masonry up until such edifices and houses were the proper height."[13] The statement is very clear; the adobes were placed "from the stone masonry up" until the planned height was reached. On the stone walls of the Qorikancha there are no vestiges of adobes; therefore the walls seem low to us and the interior space of the surviving chambers is deceptive.

Adobe was used in other buildings of great importance, like the Temple of Wiraqocha and the one at Huaytará analyzed in the preceding chapter. Centuries of constant exposure to the weather and the erosive action of the rain have caused minor damage compared to what man has done.

The stone enclosure walls that were going to bear the roof display various building techniques; besides the rustic *pirca*, there are those that present little modification in the dressing of the stones. Although the outside almost always received greater care, walls frequently have a double structure with a rustic fill in the middle (*fig. 297*). Double walls that are carefully finished on the

299. Cuzco. Fragment of the wall of Hatunkancha. Note the pronounced slant, equivalent to 10 percent per meter in relation to a plumb.

inside and outside are almost always composed of superimposed courses of blocks that did not receive the same attention at the central join, which was not visible. There are good examples of this type of wall at Pisaq (*fig. 298*).

The walls that support the roof, especially the long walls of the rectangular plan, frequently have an inward slant (*fig. 299*). This inclination could be the result of experience derived from observing the reaction of the wall to the tangential thrust of the inclined poles of the roof slopes. The slanted wall absorbs the thrust better and helps counteract it (*fig. 300*). We have observed that the inclination averages 10% per meter in relation to a plumb. That is, the top edge of a wall 3 meters high would be 30 centimeters out from the base.

All these walls have doorways, niches, and, to a lesser extent, windows. The lintels of these openings are generally of two types: finely cut monoliths or sections of tree trunk tied with braided plant-fiber rope. There are also monolithic lintels set directly into adobe walls, as at Ollantaytambo.

3. In dealing with domestic architecture, we noted that the one-room dwelling with a rectangular plan and no gables had a hip roof formed by a framework of branches covered with some thatching material. This was the most common type of roof used by the highland cultures long before the Inca expansion, and a roof with similar characteristics also served to cover circular houses. It is the most modest type of roof, used on rural houses in remote areas, and surely never caused any technical problems to the builders.

On the other hand, technical problems must have arisen in the important structures that the Incas built for their temples, palaces, or other state dependencies. No one fails to note the great contrast between the structure of the walls and the roofs. The walls of cut stones have an eternal quality that contrasts with the materials and techniques used to cover the interior spaces. Therefore it was in the framing of the roofs, which were always thatched, that the search was concentrated in an effort to perfect formulae that would provide greater durability, attain larger covered areas, and, at the same time, respond to certain aesthetic exigencies. Unfortunately, not a single example has sur-

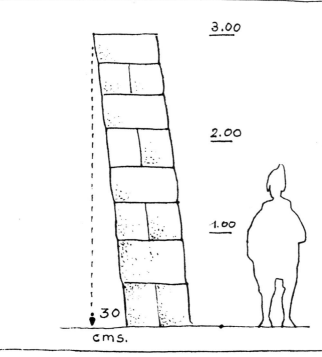

3.00

2.00

1.00

30

cms.

300. The tangential thrust (arrows) against the walls. Slanted walls counteract and absorb part of the thrust. The timbers of the roof slopes are subject to inflection.

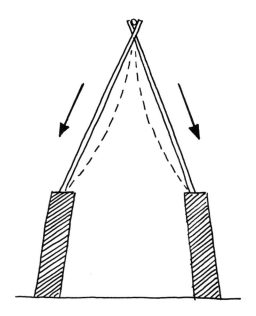

vived to permit us to make a well-founded judgment. Squier left us the following description of the roof of the *sunturwasi* that he saw in Azangaro, which had lasted more than three centuries:

The dome of the Sondor-huasi is perfect, and is formed of a series of bamboos of equal size and taper, their larger ends resting on the top of the walls; bent evenly to a central point, over a series of hoops of the same material and of graduated sizes. At the points where the vertical and horizontal supports cross each other, they are bound together by fine cords of delicately braided grass, which cross and recross each other with admirable skill and taste. Over this skeleton dome is a fine mat of the braided epidermis of the bamboo or rattan, which, as it exposes no seams, almost induces the belief that it was braided on the spot. However that may be, it was worked in different colors, and in panellings conforming in size with the diminishing spaces between the framework, that framework itself being also painted. I shall probably shock my classical readers, and be accounted presumptuous, when I venture a comparison of the Azangaro dome, in style and effect, with that of the cella of the Temple of Venus, facing the Coliseum, in the Eternal City. Over this inner matting is another, open, coarse, and strong, in which was fastened a fleece of finest ichu, which depends like heavy fringe outside the walls. Next comes a transverse layer of coarser grass or reeds, to which succeeds ichu, and so on, the whole rising in the centre so as to form a slightly flattened cone. The projecting ends of the ichu layers were cut off sharply and regularly, producing the effect of overlapping tiles.[14]

The description of the complex assemblage of the parts suggests that the lack of carpentry tools noted by Garcilaso must not have proved an insurmountable obstacle in the achievement of frameworks both sturdy and, certainly, of pleasing appearance. The Incas had no nails, nor did they rabbet the wooden pieces, because all were "tied with grass ropes." That custom has been retained in modern rural dwellings in many highland places and was also applied in many important colonial buildings from the sixteenth century on. For example, the roofs of various churches built around Cuzco have the wooden parts tied with braided strips of hide. Although the system of principal rafters, struts, and cross-

301. The horizontal stud eliminates the inflection, but since it is tied it also functions as a crossbeam and reduces the tangential thrust.

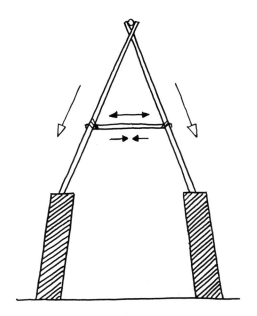

beams was imported from Spain, local techniques were used to consolidate the structure. It is also worth emphasizing that the timbers preserved their round section and were not planed or trimmed.

Garcilaso said that "they did not know how . . . to extend crossbeams from one wall to another," which must have presented a very serious problem in counteracting the tangential thrust on the long walls. We have already mentioned that this thrust might explain the use of walls with an inward slant, an expedient that helps somewhat to counteract the thrust. It is also possible that the steep pitch of the roof was made not only to aid in shedding rainwater but also to reduce the tangential thrust, for the sharper the angle at the ridgepole, the less the effect of the thrust on the walls.

Now, if it is doubtful that crossbeams were used, it is probable, on the other hand, that wooden crossbars like struts were used to avoid inflection of the long poles that acted as rafters. If not, it is hard to understand how the builders could have constructed frameworks capable of covering areas of thousands of square meters, as in the great *kallanka*. We may further observe that because all the wooden parts were tied, the crossbar that acted as a strut would also function as a crossbeam, since it closed the triangular form and, consequently, reduced the tangential thrust (*fig. 301*). In discussing the Temple of Wiraqocha in Raqchi, we mentioned the crossbeams that must have bound the horizontal beam that lay along the columns. In this particular case, it seems that these structural elements had a specific function as crossbeams rather than struts.

Surely the gables on the short sides of the rectangular plan provided greater stability to the wooden frameworks when the ridgepole was supported directly on their apex. To a certain extent this fact explains the great number of stone or adobe gables in Inca structures.

Garcilaso observed that:

They set loose on the walls all the timbers that served as framing; for the top of [the frame] in place of [using] nails, they tied it with strong ropes that they make of a long soft grass that resembles

302. Machu Picchu. Cylindrical stone pegs for tying down the roof.

303. The stone peg may have its antecedents in the projecting timber that rural houses still have.

esparto. On these first timbers they place those that served as purlins and rafters, also tied one to another and that to another; over all they laid the covering of grass, in such quantity that the [roofs of the] royal edifices of which we are speaking were almost a fathom thick, if not more. The roof itself served as a cornice for the wall, so that it would not get wet. It extended more than a *vara* beyond the wall, to shed water; they clipped all the grass that extended beyond the walls very evenly.[15]

According to Garcilaso's description, we find that the principal poles of the roof slopes rested directly on the long walls and were then tied at the level of the ridgepole to form the frame.

Cylindrical stone pegs were often placed on the outside of the gables, following their slope, and apparently served for tying the vertical poles of the roof slopes that were outside of the gable walls (*fig. 302*). These poles, one for each slope of the gables, were important in the roof structure, because, had they not been there, it would have been difficult, considering the thickness of the gable wall, to finish and tie on the horizontal poles at the ends of the house. Today in many rural houses the peasants continue to fasten the ends of the beams that support the roof to wooden pegs embedded in the adobe gables, used in much the same way as the ancient stone pegs (*fig. 304*).

Besides the stone pegs, one less frequently finds stone rings set into the top of the gable wall in a row down the middle of the slopes (*fig. 305*). These rings also served to tie on the horizontal timbers (*fig. 306*).

In the *masma*-type house, where the principal timbers of one slope rested on a wooden beam that extended from one extreme of the dwelling to the other, the lowest stone peg served to fasten that beam and secure it against tangential thrust.

Besides the cylindrical stone pegs located along the outside slope of the gables, there are also some of the same size and shape set into the inside walls, all at the same height and frequently positioned between niches (*fig. 307*). Their function has also received multiple interpretations, although we know nothing definite; the theory most generally accepted is that they served as hangers. Because of their similarity to the outside pegs, however, they may have served to tie down the roof from the inside (*fig. 308*). This hypothesis creates some problems, since inside the so-called Mausoleum at Machu Picchu, where the roof is formed by the cave itself, there are some pegs that, naturally, have no relationship to the nonexistent roof and, instead, suggest having served as hangers (*fig. 309*). On the other hand, it is rather striking that the majority of examples with pegs on the inside of rooms are structures without gables, and the pegs are on all four walls. Might they have served to fasten the roof and secure it against the top of the walls? It is not improbable. A solution of this type could serve for the chambers without gables, which almost always had pyramidal roofs. Four of the six chambers of the Qorikancha had pyramidal roofs. There is also a comment of Garcilaso's that he saw in the Valley of Yucay a "*cuadra* [great room] . . . more than seventy feet square covered in the form of a pyramid; the walls were three *estados* high and the roof more than twelve *estados*. . . ."[16] According to this information, above walls about 5 meters high there rose a hip roof

304. Urubamba Valley. Today's rural house with the roof tied to
wooden pegs.

305. Machu Picchu. One of the stone rings on the gable slope.

306. Possible use of the stone pegs and rings in the structural system of the roof

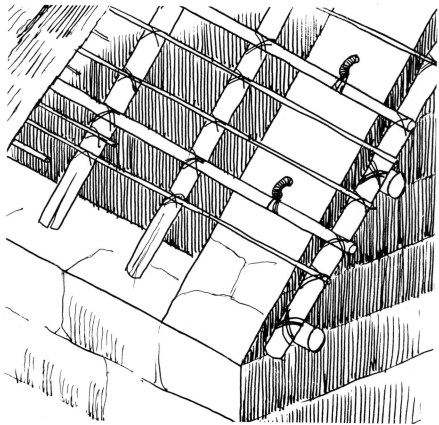

307. Machu Picchu. Stone pegs inside a room.
308. Possible method of tying the roof to pegs located inside a room

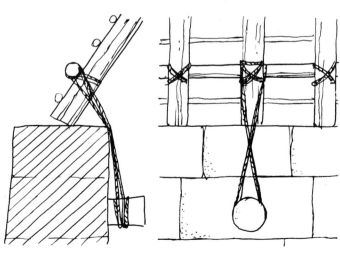

309. Machu Picchu. The pegs of so-called Mausoleum may have served as hangers, since the roof of the cave is entirely of stone.

310. According to Garcilaso there was, in Yucay, a structure with a pyramidal roof of considerable size. How was that roof fastened to the walls?

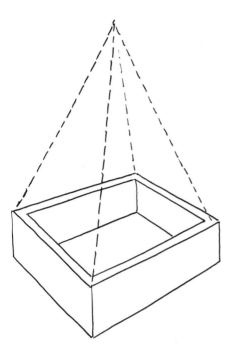

307. Machu Picchu. Stone pegs inside a room.
308. Possible method of tying the roof to pegs located inside a room

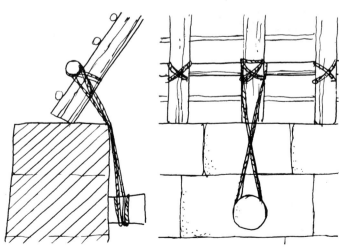

309. Machu Picchu. The pegs of so-called Mausoleum may have
   served as hangers, since the roof of the cave is entirely of stone.

310. According to Garcilaso there was, in Yucay, a structure with a
   pyramidal roof of considerable size. How was that roof fastened
   to the walls?

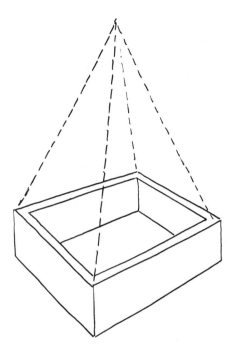

311. Machu Picchu. Pegs in the inner corner of a room.

some 20 meters high (*fig. 310*). How was that lofty wooden framework fastened to the top of the walls? Did it simply rest there? It is hard to give a positive and convincing explanation; nevertheless it is probable that the inner pegs had the function of securing the wooden frame against the top of the walls. Such use would not have prevented their also serving as hangers. In various buildings without gables there are, in each inner corner, two pegs placed very close together (*fig. 311*), almost as if in an endeavor to double the strength of the fastening on the four corner points where the hip rafters that join the two adjacent slopes always rest.

In two-story houses, the frame for the upper floor was made of timbers with one extreme resting on a setback in the back wall and the other on the top of the front wall. On these main beams it is probable that, lacking boards, the builders laid down plaited slender branches, which were then covered with earth. Houses with upper stories were dealt with in chapter 3. They are mentioned here only to note the type of frame between one floor and the next.

A final point related to structural systems is that of isolated support. We have seen that the Incas made great use of timbers set into the floor to support the ridgepole, as in the *kallanka*. They also used both square and rectangular pillars of stone and of adobe. *Masma*-type houses frequently have a central pillar built of stones; at Machu Picchu these pillars also occur in the form of monoliths, while on the coast, as at Pachacamac, they are adobe. On the other hand, the only example we have of cylindrical columns is at the Temple of Wiraqocha at Raqchi.

Aesthetics

For an aesthetic appreciation of Inca architecture, the special conditions that influenced the formation of its easily identifiable character must be considered. It is not a character that emerged from creative impulses or the restless search for new formal, plastic, or spatial expressions, but quite the contrary. State construction, from the types of dwellings to the patterns that define the urban establishments, is regulated by norms that necessarily

312. Cuzco. Double-jamb doorway on Romerito Street.

contribute to reaffirming the similarity of forms, the simplification of technology, and the use of familiar spatial concepts. Craig Morris noted the "compulsory" and "imposed" nature of Inca architecture in the administrative centers of the *qhapaq-ñan*. A similar imposition, perhaps softened, but always with specific guidelines, could determine the uniform nature of the buildings constructed under state auspices. More than a century and a half ago, as acute an observer as Humboldt said: "It is impossible to examine a single edifice of the Incas attentively without recognizing the same type in all the rest that exist throughout the Andes, extending over four hundred leagues, from one thousand to four thousand meters above sea level. It seems as if a single architect built this great number of monuments."[17] In fact, a single architect did build that great number of monuments. A single architect—the state—selected and imposed the limited repertoire of technical and formal solutions. For a state organization like the Inca one, practical solutions probably received more attention than formal problems. Therefore an aesthetic analysis of Inca architecture comes up against the impositions that contributed to the uniformity of what we try to appreciate visually today.

In fact, the formal decorative and ornamental repertoire is minimal. Although there was great mastery of stonemasonry, that ability was used to establish the prestige of the edifice. That is, as the importance of the function or meaning of the building increased, so also the excellence (or complexity) of the finish and fit of the stones increased. In short, it is a universal formula. The difference here is that among the Incas no "time was wasted" on moldings, cornices, pilasters, or any kind of geometric, phytomorphic, zoomorphic, or anthropomorphic ornamentation. We do not need to make comparisons with Old World cultures. It is sufficient, without leaving the pre-Columbian cultures, to note the "baroque" quality of Maya façades, the rich decorations in clay on the buildings of Chanchan and, in the highlands, the unexcelled quality of Tiwanaku.

From Ecuador to Bolivia the characteristics of Inca architecture are fitted to the pattern imparted by that great architect

that was the state. State employees charged with directing the
works received a brief and precise training in Cuzco and then,
anywhere in Tawantinsuyu, they applied the official norms. Thus
the formal identifying characteristics multiplied and the normative
typology was affirmed.

In the stone walls of buildings we find the following trapezoidal elements predominating:

A. *Doorways.* They may have single or double jambs, are
usually of considerable height in important buildings, and have
monolithic lintels (*fig. 312*). We are not sure what the doors
were like or how they functioned. In some doorways (the majority do not have this feature), there is, on each side of the inner
part, a hole with a cylindrical stone fastener that surely served
for tying and securing the door, which was probably made of
interlaced poles (*fig. 313*). It is interesting to note, without suggesting further implications, that the same system of closure also
appears in Maya temples at Palenque.

B. *Windows.* They are rarer in cold regions and more frequent in temperate zones, like the Urubamba River Valley. In
various settlements of that region there are several buildings with
a number of windows. Doubtless the most famous are those of
the Temple of the Three Windows at Machu Picchu (*fig. 314*).

C. *Niches.* The trapezoidal niche (*fig. 315*) is the most
repetitive formal stamp of Inca architecture and that which most
identifies the presence of Inca structures in conquered territories.
Utilitarian or decorative, the niches alternate in rhythmic sequences on innumerable walls. They are of various shapes and
sizes: simple, with double jambs, with a central window, as tall
as a man.

There is, of course, a variety of voluminal forms, like the
usnu and the fortresses, but here we wish to emphasize the limita-
tion of architectural elements visible on the wall surfaces. The
alternative compositions were limited and did not manage to
impose themselves on the value that, in most cases, emanates from
the simplicity and force of the wall. In fact, what has most attracted the attention of all who have visited Inca monuments in
the last five centuries is the walls and the astounding ability of

314. Machu Picchu. One of the openings of the "Temple of the Three Windows."

315. Pisaq. The trapezoidal niche is the formal element most
identified with Inca architecture.

316. Mycenae. Wall built about 1500 B.C.

317. Cuzco. The horizontal arrangement of the stone blocks in
    Callejón de Loreto.

the masons to shape and fit the stones, no matter how complicated
the shape or how great the size of the blocks. This ability is outstanding, particularly considering the fact that they had neither
iron tools nor draught animals. All this is true; they had, however,
the *mit'a*, which, for our purposes, could be more important than
iron tools and draught animals. Thousands of stonecutters, alternating with one another uninterruptedly in pounding stones with
other harder stones, pulverizing the rock, achieved a great amount
of work in less time and with greater ease than may be imagined.

In other periods of architectural history, we find works impressive for their size, for their perfection, and for their artistic
quality. There are thirty centuries between a Mycenaean wall
(*fig. 316*) and an Inca one, but in both the perfect fitting of the
stones is striking. It would be foolish, however, to ask ourselves,
"how could they do it?" With the backing of an all-powerful
organization that has no manpower problems and that can gather
in a moment one or ten thousand workers, the potential for erecting impressive works is almost limitless.

As we have commented, there is a hierarchy in the quality
of the finish that relates to the importance of the building. Thus
it is easy to understand that the walls of the Qorikancha attained
an excellence that only the temple category could command. The
sloping walls of the Cuzco *kancha* are also walls of high rank;
the horizontal line of the stone courses is carefully maintained
while, on the other hand, the vertical separation between one
block and the next is not regulated by any module that would
require cutting stones into equal sizes (*fig. 317*).

The scarcity of formal architectonic elements is compensated
for by the variety in shape and technique of the stone blocks; a
variety dictated not only by the prestige of the structure but also
by the complex solutions that seem to seek—as in the textiles—the
most difficult means of achieving an easily attainable result. There
is no worthwhile rational explanation when one suspects that they
enjoyed difficulties. The walls with polygonal stones, like those
of Hatunrumiyoq or Saqsaywaman, and the absurd shapes of
thousands of stones in an infinity of different places present questions with no easy answers. Did the mason have free inspiration
and freely disposable time? Is there any rational explanation for

324

this fit of lapidary fanaticism? Might it not be that at some time there was an excess of manpower and, in order not to have it idle, they sought complex and slow solutions? Was there an official state aesthetics? It is hazardous to attempt acceptable responses; even though satisfactory, they lack evidence to support them. If, in fact, the state guidelines were intended to simplify shapes and building systems, the inexhaustible solutions of the masons appear contradictory. What appears absurd to us today may have had a mystical content. But to our understanding, only the excess of human energy resulting from the *mit'a* could explain the number of works that required great devotion of time and manpower for their execution.

Besides the official formal repertoire, there was probably a shared "pleasure" in achieving certain visual effects in the stone walls—effects that were limited but sufficient to indicate an aesthetic preoccupation related to the norms of architectural identification. The treatment of the rounded stones on the corners of enclosures (*fig. 318*); the great puffed stones of Saqsaywaman with their sunken joints, which swell like fresh adobes when they are piled up (*fig. 319*); the entasis of the curved wall of the Qorikancha; the perfectly horizontal stone courses that accentuate the effect of perspective; the plastic combination of the stones of Hatunrumiyoq; the system of gradually decreasing size (*fig. 320*) that reaches the top of the wall with the musical rhythm of a finale; and the monolith that simulates two or three blocks to avoid altering the proportion of the composition (*fig. 321*)—all these demonstrate that the guidelines were not simply practical. Possibly these "virtuosities" were manifested when sensitivity could reveal itself, that is, in times when excess supplies of tributary energy permitted the following justifying byword: "anything as long as they work."

And probably there was delight among the masons when they invented solutions that we cannot explain today. Why should they incorporate an existing boulder into the wall of a house like the one at Torontoy (*fig. 322*)? What meaning can we give to the many protuberances that appear on the walls (*fig. 323*)? It is said that they served as an aid in moving the blocks during the construction. But why were some removed and others left? The

320. Cuzco. Wall with stone blocks that gradually decrease in size toward the top.

321. Cuzco. Monolith that simulates three stones in the "fortress" of
Saqsaywaman.

322. Torontoy. Monolith (outlined in black) adapted to the
structure of a house.

323. Protuberances on an Inca wall
324. Athens. Stone protuberances found on the base of the Acropolis.

walls of ancient Egypt and Greece had similar protuberances (*fig. 324*). Did they have the same meaning? What? In reality we know very little yet about Inca architecture and about the relationship between the state and building activities. As far as sensibility is concerned—as to what extent the phenomenon we now call Inca architecture was valued—we know almost nothing.

All these fanatically perfect walls cannot mean to us what they meant to the Incas. Indeed, our evaluation is probably totally different. In spite of the fact that our view of the past seeks to find in historical stratification the explanation that may satisfy our interpretation, we are aware that each epoch preceding ours saw the same problem with different eyes. And yet, there is an understanding, unchanging and satisfactory for all—a common accord—admiration for the culture that achieved this incredible result in only eighty years.

NOTES

1: Technical and Formal Antecedents

1. Morris, 1972.
2. Ibid.
3. Zuidema, 1968.
4. Rowe, 1944 and 1968.
5. Squier, 1877; Wiener, 1880; Angrand, 1972.
6. Rowe, 1944, p.9.
7. We concur with Rowe (1945, pp.270, 277) in his interpretation of Cabello Valboa.
8. Rowe, 1946, p.229.
9. Rowe, 1944, p.9.
10. Ibid., p.59.
11. Diez de San Miguel, 1964. The ruler of the Incas was called simply, the Inca. In this translation we have consistently differentiated between "the Inca," as a ruler, and "the Incas," who were the other members of the ethnic group that built the Inca empire.
12. Murra, 1964, p.425.
13. Diez de San Miguel, 1964, p.39.
14. Ibid., pp.80–81.
15. Ibid., p.92.
16. Ibid., p.106.
17. Ibid., p.116.
18. Ibid., p.204.
19. Espinoza Soriano, 1967, p.40.
20. Mori and Alonso Malpartida, 1967, p.306.
21. Ortiz de Zúñiga, 1967 and 1972.
22. Ortiz de Zúñiga, 1967, p.37.
23. Cieza de León, cap. CV, 1922, p.326.
24. Posnansky, 1945, 1958; Bennett, 1934; Ponce Sanginés, 1961, 1972.
25. Squier, 1877, p.277.
26. d'Orbigny, 1945; Posnansky, 1945; Kiss, 1937; Torres de Kuljis, ms.; Mesa and Gisbert, 1972; Ponce Sanginés, 1971.
27. Cieza de Léon, cap. CV, 1922, p.326.

2: Urban Settlements

1. Lanning, 1967, p.140.
2. Ibid., p.116.
3. Lumbreras, 1969, p.235.
4. Gasparini, 1972.
5. Menzel, 1964, pp.66–67.
6. Mesa and Gisbert, 1970, p.300.
7. Menzel, 1964, p.67.
8. Isbell, 1972, p.55.
9. Menzel, 1964, p.67.
10. Ibid., pp.70–71.
11. Morris, 1974a, p.138.
12. Rowe, 1967, p.306.
13. Lumbreras, 1969, p.262.
14. Rowe, 1967, p.311; Lanning, 1967, p.139.
15. Rowe, 1967, p.306.
16. Espinoza Soriano, 1973.
17. Rowe, 1957, p.46.
18. Betanzos, cap. XVI, 1880, p.108.
19. Ibid., pp.110–11.
20. Rowe, 1968, p.60.
21. Garcilaso de la Vega, lib. 7, cap. XI, 1945, tomo II, p.112.
22. Garcilaso de la Vega, lib. 7, cap. VIII, 1945, tomo II, pp.104–106.
23. Rowe, 1968, note 12, p.66.
24. Noticia del Peru, 1938, p.239. Porras Barrenechea (1961) gives Miguel de Estete as the source of the *Noticia del Perú*. According to Rowe, the name of the author is not known, but it is not Estete. Estete arrived in Peru with Hernando Soto, joining Pizarro at Puna. The author of the *Noticia* speaks as an eyewitness to the events that took place along the Ecuadorian coast from Coaque south; evidently it was someone who arrived before Estete, perhaps on Pedro Gregorio's boat.
25. Noticia del Peru, 1938, p.241.
26. Sancho de la Hoz, cap. XVII, 1938, p.177.
27. Ibid., p.179.
28. Pizarro, 1944, p.77.
29. Molina, 1943, p.33. According to Rowe (personal communication), the author of the 1553 account is not Cristóbal de Molina, but probably Bartolomé de Segovia, as Porras Barrenechea (1943, pp.91–92) has suggested. The manuscript bears no author's name, and the attribution to Cristóbal de Molina is an error committed many years ago. We use the name of Cristóbal de Molina here to avoid confusing the bibliographical references.
30. Lanning, 1967, pp.162–63; Rowe, 1967, p.310.
31. Hardoy, 1973, p.445.
32. Garcilaso de la Vega, lib. 7, cap. X, 1945, tomo II, pp.109–10.
33. Ibid., p.110.
34. Betanzos, cap. XIII, 1880, p.81.
35. Noticia del Peru, 1938, p.239.
36. Zuidema, 1964.

37. Sancho de la Hoz, cap. XVII, 1938, pp. 176–77.

38. Bayón, 1972, pp.239–40.

39. Ibid., p.242.

40. Cieza de Léon, cap. XLIV, 1922, p.154.

41. Bonavia, 1972b, p.84.

42. Kendall, 1974.

43. Rowe, ms., p.2.

44. Fejos, 1944; Bingham, 1930; and in various other works on the subject.

45. Bingham, 1930.

46. Valcárcel, 1964.

47. John H. Rowe, personal communication.

48. Alcina Franch, 1970, p. 100.

49. *Mawk'allaqta* means "damaged town," and is a common name for ancient sites.

50. Cieza de León, cap. XL, 1922, p.133.

51. Cieza de León, cap. XLI, 1922, p.140.

52. Cieza de León, cap. XLII, 1922, pp.145–46.

53. Ibid., p.146.

54. Cieza de León, cap. XLIV, 1922, p.154.

55. Ibid., p.155.

56. Cieza de León, cap. LXXVII, 1922, p.255.

57. Cieza de León, cap. LXXX, 1922, p.264.

58. Cieza de León, cap. LXXXIII, 1922, p.274.

59. Cieza de León, cap. LXXXIX, 1922, p.286.

60. Molina, 1943, pp.21–22. See note 29.

61. Morris, 1974a.

62. Wedin, 1963.

63. John V. Murra, personal communication.

64. Morris, 1974a.

65. Uhle, 1969.

66. Vázquez de Espinoza, cap. 43, 1948, p.453.

67. Harth-terré, 1964.

68. Morris and Thompson, 1970.

69. Morris, 1974b.

70. Ibid., 1966.

71. Cieza de León, cap. LXXXIX, 1922, p.287.

72. Angrand, 1972, lám. 237, p.261.

73. Cieza de León, cap. LXXXIX, 1922, pp.287–88.

74. Wiener, 1880, p.265.

75. Cieza de León, cap. XCIX, 1922, p.311.

76. Murra, 1964, p.422.

77. Harth-terré, 1933.

78. Menzel, 1967, p.220.

3: Domestic Architecture

1. Rowe, 1946, p.222.

2. *Wasi* means house in general, not just a peasant house.

3. Espinoza Soriano, 1974, p.238. Italics in original.

4. Cieza de León, cap. XLIV, 1922, p.157.

5. Garcilaso de la Vega, lib. 6, cap. IV, 1945, tomo II, p.15. According to Rowe (personal communication) the Incas did not make their adobes in molds, but rather by hand and, therefore, they varied in size. Garcilaso's statements about the sizes are also incorrect.

6. Šolc, 1969, pp.83–84.

7. Ibid., p.80.

8. Garcilaso de la Vega, lib. 6, cap. IV, 1945, tomo II, p.15.

9. Rowe, 1946, p.222.

10. Garcilaso de la Vega, lib. 7, cap. X, 1945, tomo II, pp.110–11.

11. Lavallée, 1974, p.102.

12. Thompson, 1974, p.102.

13. Thompson, 1972a.

14. Bonavia, 1972a, p.94.

15. Thompson, 1968, p.117.

16. Mesa and Gisbert, 1966, pp.492–93.

17. There are some examples of doors with lintels that form a corbeled vault.

18. Trimborn, 1969.

19. Trimborn, 1973, p.189.

20. Matos Mendieta, 1972, p.371.

21. Villar Córdova, 1935.

22. John V. Murra, personal communication.

23. There is a good description of the Sillustani *chullpas* in Squier (1877, pp.376–83).

24. Rowe, 1946, p.226.

25. Cobo, lib. 14, cap. XVIII, 1956, tomo 92, p. 273. The *estado* is a measurement based on the average height of a man, and it used to be approximately six feet. The Castilian foot equals approximately 28 centimeters.

26. Squier, 1877, pp.381–82.

27. Garcilaso de la Vega, lib. 7, cap. XXIX, 1945, tomo II, p.152.

28. Valcárcel, 1964.

29. Pardo, 1957, p.232.

30. Kubler, 1975, p.329.

31. Arellano López, 1975.

4: The Architecture of Power

1. Cieza de León, cap. LI, 1967, p.169.

2. Morris, 1972.

3. Prescott, 1942, p.238.

4. Cieza de León, cap. LXXXI, 1922, p.267.

5. Garcilaso de la Vega, lib. 6, cap. IV, 1945, tomo II, pp.14–15.

6. Garcilaso de la Vega, lib. 7, cap. IX, 1945, tomo II, p.108.

7. Garcilaso de la Vega, lib. 7, cap. X, 1945, tomo II, pp.109–11.

8. Pachakuti Yamqui Salcamaygua, 1879, p.259; Gonçález Holguín, 1952, p.58.

9. Morris, 1974a.

10. Molina, 1943, pp.22–23.

11. Morris, 1966.

12. Murra and Hadden, 1966, p. 136.

13. Diez de San Miguel, 1964, p.81.

14. Nordenskiöld, 1915.

15. Lara, 1967, p.46.

16. Terán, 1973.

17. Alcina Franch, 1970, p.100.

18. Cobo, lib. 13, cap. XII, 1956, tomo 92, pp.167–68.

19. Garcilaso de la Vega, lib. 3, cap. XX, 1945, tomo I, p.172.

20. Cieza de León, cap. XIV, 1967, p.42.

21. Rowe, 1944.

22. Ladrón de Guevara Avilés, 1967, pp.73–74.

23. Uhle, 1930, p.293.

24. Garcilaso de la Vega, lib. 3, cap. XXI, 1945, tomo I, pp.173–74.

25. Cieza de León, cap. XXVII, 1967, p.92.

26. Rowe, 1944, p.29.

27. Cieza de León, cap. XXVII, 1967, p.91.

28. Garcilaso de la Vega, lib. 3, cap. XXIV, 1945, tomo I, p.180.

29. Zuidema, 1968.

30. Garcilaso de la Vega, lib. 5, cap. XXII, 1945, tomo I, p.271; Cieza de León, cap. XCVIII, 1922, p.309.

31. Garcilaso de la Vega, lib. 5, cap. XXII, 1945, tomo I, pp.271–73.

32. Duviols, 1971, p.97.

33. Ramos Gavilán, lib. 1, cap. XVIII, 1976, p.62.

34. Mesa and Gisbert, 1972, p.134.

35. Cieza de León, cap. XXII, 1967, p.77.

36. Cieza de León, cap. XLIV, 1922, p.158.

37. Cieza de León, cap. LXXXI, 1922, p. 268.

38. Cieza de León, cap. LVII, 1922, p.205.

39. López, 1953, p.354. The account quoted is not by Blas Valera, in spite of this attribution by Cornejo Bouroncle. It is commonly cited as the work of an "Anonymous Jesuit." José Durand has identified the probable author, a personal friend of Valera's named Luis López. (Information from John H. Rowe.)

40. Cobo, lib. 13, caps. XIII–XVI, 1956, tomo 92, pp.169–86.

41. López, 1953, p.355.

42. Cabello Valboa, tercera parte, cap. 21, 1951, p.365.

43. Cobo, lib. 13, cap. XIV, 1956, tomo 92, p.177.

44. Guaman Poma de Ayala, 1936.

45. Molina, 1943, p.22.

46. Guaman Poma de Ayala, 1936.

47. Cieza de León, cap. LXIV, 1967, p.215.

48. Thompson, 1972b, p.78.

49. Zuidema, 1968, p.48.

50. Jerez, 1938, p.54.

51. Cited in Shea, 1966, p.110.

52. Cabieses, ms.

53. See the plan of the Willka Waman complex, fig. 106.

54. Angrand, 1972, p.262, lám. 240; Wiener, 1880, p.266.

55. The plan of Willka Waman in chapter 2 (fig. 106) indicates that the usnu was enclosed by a rectangular structure. This plan is based on field observations. More recently, however, the Peruvian architect Agurto has drawn up a topographic plan indicating that the form of the compound is indeed trapezoidal.

56. Cieza de León, cap. LXXXIX, 1922, p.287.

57. See the plan of the Huánuco Pampa complex, fig. 98.

58. Sancho de la Hoz, cap. XVII, 1938, p.178.

59. Pardo, 1970, p.105.

60. All the preceding quotations are from extracts published by Valcárcel, 1934, pp.14–17.

61. Valcárcel, 1935, p.174.

62. Ibid., 1934, p.17.

63. Ibid., p.19.

64. Ibid., 1935, p.174.

65. Ibid., 1934, p.20.

66. Ibid., 1935, p.174.

67. Ibid., p.176. The author of the *Noticias cronológicas*, also called the *Anales del Cuzco*, is Diego de Esquivel y Navía. The work was completed in 1746. (Information from John H. Rowe.)

68. Valcárcel, 1934, p.20.

69. Ibid., 1935, p.176.

70. Cieza de León, cap. LI, 1967, p.172.

71. Kalafatovich, 1970, p.64.

72. Ibid.

73. Rowe, 1946, p.226.

74. Bedoya Maruri, 1974.

75. Cabieses, ms.
76. See fig. 212.
77. Murra, 1975, p.23.
78. Thompson and Murra, 1966.
79. Cieza de León, cap. XLIV, 1922, p.153.
80. Ibid., p.155.
81. Cieza de León, cap. LXXIV, 1922, p.275.
82. Byrne de Caballero, ms.
83. See Kosok, 1965; Regal, 1970.

5: TECHNICAL AND AESTHETIC PROBLEMS

1. Garcilaso de la Vega, lib. 6, cap. I, 1945, tomo II, p.7.
2. Garcilaso de la Vega, lib. 2, cap. XXVIII, 1945, tomo I, p.125.
3. Ibid., pp.125–26.
4. Garcilaso de la Vega, lib. 6, cap. I, 1945, tomo II, p.8.
5. Garcilaso de la Vega, lib. 6, cap. IV, 1945, tomo II, p.15.
6. This statement is important because it indicates that the timbers preserved their round section. They were simply cut to the necessary length and their bark removed.
7. Garcilaso de la Vega, lib. 2, cap. XXVIII, 1945, tomo I, p.126.
8. Ibid.
9. Ibid., p.127.
10. Cieza de León, cap. CXIV, 1922, p.346.
11. See p.00.
12. John H. Rowe, personal communication.
13. Betanzos, cap. XVI, 1880, p.109.
14. Squier, 1877, pp.394–95.
15. Garcilaso de la Vega, lib. 6, cap. IV, 1945, tomo II, p.15.
16. Ibid. See note 25 to chapter 3.
17. Humboldt, 1810.

REFERENCES

Alcina Franch, José
1970 Excavaciones en Chinchero (Cuzco): Temporadas 1968 y 1969. *Revista Española de Antropología Americana* [Trabajos y Conferencias], vol. 5, pp.99–121. Madrid.

Angrand, Léonce
1972 *Imagen del Perú en el siglo XIX*. Lima: Editor Carlos Milla Batres.

Arellano López, Jorge
1975 *La ciudadela prehispánica de Iskanwaya*. Atlas. Prólogo y bibliografía de Carlos Ponce Sanginés. Centro de Investigaciones Arqueológicas, n.s., Publication no. 6. La Paz, Bolivia.

Bayón, Damián
1972 Las vistas antiguas del Cuzco en la Biblioteca Nacional de París. In *Verhandlungen des XXXVIII. Internationalen Amerikanistenkongresses, Stuttgart-München August 12–18, 1968*, vol. IV, pp.239–46. Munich: Klaus Renner Verlag.

Bedoya Maruri, Angel N.
1974 *La arqueología en la región interandina de Ecuador*. Puebla, Mexico: Editorial José M. Cajica.

Bennett, Wendell C.
1934 Excavations at Tiahuanaco. *Anthropological Papers of the American Museum of Natural History*, vol. XXXIV, part III, pp.359–494. New York.

Betanzos, Juan de
1880 *Suma y narración de los Incas* . . . [1551]; publícala Marcos Jiménez de la Espada. Biblioteca Hispano-Ultramarina, vol. V, second paging. Madrid: Imprenta de Manuel G. Hernández.

Bingham, Hiram
1930 *Machu Picchu, a citadel of the Incas. Report of the explorations and excavations made in 1911, 1912 and 1915 under the auspices of Yale University and the National Geographic Society*. Memoirs of the National Geographic Society. New Haven: Yale University Press.

Bonavia, Duccio
1972a La ceja de selva: Colonizadores y avanzadas. In *Pueblos y Culturas de la Sierra Central del Perú*, ed. Duccio Bonavia and Rogger Ravines, pp. 90–99. Lima: Cerro de Pasco Corporation.
1972b Factores ecológicos que han intervenido en la transformación urbana a través de los últimos siglos de la época precolombina. In *XXXIX Congreso Internacional de Americanistas, Lima, 1970, Actas y Memorias*, vol. 2, pp. 79–97. Lima: Instituto de Estudios Peruanos.

Byrne de Caballero, Geraldine
La arquitectura del almacenamiento en la logística incaica. Universidad Mayor de San Simón, Cochabamba, Bolivia. 1975.

Cabello Valboa, Miguel
1951 *Miscelánea antártica; una historia del Perú antiguo* [1586]. Lima: Instituto de Etnología, Universidad Nacional Mayor de San Marcos.

Cabieses, Fernando
Machu Picchu, apuntes etnohistóricos. Lima. 1974.

Cieza de León, Pedro de
1922 *La crónica del Perú* [1550]. Los Grandes Viajes Clásicos, no. 24. Madrid: Calpe.
1967 *El señorío de los Incas (2ª. parte de la Crónica del Perú)* [1553]. Lima: Instituto de Estudios Peruanos.

Cobo, Bernabé
1956 *Historia del Nuevo Mundo* [1653]. Biblioteca de Autores Españoles, vols. 91 and 92. Madrid: Ediciones Atlas.

Diez de San Miguel, Garci
1964 *Visita hecha a la provincia de Chucuito por Garci Diez de San Miguel en el año 1567*. Documentos Regionales para la Etnología y Etnohistoria Andinas, vol. I. Lima: Casa de la Cultura del Perú.

d'Orbigny, Alcides
1945 *Viaje a la América Meridional* [1844]. Buenos Aires: Editorial Futuro.

Duviols, Pierre
1971 *La lutte contre les religions autochtones dans le Pérou colonial. "L' extirpation de l'idolâtrie" entre 1532 et 1660*. Lima: Travaux de l'Institut Français d'Etudes Andines, vol. XIII.

Espinoza Soriano, Waldemar
1967 El primer informe etnológico sobre Cajamarca. Año de 1540. *Revista Peruana de Cultura*, nos. 11–12 (enero–junio), pp.5–41. Lima.
1973 *La destrucción del imperio de los Incas; la rivalidad política y señorial de los curacazgos andinos*. Lima: Ediciones Retablo de Papel.
1974 Colonias de mitmas múltiples en Abancay, siglos XV y XVI; una información inédita de 1575 para la etnohistoria andina. *Revista del Museo Nacional*, vol. XXXIX (1973), pp.225–99. Lima.

Fejos, Paul

1944   *Archeological explorations in the Cordillera Vilcabamba, southeastern Peru*. Viking Fund Publications in Anthropology, no. 3. New York.

Garcilaso de la Vega, "el Inca"

1945   *Comentarios reales de los Incas* [1604]. Edited by Angel Rosenblat. 2d ed. 2 vols. Buenos Aires: Emecé Editores.

Gasparini, Graziano

1972   *América, barroco y arquitectura*. Caracas: Ernesto Armitano Editor.

Gonçález Holguín, Diego

1952   *Vocabvlario de la lengva general de todo el Perv llamada lengua Qquichua o del Inca* [1608]. Lima: Edición del Instituto de Historia, Universidad Nacional Mayor de San Marcos.

Guaman Poma de Ayala, Felipe

1936   *Nueva corónica y buen gobierno (codex péruvien illustré)* [1615]. Paris: Travaux et Mémoires de l'Institut d'Ethnologie, XXIII.

Hardoy, Jorge E.

1973   *Pre-Columbian cities*. Translated by Judith Thorne. New York: Walker and Company.

Harth-terré, Emilio

1933   Incahuasi. Ruinas incaicas del valle de Lunahuaná. *Revista del Museo Nacional*, vol. II, no. 2, pp.99–125. Lima.

1964   El pueblo de Huánuco Viejo. *El Arquitecto Peruano*, nos. 320–21, pp.21–40. Lima.

Humboldt, Alexander von

1810   *Vues des cordillères, et monumens des peuples indigènes de l'Amérique*. Paris: F. Schoell.

Isbell, William H.

1972   Huari y los orígenes del primer imperio andino. In *Pueblos y Culturas de la Sierra Central del Perú*, ed. Duccio Bonavia and Rogger Ravines, pp.52–65. Lima: Cerro de Pasco Corporation.

Jerez, Francisco de

1938   Verdadera relación de la conquista del Perú y provincia del Cuzco, llamada la Nueva Castilla . . . [1534]. In *Los cronistas de la conquista*. Biblioteca de Cultura Peruana, 1st ser., no. 2, pp.15–115. Paris: Desclée, De Brower.

Kalafatovich, Carlos

1970   Geología del grupo arqueológico de la fortaleza de Saccsayhuaman y sus vecindades. *Revista Saqsaywaman*, no. 1 (julio), pp.61–68. Cuzco.

Kendall, Ann

1974   Architecture and planning at the Inca sites in the Cusichaca area. *Baessler-Archiv*, Neue Folge, Band XXII (XLVII. Band), pp.73–137. Berlin.

Kiss, Edmund

1937   *Das Sonnentor von Tihuanaku und Hörbigers Welteislehre*. Leipzig: Koehler & Amelang.

Kosok, Paul

1965   *Life, land and water in ancient Peru*. New York: Long Island University Press.

Kubler, George

1975   *The art and architecture of ancient America; the Mexican/Maya/and Andean peoples*. 2d ed. The Pelican History of Art. Harmondsworth, Middlesex: Penguin Books.

Ladrón de Guevara Avilés, Oscar

1967   Trabajos de restauración en el Ccoricancha y templo de Santo Domingo. Prólogo del Dr. Luis A. Pardo. *Revista del Museo e Instituto Arqueológico de la Universidad Nacional del Cuzco*, año XIV, no. 21 (junio), pp. 29–93. Cuzco.

Lanning, Edward P.

1967   *Peru before the Incas*. Englewood Cliffs: Prentice Hall, Spectrum.

Lara, Jesús

1967   *Inkallajta; Inkaraqay*. Biblioteca IV Centenario. La Paz-Cochabamba, Bolivia: Editorial Los Amigos del Libro.

Lavallée, Danièle

1974   Estructura y organización del habitat en los Andes centrales durante el Período Intermedio Tardío. *Revista del Museo Nacional*, vol. XXXIX (1973), pp.91–116. Lima.

López, Luis

1953   Relación de las costumbres antiguas de los naturales del Piru [1594]. *Revista del Archivo Histórico del Cuzco*, año IV, no. 4, pp.346–415. Cuzco. [Author mistakenly given as Blas Valera]

Lumbreras, Luis Guillermo

1969   *De los pueblos, las culturas y las artes del antiguo Perú*. Lima: Moncloa-Campodonico, Editores Asociados.

Matos Mendieta, Ramiro

1972   Wakan y Wamalli. Estudio arqueológico de dos aldeas rurales. In *Visita de la Provincia de León de Huánuco en 1562, Iñigo Ortiz de Zúñiga, visitador*, vol. II, pp.367–

82. Huánuco, Peru: Universidad Nacional Hermilio Valdizón.

Menzel, Dorothy
1964 Style and time in the Middle Horizon. *Ñawpa Pacha 2*, pp.1–105. Berkeley.
1967 The Inca occupation of the south coast of Peru. In *Peruvian Archaeology*, ed. John Howland Rowe and Dorothy Menzel, pp.217–34. Palo Alto: Peek Publications.

Mesa, José de, and Gisbert, Teresa
1966 Los Chipayas. In *Anuario de Estudios Americanos, XXIII*. (Publicaciones de la Escuela de Estudios Hispano-Americanos de Sevilla, no. general CLXXIV), pp.479–506. Seville.
1970 Culturas de los Andes. In *Historia del Arte Salvat*, vol. 1, fascicle 124. Barcelona: Salvat Editores.
1972 La arquitectura incaica en Bolivia. *Boletín del Centro de Investigaciones Históricas y Estéticas*, no. 13 (enero), pp.129–68. (Facultad de Arquitectura y Urbanismo, Universidad Central de Venezuela.) Caracas.

Molina, Cristóbal de [Bartolomé de Segovia]
1943 Relación de muchas cosas acaecidas en el Perú . . . en la conquista y población de estos reinos . . . que . . . más se podrá decir "destrucción del Perú . . ." [ca. 1558]. In *Las crónicas de los Molinas*. Los Pequeños Grandes Libros de Historia Americana, 1st ser., vol. IV, first paging, pp.1–78. Lima: Lib. e Imp. D. Miranda.

Mori, Juan de, and Alonso Malpartida, Hernando
1967 La visitación de los pueblos de los indios [1549]. In *Visita de la Provincia de León de Huánuco en 1562, Iñigo Ortiz de Zúñiga, visitador*, vol. I, pp.289–310. Huánuco, Peru: Universidad Nacional Hermilio Valdizán.

Morris, Craig
1966 El *tampu* real de Tunsucancha. *Cuadernos de Investigación*, no. 1, Antropología, pp.95–107. (Universidad Nacional Hermilio Valdizán.) Huánuco, Peru.
1972 The identification of function in Inca architecture and ceramics. In *XXXIX Congreso Internacional de Americanistas, Lima, 1970, Actas y Memorias*, vol. 3, pp.135–44. Lima: Instituto de Estudios Peruanos.
1974a Establecimientos estatales en el Tawantinsuyu: Una estrategia de urbanismo obligado. *Revista del Museo Nacional*, vol. XXXIX (1973), pp.127–41. Lima.

1974b Reconstructing patterns of non-agricultural production in the Inca economy: Archaeology and documents in institutional analysis. In *Reconstructing Complex Societies: an Archaeological Colloquium*, ed. Charlotte B. Moore, pp.49–60. Supplement to the *Bulletin of the American Schools of Oriental Research* No. 20. [Missoula, Montana].

Morris, Craig, and Thompson, Donald E.
1970 Huánuco Viejo: An Inca administrative center. *American Antiquity*, vol. 35, no. 3 (July), pp.344–62. Washington.

Murra, John V.
1964 Una apreciación etnológica de la Visita. In *Visita hecha a la provincia de Chucuito por Garci Diez de San Miguel en el año 1567*, pp.419–44. Documentos Regionales para la Etnología y Etnohistoria Andinas, vol. I. Lima: Casa de la Cultura del Perú.
1975 *Formaciones económicas y políticas del mundo andino*. Lima: Instituto de Estudios Peruanos.

Murra, John V., and Hadden, Gordon J.
1966 Apéndice. Informe presentado al Patronato Nacional de Arqueología sobre la labor de limpieza y consolidación de Huánuco Viejo (20 de julio a 23 de noviembre 1965). *Cuadernos de Investigación*, no. 1, Antropología, pp.129–44. (Universidad Nacional Hermilio Valdizán.) Huánuco, Peru.

Nordenskiöld, Erland
1915 Incallacta, eine befestigte und von Inca Tupac Yupanqui angelegte Stadt. *Ymer*, Trettiondefemte årgången [v. 35], Häft 2, pp.169–85. Stockholm.

Noticia del Peru
1938 Noticia del Peru. In *Los cronistas de la conquista*. Biblioteca de Cultura Peruana, 1st ser., no. 2, pp.195–251. Paris: Desclée, De Brouwer.

Ortiz de Zúñiga, Iñigo
1967 *Visita de la provincia de León de Huánuco en 1562, Iñigo Ortiz de Zúñiga, visitador*. Vol. I, *Visita de las cuatro Waranqa de los Chupachu*. Documentos para la Historia y Etnología de Huánuco y la Selva Central, vol. I. Huánuco, Peru: Universidad Nacional Hermilio Valdizán.
1972 *Visita de la provincia de León de Huánuco en 1562, Iñigo Ortiz de Zúñiga, visitador*. Vol. II, *Visita de los Yacha y mitmaqkuna cuzqueños encomendados en Juan Sanchez Falcon*. Documentos para la Historia y Etnología de

Huánuco y la Selva Central, vol. II. Huánuco, Peru: Universidad Nacional Hermilio Valdizán.

Pachacuti Yamqui Salcamaygua, Joan de Santacruz
1879   Relación de antigüedades deste reyno del Pirú [early seventeenth century]. In *Tres relaciones de antigüedades peruanas*, pp.229–328. Madrid: Ministerio de Fomento.

Pardo, Luis A.
1957   *Historia y arqueología del Cuzco.* 2 vols. Cuzco: Published by the author.
1970   La fortaleza de Saccsayhuaman. *Revista Saqsaywaman*, no. 1 (julio), pp.89–157. Cuzco.

Pizarro, Pedro
1944   *Relación del descubrimiento y conquista de los reinos del Perú y del gobierno y orden que los naturales tenían . . .* [1571]. Buenos Aires: Editorial Futuro.

Ponce Sanginés, Carlos
1961   *Informe de labores (Octubre 1957–Febrero 1961).* Centro de Investigaciones en Tiwanaku, Publication No. 1. La Paz, Bolivia.
1971   *Procedencia de las areniscas utilizadas en el templo pre-colombino de Pumapunku.* Academia Nacional de Ciencias de Bolivia, Publication No. 22. La Paz, Bolivia.
1972   *Tiwanaku: Espacio, tiempo y cultura; ensayo de síntesis arqueológica.* Academia Nacional de Ciencias de Bolivia, Publication No. 30. La Paz, Bolivia.

Porras Barrenechea, Raúl
1943   Los dos Cristóbal de Molina. In *Las crónicas de los Molinas.* Los Pequeños Grandes Libros de Historia Americana, 1st ser., vol. IV, second paging, pp.85–98. Lima: Lib. e Imp. D. Miranda.
1961   *Antología del Cuzco.* Lima: Librería Internacional del Perú.

Posnansky, Arthur
1945   *Tihuanacu: la cuna del hombre americano. Tihuanacu: the cradle of American man.* Vols. I and II. New York: J. J. Augustin.
1958   *Tihuanacu: la cuna del hombre americano. Tihuanacu: the cradle of American man.* Vols. III and IV. La Paz, Bolivia: Ministerio de Educación.

Prescott, William H.
1942   *History of the conquest of Peru* [1847]. Everyman's Library. London: J. M. Dent & Sons Ltd. and New York: E. P. Dutton & Co.

Ramos Gavilán, Alonso
1976   *Historia de Nuestra Señora de Copacabana. Segunda edición completa, según la impresión príncipe de 1621.* La Paz: Academia Boliviana de la Historia.

Regal, Alberto
1970   *Los trabajos hidráulicos del Inca en el antiguo Perú.* Prólogo de Luis E. Valcárcel. Lima: Imp. "Gráf. Industrial."

Rowe, John Howland
1944   *An introduction to the archaeology of Cuzco.* Papers of the Peabody Museum of American Archaeology and Ethnology, Harvard University, vol. XXVII, no. 2. Cambridge.
1945   Absolute chronology in the Andean area. *American Antiquity*, vol. X, no. 3 (January), pp.265–84. Menasha.
1946   Inca culture at the time of the Spanish conquest. *Handbook of South American Indians.* Bureau of American Ethnology, Bulletin 143, vol. 2, pp.183–330. Washington.
1957   La arqueología del Cuzco como historia cultural. *Revista del Museo e Instituto Arqueológico de la Universidad Nacional del Cuzco*, año X, nos. 16–17 (diciembre), pp. 34–48. Cuzco.
1967   Urban settlements in ancient Peru. In *Peruvian Archaeology*, ed. John Howland Rowe and Dorothy Menzel, pp. 293–320. Palo Alto: Peek Publications.
1968   What kind of a settlement was Inca Cuzco? *Ñawpa Pacha 5*, pp.59–76. Berkeley.
ms.   Informe del Dr. John Howland Rowe al Arq. José de Mesa Figueroa sobre las obras de P'isaq. Cusco, 22 de septiembre de 1975.

Sancho de la Hoz, Pedro
1938   Relación para S.M. de lo sucedido en la conquista y pacificación de estas provincias de la Nueva Castilla y de la calidad de la tierra . . . [1534]. In *Los Cronistas de la Conquista.* Biblioteca de Cultura Peruana, 1st ser., no. 2, pp.117–93. Paris: Desclée, De Brower.

Shea, Daniel
1966   El conjunto arquitectónico central en la plaza de Huánuco Viejo. *Cuadernos de Investigación*, no. 1, Antropología, pp.108–16. (Universidad Nacional Hermilio Valdizán.) Huánuco, Peru.

Šolc, Václav
1969   *Los Aymaras de las islas del Titicaca.* Mexico: Instituto Indigenista Interamericano, Social Anthropology series, 12.

Squier, Ephraim George
1877 *Peru: incidents of travel and exploration in the land of the Incas.* New York: Harper & Brothers.

Terán, Roberto
1973 "La ciudadela de Incallacta," *El Diario*, 5 agosto 1973. Cochabamba.

Thompson, Donald E.
1968 An archeological evaluation of ethnohistoric evidence on Inca culture. In *Anthropological Archeology in the Americas*, ed. Betty J. Meggers, pp.108–20. Washington: The Anthropological Society of Washington.

1972a Etnias y grupos locales tardíos. In *Pueblos y Culturas de la Sierra Central del Perú*, ed. Duccio Bonavia and Rogger Ravines, pp.66–75. Lima: Cerro de Pasco Corporation.

1972b La ocupación incaica en la sierra central. In *Pueblos y Culturas de la Sierra Central del Perú*, ed. Duccio Bonavia and Rogger Ravines, pp.76–89. Lima: Cerro de Pasco Corporation.

1974 Investigaciones arqueológicas en los Andes orientales del norte del Perú. *Revista del Museo Nacional*, vol. XXXIX (1973), pp.117–25. Lima.

Thompson, Donald E., and Murra, John V.
1966 Puentes incaicos en la región de Huánuco Pampa. *Cuadernos de Investigación*, no. 1, Antropología, pp.79–94. (Universidad Nacional Hermilio Valdizán.) Huánuco, Peru.

Torres de Kuljis, Martha
ms. La arquitectura nacional a través de la historia. Paper presented to the Primer Congreso de Historiadores Bolivianos, La Paz, Bolivia, 1970.

Trimborn, Hermann
1969 Die Chullpas von Atiquipa. In *Verhandlungen des XXXVIII. Internationalen Amerikanistenkongresses*, Stuttgart-München August 12–18, 1968, vol. I, pp.393–405. Munich: Klaus Renner Verlag.

1973 La falsa bóveda en las antiguas culturas costeras del antiguo Perú. *Revista del Museo Nacional*, vol. XXXVIII (1972), pp.185–90. Lima.

Uhle, Max
1930 El Templo del Sol de los Incas en Cuzco. In *Proceedings of the Twenty-third International Congress of Ameri-* canists, held at New York, September 17–22, 1928, pp. 291–95. New York.

1969 Las ruinas de Tomebamba. In *Estudios sobre historia incaica*. Comentarios del Peru, 11, pp.81–122. Lima: Universidad Nacional Mayor de San Marcos.

Valcárcel, Luis E.
1934 Sajsawaman redescubierto. *Revista del Museo Nacional*, vol. III, nos. 1–2, pp.3–36. Lima.

1935 Sajsawaman redescubierto (IV). *Revista del Museo Nacional*, vol. IV, no. 2, II semestre, pp. 161–203. Lima.

1964 *Machu Picchu, el más famoso monumento arqueológico del Perú*. Biblioteca de América. Libros del Tiempo Nuevo, 11. Buenos Aires: Editorial Universitaria de Buenos Aires.

Vázquez de Espinosa, Antonio
1948 *Compendio y descripción de las Indias Occidentales [1629]. Transcrito del manuscrito original por Charles Upson Clark*. Washington: Smithsonian Miscellaneous Collections, vol. 108 (whole volume).

Villar Córdova, Pedro Eduardo
1935 *Las culturas pre-hispánicas del Departamento de Lima*. 1st ed. Auspiciado por la H. Municipalidad de Lima. (Homenaje al IV Centenario de la Fundación de Lima: o antigua "Ciudad de los Reyes"). Lima.

Wedin, Åke
1963 *La cronología de la historia incaica: estudio crítico*. Madrid: Instituto Ibero-Americano Gotemburgo Suecia.

Wiener, Charles
1880 *Pérou et Bolivie: récit de voyage suivi d'études archéologiques et ethnographiques et de notes sur l'écriture et les langues des populations indiennes*. Paris: Librairie Hachette et Cie.

Zuidema, Reiner Tom
1964 *The ceque system of Cuzco: The social organization of the capital of the Inca*. Translated by Eva M. Hooykaas. Leiden: E. J. Brill. (International Archives of Ethnography, Supplement to Vol. L.)

1968 La relación entre el patrón de poblamiento prehispánico y los principios derivados de la estructura social incaica. In *XXXVII Congreso Internacional de Americanistas, República Argentina—1966, Actas y Memorias*, vol. I, pp. 45–55. Buenos Aires.

GLOSSARY

(A) designates words in Aymara,
(R) words in Runasimi.

alasaa (A): Upper division, equivalent to *hanansaya*.

Amarukancha (R): Houses of Wayna Qhapaq in Cuzco. Where the church of the Society of Jesus now stands.

Antisuyu (R): One of the four parts forming the Inca empire.

aqllakuna (R): "Chosen women." Women specially chosen to perform certain duties.

aqllawasi (R): House of the "chosen women," sometimes referred to as convents.

ayllu (R): Social division; lineage.

Aymara: Ethnic group occupying much of the territory of ancient Qollasuyu; the language of this group, which belongs to the Haqaru linguistic family.

barrio: Informal division of a city or town; neighborhood, district, precinct.

cacicazgo: Territory governed by a cacique.

cacique: Political leader, chief.

cañas: Equestrian exercise similar to jousting.

Cassana (R): Royal houses of Pachakuti located on the plaza of Haucaypata in Cuzco.

ceque (R): Imaginary lines (connected with ceremonial) that radiated out from Cuzco.

ch'ampa (R): Sod blocks cut directly from the ground and used in building.

Chanka: Ethnic group that lived north of Cuzco. They were routed by Pachakuti.

chicha: Alcoholic beverage made by fermenting maize.

Chinchaysuyu (R): One of the four parts forming the Inca empire.

Chipaya: Ethnic group living in the department of Oruro, Bolivia.

chullpa (R): Burial structure with circular or quadrangular plan. Interior has a false vault.

Chunchulmayo (R): "Gut River" in Cuzco.

chuño (R): Dehydrated potatoes prepared by freezing and sun drying.

Coracora (R): Royal houses on the plaza of Haucaypata in Cuzco.

Cuntisuyu (R): One of the four parts forming the Inca empire.

Cuyusmanco (R): Royal houses to the north of the plaza of Cuzco. Related to Inka Wiraqocha.

guaca: See wak'a.

hanan (R): Upper; hence *hanan Cuzco*, upper Cuzco.

hanansaya (R): Upper section in the dual division or moiety system. Equivalent to *alasaa*.

Haqaru: Linguistic family to which Aymara belongs.

hihuana (R): Hard black stone used to dress other stones, mentioned by Garcilaso de la Vega. Almost certainly a misprint for *hihuaya*.

huaca: See wak'a.

hurin (R): Lower; hence *hurin Cuzco*, lower Cuzco.

hurinsaya (R): Lower section in the dual division or moiety system. Equivalent to *masaa*.

ichu: A high-altitude bunch grass. The material most commonly used as roof thatch. Spanish borrowed from Runasimi.

inkawasi (R): House of the Inca, a common name.

intiwatana (R): "Place where the sun is tied." A term recently made popular. The so-called *intiwatana* may have been *usnu*.

kallanka (R): Large unpartitioned hall with wooden pillars to support the roof. Served as temporary lodging for individuals rather than families.

kancha (R): Group of several roofed chambers inside a walled compound; also means enclosure.

k'añeri (A): Woolen blankets woven by women.

Kawki: A dialect of Aymara still spoken in Tupe, Peru.

khipu (R): System of knotted cords used for record keeping.

khipu kamayoq (R): Specialist who knots and interprets *khipu*.

Lupaqa: Ethnic group living near Lake Titicaca.

mamacuna (R): Chosen women dedicated to religious service.

masaa (A): Lower division, equivalent to *hurinsaya*.

masma (R): One-room building with one of the long sides open.

mawk'allaqta (R): "Damaged town," a name commonly given to archaeological sites.

mit'a (R): Compulsory labor tribute given to the state in rotation; never permanent.

mitimaes: Groups settled by the state in plan of enforced colonization. Spanish version of Runasimi term *mitmakuna*.

ñusta (R): Young unmarried woman of one of the royal *ayllu;* princess.

pachaca (R): Group of one hundred taxpayers.

panaqa (R): Royal "corporation" or *ayllu* composed of the descendants of an Inca, except for his successor.

p'atjati (A): Sleeping platform some 30 centimeters high.

phutu (A): Niche.

pirca: Dry laid fieldstone masonry. Spanish term derived from the Runasimi *perqa*, meaning wall.

pukara (R): Fortress.

Pumac Chupan (R): "Puma's tail"; location in Cuzco at the confluence of the Huatanay and Tullumayo rivers.

puñuna-pata (R): Sleeping platform (see *p'atjati*).

putuku: Rural Chipaya house built of sod blocks that rise to form a false vault.

qhapaq-ñan (R): Royal highway; the road connecting Cuzco and Quito.

Qolla: Inhabitant of Qollasuyu.

Qollasuyu (R): One of the four parts forming the Inca empire.

qollqa (R): Storehouse.

Qorikancha (R): "Golden Enclosure," called the Temple of the Sun since the conquest. It was the highest ranking religious structure. Located in Cuzco.

Quechua: Ethnic group that occupied a territory near Cuzco.

Runasimi (R): Official language of the Incas. Second official language of modern Peru.

sucanka (R): Small towers that marked the position of the sun.

sunturwasi (R): Circular structure.

suyu (R): Quarter (in the sense of region).

tampu (R): Rest station. There was a *tampu* on the road at the end of each day's travel.

tapia: Tamped earth construction using forms.

Tawantinsuyu (R): "Land of the four quarters." The Inca empire.

tinkuy (R): Place of pleasant encounter in the symbolic sense, where the *hurin* and *hanan* divisions meet. Does not eliminate rivalries.

tola: Any of several species of resinous bushy plants used as fuel.

usnu (R): May be a stepped structure, a platform, base of a throne, place intended for high ranking personages. May also be an altar.

vara: Measurement equal to about 85 centimeters.

wak'a (R): Something sacred, may be a hill, a river, a stone, etc.

Wanka: Ethnic group that lived in the region of the Mantaro River.

wasi (R): House.

CREDITS FOR PHOTOGRAPHS
AND PLANS
(Listed by figure numbers)

Alcina Franch, José: 203
Angrand, Leonce (book edited by C. Milla Batres): 100, 265
Arellano López, Jorge: 182
Bouchard, J. F.: 89
British Museum, London: 51
Crespo Toral, Hernán: 285, 286, 287, 291
Gasparini, Paolo: 2, 114, 116, 119, 120, 138, 139, 140, 144, 281
Gisbert, Teresa, and Mesa, José de (courtesy of): 104, 125, 129, 133, 179, 191, 192, 194, 195, 196, 252
Guaman Poma de Ayala, Felipe: 257, 258, 260, 261
Guillén, Abraham: 24, 26, 30, 32, 45, 57, 67, 68, 70, 71, 87, 88, 111, 113, 124, 141, 145, 147, 148, 166, 168, 208, 220, 253, 263, 268, 283, 289, 292, 293, 312, 322
Harth-terré, Emilio: 31, 112, 120, 282
Hiram Bingham Collection, Yale University: 53, 63, 173, 174(a), 175, 201
Instituto Nacional de Cultura, Peru (plans provided by): 52, 75, 142, 210, 221, 222, 276, 279
Jiménez Borja, Arturo: 170
Kendall, Ann: 64
Matos Mendieta, Ramiro: 130
Morris, Craig: 90, 92, 93, 189
Mujica, Elías: 4
Murra, John V. (courtesy of): 184
Rex González, Alberto: 105
Rowe, John H.: 209
Servicio Aerofotográfico Nacional, Lima (Peru): 36, 39, 61, 73, 78, 96, 278

Squier, Ephraim G. (from the book of): 8, 38(a), 122, 250, 251, 256
Velasco Cáceres, Emma (courtesy of): 223
Von Hagen, Victor W.: 146
Wiener, Charles (from the book of): 266
Yale University, Department of Anthropology: 10, 15, 19, 20, 21(a), 22, 254, 255

Graziano Gasparini and Luise Margolies: frontis., 1, 3, 5, 6, 7, 9, 11, 12, 13, 14, 16, 17, 18, 21(b), 23, 25, 27, 28, 29, 33, 34, 35, 37, 38(b), 40, 41, 42, 43, 44, 46, 47, 48, 54, 55, 56, 59, 60, 62, 65, 66, 69, 72, 74, 76, 77, 79, 80, 81, 82, 83, 84, 85, 86, 91, 94, 95, 97, 98, 99, 101, 102, 103, 106, 107, 108, 109, 115, 117, 118, 121, 123, 126, 127, 128, 131, 132, 134, 135, 136, 137, 143, 149, 150, 151, 152, 153, 154, 155, 156, 157, 158, 159, 160, 161, 162, 163, 164, 165, 167, 169, 171, 172, 174(b), 176, 177, 178, 179, 181, 183, 185, 186, 187, 188, 190, 193, 197, 198, 199, 200, 202, 204, 205, 206, 207, 211, 212, 213, 214, 215, 216, 217, 218, 219, 224, 225, 226, 227, 228, 229, 230, 231, 232, 233, 234, 235, 236, 237, 238, 239, 240, 241, 242, 243, 244, 245, 246, 247, 248, 249, 259, 262, 264, 267, 269, 270, 271, 272, 273, 274, 275, 277, 280, 288, 290, 294, 295, 296, 297, 298, 299, 300, 301, 302, 303, 304, 305, 306, 307, 308, 309, 310, 311, 313, 314, 315, 316, 317, 318, 319, 320, 321, 323, 324
Collection of the authors: 49, 50
The plans corresponding to the following figure numbers were redrawn by the authors: 52, 75, 90, 105, 112, 142, 170, 182, 189, 203, 210, 221, 222, 276, 279, 282

INDEX